TENNESSEE

American Historical Press
Sun Valley, California

TENNESSEE

THE VOLUNTEER STATE

AN ILLUSTRATED HISTORY

DR. ROBERT E. CORLEW
&
WILLIAM B. WHEELER

© 2008 American Historical Press
All Rights Reserved
Published 2008
Printed in South Korea

Library of Congress Catalogue Card Number: 2008008933611

ISBN: 978-1-892724-58-8

Bibliography: p. 240
Includes Index

CONTENTS

Chattanooga built upon the industrial base that the Federal Army of Occupation had left the town following the Civil War. In fact, Chattanooga advertised for carpetbaggers to move there and keep its industries running. This bucolic view by Harry Fenn shows the town as it appeared from Lookout Mountain shortly after the war. Courtesy, James A. Hoobler

PREFACE

History, as Isaac Watts wrote 250 years ago, is as an "ever rolling stream" where events occur and soon are forgotten—unless recorded for posterity. For millions of years men lived without historians who wrote ponderous history books, but within the past few hundred years, with the development of printing and modern methods of book production, they have become inundated with both fact and fiction depicting past events. Many historical accounts have enriched our lives and provided a lamp by which we may chart a path into the future.

This book is little more than an outline of some of the important developments in Tennessee during the past 200 years. What we have written comes from the records and artifacts left by those who have gone before us, and consists mainly of the activities and institutions of the early Europeans and their descendants. As to what occurred and how man lived in Tennessee before the Europeans came, we must leave in large measure to conjecture.

The many pages of illustrative materials make this book useful and unique and bear out the old adage that a picture sometimes is worth a thousand words. We are indebted to Mr. Jim Hoobler for the careful selection of the illustrative materials, to Professor John McDaniel for a very thorough reading and sound constructive criticism of the manuscript, and to Mary Saille Corlew for careful proofreading.

On January 8, 1815, General Andrew
Jackson's troops defeated the British forces of
General Sir Edward Packenham at Chalmette,
below New Orleans. This ended the British
threat against the United States, and propelled Jackson into national prominence.
Courtesy, Tennessee State Museum

TENNESSEE IN EARLY TIMES

To 1815

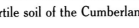

It was "nothing . . . but a howling wilderness" to a small group of soldiers who in December 1768 traversed the secluded valleys of present-day Tennessee between the Cumberland and Unaka mountains. But a few weeks later, the same soldiers reported that several dozen cabins were being developed, and they were amazed to see them "on every spot where the range was good."

So great was the exodus from the eastern states during the next few years that by 1791 more than 35,000 people had moved to the area soon to become Tennessee. Two major settlements developed. The first, in the state's northeast corner, consisted primarily of cabins located along the Holston, Nolichucky, and Watauga rivers. Because water was so vital—for transportation as well as food and drink—both sides of these rivers soon became dotted with homes. Communication with the royal administrations of North Carolina and Virginia was well-nigh impossible because of the distance, and as early as 1772 the people living along these rivers, realizing the necessity of organizing a government, hastily formed the "Watauga Association," and developed rules and regulations which in essence stated that the will of the majority would prevail. The Revolutionary War began three years later, and the western people, who fought both the British and the Indians, soon developed a spirit of independence not unlike that experienced by the patriots of Philadelphia in 1775.

Settlement in the second area, the fertile soil of the Cumberland or Central Basin, began 10 years after cabins first appeared along the Watauga and the Nolichucky rivers. Uriah Stone and other "long hunters" had taken to the East such glowing reports of fertile land on the Cumberland River that James Robertson, under the sponsorship of a group of businessmen known as the Transylvania Company, led a group of settlers in 1779 to the French Lick (present-day Nashville). He was joined in the following spring by John Donelson, who came by flatboat down the Tennessee River and up the Cumberland. Hastily, the two or three hundred settlers formed settlements, and these grew daily.

Long before these Tennesseans of European origin made permanent settlements, native Americans had for thousands of years hunted, fished, and fought along the rivers, valleys, and mountains. Those living in Tennessee when the first whites came were probably descendants of Ice Age hunters who had settled North America thousands of years earlier. They were the Paleo-Indians, whose Asian ancestors had crossed from the Asian to the North American continent via a broad rolling plain several hundred miles wide at the Bering Sea. In a series of migrations these Asian hunters had spread throughout Canada before turning south and ultimately reaching Tennessee. The fact that the Paleo-Indians shared many physical characteristics with the Asians has convinced scholars of their origin. Archaeologists have discovered such an abundance of Paleolithic fluted spear points and other weapons and tools that they believe a fairly substantial number

of people inhabited the Tennessee Valley during this period.

With the ending of the Ice Age, a new Indian culture, which archaeologists call the Archaic, emerged. Radiocarbon dating has placed the time of the Archaic Indians in Tennessee as being from about 8000 to 1000 B.C. Although most moved with the seasons, members of the Archaic group were generally less nomadic than their ancestors. They established some temporary villages, domesticated the dog, and wore more elaborate attire than their predecessors.

By 1000 B.C. a new group, the Woodland Indians, had evolved. Far more sophisticated than their ancestors, they began to supplement hunting and gathering with primitive agriculture, and cultivated maize, squash, and beans. They used bows and arrows as well as spears in hunting and fighting, and developed pottery for use in preparing foods. Their

belief in the hereafter may have been responsible for their development of burial mounds. These dome-shaped earthen tombs are scattered throughout present-day Tennessee.

A new culture characterized by a more sophisticated life-style developed approximately 500 years before Columbus sailed the Caribbean, and it supplanted the Woodland group. Because the Indians were concentrated along the Mississippi River, they became known as the Mississippians. They developed villages and towns, cultivated corn and other vegetables, centralized government and religion, and built taller and more elaborate mounds than had their predecessors. The mounds became substructures for religious and community buildings, and some—such as the Pinson Mound in Madison County—reached a height of 70 feet or more.

These were the prehistoric Indians, who lived before the time of written records. The "historic" Indians were encountered by the European explorers who first came to Tennessee some 50 years after Columbus' discovery. The explorers left written accounts of those Indians with whom they came in contact.

The first European to set foot on Tennessee soil was the Spanish conquistador Hernando de Soto, who arrived in Florida in 1539 with an army of 600 men. In July of the following year he entered East Tennessee and tracked along the Hiwassee River in search of gold and other treasures. After making camp in the vicinity of Chattanooga, he moved in a southwesterly direction, and may have crossed the Mississippi River near present-day Memphis. A second Spanish party, led by Juan Pardo, explored the Chattanooga area in the mid-1560s. De Soto reported many contacts with the Indians, treated them cruelly, and robbed them of such material wealth as he could readily find. He died two years after his arrival in Tennessee, but Pardo and other Spaniards lived to develop profitable trade relations with the Cherokees and other tribes.

The Tennessee Indians at the time of

Left: *The variety of shapes of these projectile points demonstrates the specialized hunting techniques of the Archaic Culture Indians, who inhabited Tennessee between 8,000 and 1,000 B.C. Courtesy, Tennessee State Museum, Vanderbilt University Gates P. Thruston Collection*

Lower left: *The first Europeans to visit what is now Tennessee in 1540 were the men on the de Soto Expedition. They are believed to have entered Tennessee in 1540 near Chattanooga, and again near Memphis. They lived peacefully with the Mississippian peoples at Chiaha, near present-day Chattanooga, but at the Chickasaw Bluffs, on the Mississippi River, they burned an Indian town. That incident is depicted in this mural in the Tennessee Governor's Office. Courtesy, The Office of the Governor*

Above: *At times whimsical, at times even grotesque, the effigy pottery of the Mississippian culture (A.D. 1000 to 1500) shows the great mastery of fired clay techniques that these people had attained. Courtesy, Tennessee State Museum, Vanderbilt University Gates P. Thruston Collection*

Left: Farming developed in Tennessee during the Woodland Culture period, from 1000 B.C. to A.D. 1000. These prehistoric peoples learned to raise corn, beans, and squash. Painting by Carlyle Urello. Courtesy, Tennessee State Museum

Far left: A belief in an afterlife by the prehistoric Indians is believed to have been responsible for the development of burial mounds during the Woodland Culture period, between 1000 B.C. and A.D. 1000. Painting by Carlyle Urello. Courtesy, Tennessee State Museum

Left: Early man hunted mastodons that roamed the hills and valleys of Tennessee during the late ice age. Bones of the animals and the spear points of their hunters have been found in areas of the state. After a painting by Charles R. Knight. Courtesy, Library Services Department, American Museum of Natural History

Far left: Ceremonial mound complexes were the administrative and religious centers of the Indians during the Mississippian Culture. Painting by Carlyle Urello. Courtesy, Tennessee State Museum

the arrival of the Europeans had a Late
Mississippian culture and were distinctly
divided into tribes. The largest and most
important group in the southeastern
United States was the Cherokee tribe,
whose "Overhill Towns" along the Little
Tennessee River and elsewhere in East
Tennessee gave them a strong claim to
the region. Both the French and the English developed a lively trade with them,
and their society and economy were
much more advanced than those of other
Tennessee tribes. They played a very important role in the lives of the people who
settled Tennessee, and they remained in
the state until forcibly expelled by the
federal government in 1838.

The Chickasaws, although not a large
tribe, were strong militarily and asserted
a claim to West Tennessee. Their principal towns were in north-central Mississippi, but the abundance of wild game in
West Tennessee drew them northward.

Central Tennessee was inhabited for
several decades by the Shawnees. Al-

though they were small in number, their
activities and interests extended over a
wide area, which caused them eventually
to lose interest in the Cumberland Valley. Finally, a coalition of Cherokees and
Chickasaws, which claimed Middle Tennessee as a hunting ground, drove the
Shawnee northward. Other tribes in and
out of Tennessee during the seventeenth
and eighteenth centuries included the
Yuchis in the east, the Natchez of the
lower Mississippi Valley, and a confeder-
ation of small tribes called the Creeks located in the south.

French and English explorers arrived
in North America early in the seventeenth century, and in 1607 several
hundred English people established
Jamestown on the James River. Within
a few decades Virginia traders followed
rivers and trails westward. By 1671 they
had crossed the Blue Ridge Mountains
and encamped in the vicinity of present-
day Radford; two years later a group under James Needham penetrated as far as
the Little Tennessee River, where they
found several Cherokee towns. Later, explorers made contact with the Indians,
and within a short time developed a lucrative trade.

While the English built Jamestown,
Frenchmen founded Quebec near the
mouth of the St. Lawrence River. They
explored the Mississippi Valley as far
south as the Gulf of Mexico. Among
them were Jacques Marquette and Louis
Jolliet—the former a Catholic priest and
the latter a fur trader—who traveled together over a large area and encamped
along the Chickasaw Bluffs in 1673 at
the present-day site of Memphis. Other
Frenchmen who came to Tennessee
during the colonial period were René
Robert Cavelier, Sieur de La Salle,
Martin Chartier, Jean Couture, and Jean
du Charleville.

La Salle, who established a fort near
Memphis that was used by later groups,
was killed by one of his men during a rebellion when he reached present-day
Texas. Chartier, who had deserted La
Salle even before the rebellion, had established a trading post at French Lick

(Nashville) and lived for several years among the Shawnees. He was succeeded in the early 1690s by Couture, who traded among the Indians throughout a wide area. Du Charleville came a few years later. In the early 1700s he was widely known for his successful trading post at French Lick.

Because of the competition for the lucrative trade that both the French and the English had developed with the Indians, conflict soon arose and became an important cause of a series of intercolonial wars. The last, the French and Indian War, began in 1754 and ended nine years later, when the French were defeated and expelled from the Mississippi Valley.

Despite the intercolonial wars, English traders and hunters continued to visit the

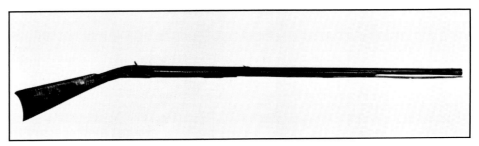

western country on a regular basis. Some, known as "long hunters," would hunt and trap in the wilderness for a season or longer. Daniel Boone was perhaps the most famous of the long hunters, and in 1760 he carved on a beech tree in present-day Washington County that he had "cilled" a "bar" in the vicinity. Thomas "Big Foot" Spencer spent an entire winter in and out of a hollow tree in present-day Sumner County, and other hunters who had penetrated to the Central Basin by mid-century included Joseph Hollingshed, Uriah Stone, and Kasper Mansker. Mansker ultimately decided to remain permanently, and he built a small fort for his family in Sumner County.

By the early 1770s dissatisfaction with oppressive colonial seaboard governments, along with economic opportunities in the West, had been responsible for the settlement of hundreds of people in the transmontane area. William Bean and a group of friends and relatives from Pittsylvania County, Virginia, are often called Tennessee's "first permanent settlers," but close behind was James Robertson, sometimes called the "Father of Tennessee," who brought family and friends destined to play major roles in the settlement of both the eastern sector and the Cumberland area of Middle Tennessee.

By 1772 four settlements consisting

of several thousand people had developed. The principal one, Watauga, was centered at Sycamore Shoals (present-day Elizabethton) and spread along the Watauga River. Just to the south, Nolichucky was formed along the Nolichucky River and its tributaries. It had developed from a settlement established in 1771 by Jacob Brown, a merchant from South Carolina. To the northwest of Nolichucky, between present-day Rogersville and Kingsport, was Carter's Valley, established by a Virginia merchant named John Carter who first lived at Watauga. Due to incessant Indian attacks, the life of Carter's Valley was short, and Carter and his party soon returned to Watauga for protection. Northwest of Watauga and east of Carter's Valley lay the North Holston settlement. It centered around Sapling Grove (present-day Bristol) where Evan Shelby built a store and stockade in 1770. According to later surveys, this settlement lay mainly in present-day Virginia.

Because these settlements were outside the bounds of the organized governments of both Virginia and North Carolina, leaders established a government of their own and called it the "Watauga Association." It consisted of a court of five members, who had both judicial and legislative functions, and included the usual county officers, like sheriff and clerk. It became the precursor of similar frontier governments, such as those found in the Cumberland settlements in 1780 and Franklin in 1784.

Continued disagreements and problems between the seaboard colonies and Great Britain resulted in the American Revolution (1775-1783). While the Wataugans probably knew little about "taxation without representation," they had endured oppressive Indian warfare and honestly believed that the British were responsible. They therefore raised a company of soldiers under the command of James Robertson, and made plans to join North Carolina in the fight. North Carolina authorities soon recognized the Wataugans as "Washington County," and asked for delegates to meet

John Sevier was a representative of "Washington County" (as Wautauga was known during the American Revolution) in the North Carolina legislature. He became Tennessee's first governor in 1796. Courtesy, Tennessee Historical Society Collection

Left: *Colonel Isaac Shelby led troops with John Sevier against British Major Patrick Ferguson's force at Sycamore Shoals in 1780. This American victory has been called the turning point of the Revolution in the South. Courtesy, Tennessee State Museum*

Above: *Tennessee volunteers mustered at Sycamore Shoals to fight the British at the Battle of Kings Mountain. Courtesy, Tennessee State Museum*

Left: *This engraving depicts the death of Major Patrick Ferguson at the Battle of King's Mountain as he led a band of British Loyalist troops against the Overmountain men. Courtesy, New York Public Library*

James Robertson led a migration of settlers to Tennessee's Central Basin in 1779. This area, 200 miles west of Wautauga, became the state's second major settlement. Courtesy, Tennessee Historical Society Collection

regularly with the North Carolina legislature. John Carter and John Sevier were chosen as representatives for the new county.

British troops at first invaded the northern colonies, particularly Massachusetts, and several years elapsed before they invaded the South. In the meantime, however, the Cherokees—led by Dragging Canoe and other young chieftains who for years had resented the continued encroachment of whites upon their land claims—and other tribes armed and encouraged by the British moved against the western settlers. For several months during the summer and fall of 1776, the Wataugans all but despaired of their lives as they sustained continued assaults. Not until the following year, after receiving aid from Virginia, North Carolina, and Georgia, were the Wataugans able to turn the Indians back. Not only had they preserved their own settlements, but they had kept open the road to Kentucky and the Illinois country.

Although some Wataugans fought in Georgia, Virginia, and South Carolina, their principal military activity was at King's Mountain. When British troops entered the southern colonies, they expected to find a great deal of Loyalist support. Major General Charles Cornwallis, who had fought with success in the North, landed at Savannah late in December 1778 and proceeded to run at large throughout Georgia and South Car-

olina. He established seaboard bases at Savannah and Charleston, and extended his line west along the Savannah River. He assigned Major Patrick Ferguson to protect his westwardly exposed left flank, and Ferguson soon wreaked havoc with many of the small settlements in the Piedmont. Patriot troops under the command of Colonel Isaac Shelby and Charles Robertson (a brother of James) met detachments of Ferguson's men in the Piedmont but were forced to retreat before superior British forces.

Frontier troops, responding to Ferguson's threat to bring his men "over the mountains, hang the leaders," and lay the "country waste with fire and sword," assembled at Sycamore Shoals on September 25, 1780, under the command of Shelby and John Sevier. Armed with rifles, they proceeded in a southwestward direction and soon encountered Ferguson at King's Mountain, a narrow ridge located in South Carolina just over the Carolina line. Ferguson, who had ordered his men to employ the bayonet instead of using precious ammunition, soon found the Americans so well camou-

flaged that he was unable to use the dreaded steel weapon effectively. After several attempts, the Americans were able to cause the British to surrender. Ferguson himself was slain.

This victory has justifiably been called the turning point of the Revolution in the South. It greatly encouraged the southern patriots and caused Cornwallis to abandon his campaign in North Carolina. By the following year he had moved northward and surrendered at Yorktown—an American victory that brought hostilities to a virtual end. In the meantime Major Robertson's army had joined General Nathanael Greene's forces, and Shelby and Sevier had joined General Francis Marion in South Carolina.

The Revolution was well underway before the second major settlement in Tennessee was established. While Charles Robertson fought the British in the east, James Robertson, his brother, resolved to plant a new settlement nearly 200 miles west of Watauga in the heart of the Central Basin. Financed by a group of eastern businessmen, led by Richard Henderson, which was interested in ac-

Left: *The April 24, 1780, arrival of the Donelson party at the Nashborough bluffs is depicted in this mural in the Governor's Office. Courtesy, The Office of the Governor*

Below left: *Fort Nashborough, the nucleus of today's Nashville, was built on the bluff of the Cumberland River, south of the French Lick salt spring. It protected most of the settlers in the Cumberland settlements. This is a scale model of the fort, which was built in 1780. Courtesy, Tennessee State Musuem*

Below: *John Donelson's journal of the voyage to the site of today's Nashville recorded the entire journey, which originated from Fort Patrick Henry. Courtesy, Tennessee Historical Society Collection*

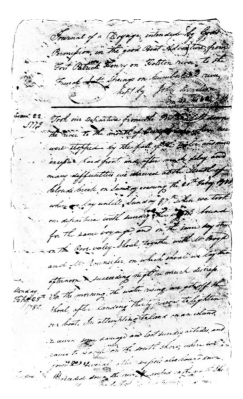

John Sevier, the future governor of Tennessee, as he appeared in about 1790 in the uniform of the North Carolina militia. Courtesy, Tennessee Historical Society Collection

than. They set out from Fort Patrick Henry in October "warmly dressed in frontier attire, long shirts of unbleached homespun linsey under buckskin jackets reaching almost to the knees," and carrying food and blankets. They walked north several miles into Virginia, and then went west through Cumberland Gap and then along Daniel Boone's Wilderness Road. Ultimately, they turned south and entered Tennessee just north of present-day Clarksville, visited briefly with Thomas Kilgore, who earlier that year had built a stockade called "Kilgore's Station," pushed on to Kasper Mansker's Station, and then to French Lick. Interestingly, they found the Cumberland River frozen and were able to cross it on the hard ice. While awaiting the arrival of other settlers, they built a fort and named it Nashborough after General Francis Nash, who had been a clerk in Judge Henderson's court before fighting in the Revolution.

John Donelson, who with his family had joined the Wataugans in 1771, was in command of the group that came by water. He had constructed a flotilla of flatboats, which transported mainly the women and children. Aboard his flagship, the *Adventure,* he and other members of his family (including his young daughter, Rachel, who later married Andrew Jackson) set forth at the head of more than a dozen small boats on December 22, 1779. His detailed journal told of the hardships encountered. Extreme cold and other problems held them up for several weeks. Early in March Mrs. Ephraim Peyton, whose husband had traveled with Robertson overland, had a baby. On the following day Donelson's party suffered the first of many Indian attacks, and experienced considerable difficulty in navigating the rocks and swift current at present-day Muscle Shoals. Almost despairing, Donelson noted that at the shoals "we did not know how soon we should be dashed to pieces, and all our troubles ended at once."

Finally, after navigating stretches of the Tennessee, Ohio, and Cumberland rivers, Donelson arrived in Nashborough

quiring western lands for speculation, Robertson and eight companions came to the Basin in the spring of 1779 to select a site somewhere in the vicinity of French Lick. He was pleased with the general area; indeed, as his daughter, Lavinia Robertson Craighead, later wrote, he returned "with such a glowing description of the country . . . that he made up a large party to go and settle on the Cumberland River where Nashville now stands."

The migration to the Basin country followed two routes, one overland and the other by water. The former was led by Robertson and consisted of some 200 men driving horses, cattle, sheep, and hogs, and included two of Robertson's brothers and his 10-year-old son, Jona-

on April 24, 1780. He confided to his journal his "satisfaction" in being able "to restore to him[self] and others their families and friends . . . and who, some time since, perhaps despaired of ever meeting again . . . "

Before the summer ended, hundreds of people had come to Nashborough—including Judge Henderson, who remained only long enough to assume an active role in forming a frontier government. Not content with settling at the small fort Robertson had built, some of the people established small stations a few miles out from Nashborough. Two hundred and fifty-six adult males joined together, however, in the formation of a government described in the Cumberland Compact.

Following the pattern of the settlers at Watauga, the Nashborough group established a tribunal of 12 judges who swore "to do equal and impartial justice . . . according to their best skill and judgment." The judges, who assumed legislative powers as well, were apportioned among the several regional settlements. Describing their "distressed situation" as occasioned by a location far removed from civilization, they asked for "immediate aid and protection" from North Carolina. It was 1783, however, before North Carolina recognized the settlements by organizing them into Davidson County (named for General Williams Davidson, who had fought in the Revolution) and began to send help. Robertson was promptly chosen as the county's representative to the North Carolina legislature, and the usual county officials were inducted into office. The following year the name of the county seat was changed to Nashville.

Westward expansion was among the first topics the leaders of the new American nation discussed after winning independence in 1783. Naturally, frontiersmen listened intently as Thomas Jefferson and other national leaders proposed the formation of several new western states to be admitted to the Union on a basis equal to the original 13.

John Sevier was among those who knew that statehood would bring enormous profits in land sales; as a statesman interested in the welfare of friends and neighbors, he also knew that statehood would bring protection from Indian warfare and, eventually, better transportation. In August 1784 leaders of the Watauga-Holston area met in Jonesboro specifically to organize a new state. They chose Sevier as chairman of their group, invited "any contiguous part of Virginia" to join them, and adjourned, determined to reassemble a few weeks later to take definite action. Although neither the Virginians nor the people of the Cumberland joined in, the Wataugans reassembled in November and again in March 1785, when they announced that "a decent respect to the opinions of mankind" necessitated that they "should manifest to the world the reasons which induced" them to take the initiative in forming a new state. Their lives, liberty, and property, they asserted, could best be protected by separation from North Carolina and acceptance into the Union as the 14th state. Naming the state Franklin, for Benjamin Franklin, they drafted a constitution and called upon the American Congress for recognition. The group chose Sevier as governor, and Landon Carter, Stockley Donelson, and William Cocke as other officials.

North Carolina officials viewed this action as nothing more than frontier rebellion by three of that state's western counties. Although some of the state's leaders had earlier expressed an interest in being rid of the responsibility for the transmontane areas, they now stated a firm intention of retaining the western lands. Governor Alexander Martin, who at first tried to placate the rebels, published a "manifesto" late in April 1785 in which he asserted that North Carolina would "regain her government over the revolting country or render it not worth possessing." Appealing to Sevier not to "tarnish the laurels . . . gloriously won at King's Mountain" or to "be hurried on by blind ambition" to gain statehood prematurely, he talked of sending troops to force the Wataugans into submission.

Fortunately, the militant governor's

William Blount served as territorial governor from 1790 to 1796. Courtesy, Tennessee Historical Society Collection

term was near its end, and he was succeeded a few weeks later by Richard Caswell, a man of mild temperament who enjoyed the confidence of the western people. He proposed that Franklin immediately disband its government and renew its allegiance to North Carolina. In return, he would pardon all who had participated in the independence movement and accept into the North Carolina General Assembly several delegates from the Franklin region. This move divided the Franklin people, and those who wished to cooperate with North Carolina joined John Tipton, a long-standing enemy of

Sevier's. Tipton was chosen immediately for membership in the North Carolina General Assembly, was appointed a colonel in the militia, and, with new confidence, undertook to enforce the will of North Carolina in the Franklin area. Hostilities developed; several people were killed or wounded, and two of Sevier's sons were captured and threatened with execution by hanging.

In the meantime developments at the national level did not favor Franklin's cause. Leaders who sought the advice of Benjamin Franklin were urged to abandon the independence movement and

This circa 1830 painting of John McNairy by John C. Grimes shows McNairy late in life. Courtesy, Tennessee Historical Society Collection

await action at the federal level. In 1787 the Constitutional Convention in Philadelphia wrote in the new federal constitution that new states could not be formed within the bounds of one of the original 13 without the respective states' permission. These developments all helped to sound the death knell of the backwoodsmen's struggle for independence. Sevier's term as governor expired in the spring of 1788, and for all practical purposes, the State of Franklin ended. Sevier was arrested by the Tipton forces and charged with treason, but he was never tried. Early in 1789 Sevier re-

newed his allegiance to North Carolina. He was elected to the North Carolina Senate and restored to his military rank as brigadier general.

Other developments soon placed Tennessee on the pathway to statehood. Soon after North Carolina ratified the federal constitution (November 21, 1789), state leaders transferred their claims to the western lands to the federal government. Congress immediately accepted the land cession, and in May 1790 President George Washington signed into law a measure establishing the "Territory of the United States south of the river Ohio." Six years later Tennessee became a state.

In 1787 Congress had provided for the territorial government of the Old Northwest, and these rules were applied to Tennessee. They provided in part that as long as a territory had a population under 60,000, it could not become a state but would have many of the rights and privileges of statehood. For example, if the population exceeded 5,000, the people could elect a member of the House of Representatives, send a delegate to Congress, and receive a federally appointed governor. When the population reached 60,000 or more, they could apply for statehood.

President Washington chose a man he knew from the Constitutional Convention, William Blount of North Carolina, as governor of the Southwest Territory. Daniel Smith of Sumner County was chosen as territorial secretary, and David Campbell, John McNairy, and Joseph Anderson as judges. The 41-year-old Blount already was a well-known land speculator, businessman, and statesman who had fought in the Revolution and represented North Carolina at the Constitutional Convention. Born of well-to-do parents, Blount and other members of his family had aggressively taken up claims to thousands of acres of western lands. As he stated after his appointment as governor, the position would not only give him an opportunity to serve his country but would also enable him to keep a close and careful eye on his land holdings so that their value might be enhanced.

Blount took up his duties with characteristic vigor. By early in the autumn of 1790, he had taken the oath of office, consulted with President Washington, and established his headquarters on the fork of the Holston and Watauga rivers—at Rocky Mount—in the home of William Cobb, a wealthy pioneer who knew influential people both in North Carolina and the less civilized hinterlands.

The Southwest Territory consisted of two major pockets of settlement separated by 200 miles of wilderness. The eastern settlements, which were divided into the counties of Greene, Hawkins, Sullivan, and Washington, had a total population of about 28,000; the Cumberland settlements, which consisted of Davidson, Sumner, and Tennessee (soon to be divided into Montgomery and Robertson) counties, had about one-fourth that number. On December 15 Blount arrived at Nashborough and was the houseguest of James Robertson for nearly two weeks. There he met with some Cumberland leaders and informed them of the change in government. He then returned to Cobb's home and took up other duties, including selecting a legislative body, attempting to settle Indian problems, planning for a census, and selecting a permanent location for a territorial capital.

The selection of a site for the capital was easily accomplished. James White had explored, purchased, and erected "White's Fort" on land located a few miles below the junction of the Holston and French Broad rivers. Blount owned land nearby, and he had no difficulty in deciding upon that general vicinity for the capital. He built a governor's "mansion" on a small hill near the river and announced that it would serve as a residence for his family as well as the territorial capitol. White immediately laid out and sold lots near the capitol, and in a short time a frontier town developed, which Blount named "Knoxville" in honor of Major General Henry Knox, Washington's secretary of war. In June of the following year (1792), Knox County was carved from Hawkins County, and Knoxville became not only the territorial capital but also the county seat. Jefferson County, also a part of Hawkins and named for the secretary of state, was created at the same time. The politically adroit Blount grouped these two counties into a military and judicial district and named it for Washington's other cabinet member, Alexander Hamilton.

A census was taken in the summer of 1791. While the mobility of the settlers made an accurate count nearly impossi-

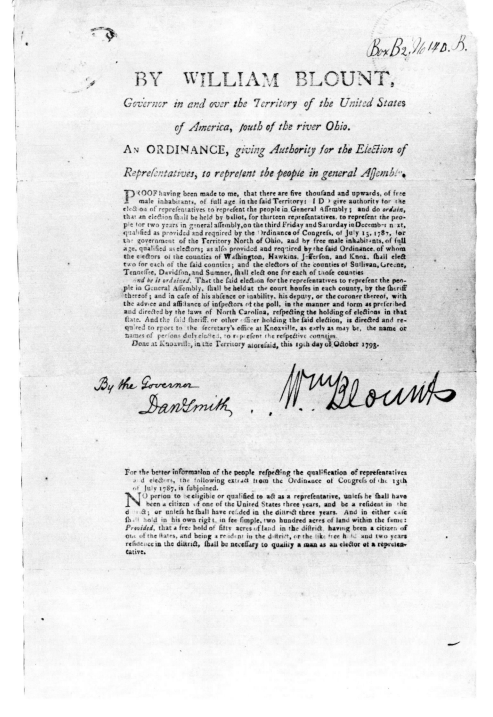

The ordinance for the election of the first Tennessee Territory legislature was signed by Governor William Blount in 1793. With this document Tennessee moved one step closer to statehood. Courtesy, Tennessee Historical Society Collection

ble, a report made to Blount in September claimed there were 35,691 people, of whom 6,271 were free white males of voting age. Nearly 3,500 were slaves, and they were concentrated largely in Knox, Hawkins, Sumner, and Davidson counties, although there were a few in each of the other counties.

Plans were made for the election of a territorial legislature only after many people had complained of Blount's tardiness

in developing them. In October 1793, 13 members were elected to a House of Representatives (only free white males who owned at least 50 acres could vote). The representatives assembled in Knoxville in February 1794 and selected 10 men, from whom President Washington could choose five to constitute the upper house. Washington promptly appointed Sevier, Stockley Donelson, and Parmenas Taylor from the eastern counties, and Griffith

This was the first map published of the new state of Tennessee (spelled Tennassee*). It was printed in Philadelphia in 1796. Courtesy, Dr. James C. Kelly*

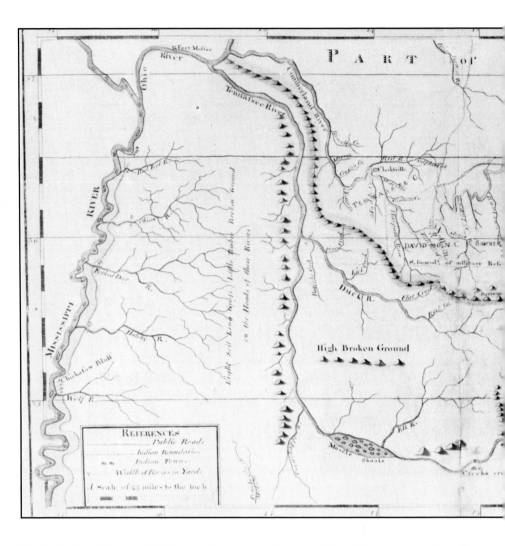

Rutherford and James Winchester from the central counties. When both houses assembled not long thereafter, they established a tax rate, provided for the collection of taxes, incorporated Knoxville, created Sevier County, and enacted other measures.

Participation in the first legislative session whetted the lawmakers' desire for statehood because all envisioned opportunities for personal and economic advancement. Blount, for example, envisioned himself as a potential U.S. senator from the new state, and others also hoped to occupy high offices.

Blount called the legislators into special session in June 1795 to consider statehood. Upon the governor's recommendation, legislators provided for a census and a poll on the question of statehood. While conducting the census the county sheriffs who undertook it asked each adult male whether it was his "wish

if, on taking the enumeration there should prove to be less than sixty thousand inhabitants, that the territory shall be admitted as a state into the Federal Union with such a number or not." The total count—subject to many disputes about its accuracy—showed a population of 77,262 and a positive vote on the statehood question of 6,504 to 2,562. All the eastern counties voted for admission under the conditions specified, but the western counties were overwhelmingly against it.

Perhaps Representative Thomas Hardeman of Davidson County had expressed the sentiments of many of the Cumberland settlers when he argued that statehood would mean increased taxes and few benefits for the people of the three central counties. Moreover, many of the Cumberland leaders feared that the eastern counties would run the affairs of state, and they looked forward to a

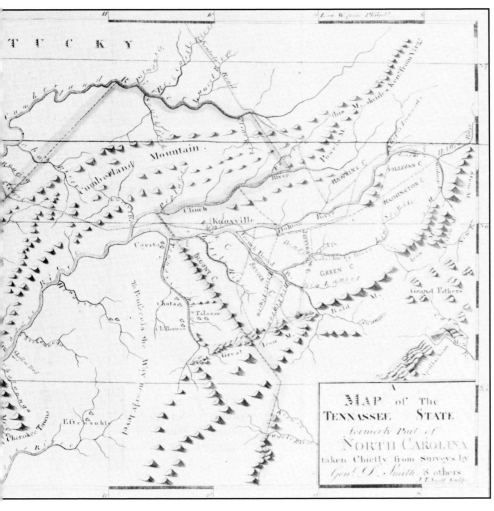

Below left: *Archibald Roane. Courtesy, Tennessee State Library & Archives*

Below center: *William Cocke served as one of Tennessee's first U.S. senators. Courtesy, Tennessee State Library & Archives*

Below right: *Joseph McMinn carried a copy of Tennessee's constitution, and a letter from territorial governor William Blount petitioning for statehood, to President George Washington in 1796. Courtesy, Tennessee Historical Society Collection*

time when they might become a state in their own right.

Governor Blount called for the election on December 18-19 of five delegates from each county who were to assemble in Knoxville in January 1796 and write a constitution preparatory to statehood. Able men were chosen, including Territorial Judges Joseph Anderson and John McNairy, and Territorial Secretary Daniel Smith. James Houston, father of Sam Houston, represented Blount County. Landon Carter, former speaker of the house of the Franklin legislature, and John Tipton, who had so vigorously opposed the Franklin movement, were among those from Washington County. James Robertson, Andrew Jackson, and Thomas Hardeman represented the Cumberland counties. In addition to Jackson, men destined to serve later as governor or represent the state in the U.S. Congress included William Cocke, Joseph McMinn, John Rhea, and Archibald Roane. Sixteen members listed their birthplaces as Virginia, eight as Pennsylvania, seven as North Carolina, four as South Carolina, and three as Maryland.

These legislators developed the foundation for the fundamental laws of Tennessee. Judge Anderson and his father-in-law, Alexander Outlaw, were joined by McMinn and Hardeman in opposing the majority, as represented by Blount, Jackson, Robertson, and Smith. They insisted upon a bill of rights and a unicameral legislature, and wanted to make belief in "the divine authority of the old and new testaments" a qualification for office holding. Fearful that the state government might gain too much power, they sought to curb the powers of both the executive and legislative bodies.

Modeled after the constitutions of North Carolina and Pennsylvania, and later described by Thomas Jefferson as "the least imperfect and most republican" he had seen, the document was completed after three weeks of deliberation. It was a conservative document when viewed from a modern standpoint. Membership in the legislature was open only to free males who were at least 21

years old and owned at least 200 acres, and had resided for three or more years in the territory. Legislators were given broad lawmaking powers which were not subject to gubernatorial veto. The chief executive's tenure was limited to three consecutive terms of two years each. Commanded to "take care that the laws shall be faithfully executed," the governor had to be at least 25 years of age and had to own at least 500 acres. Judges were to serve for life on good behavior and presided over "such superior and inferior courts of law and equity" as the legislature should create. All freemen who were at least 21 years of age and residents of a county for at least six months could vote.

Before the convention adjourned, members chose John Sevier for governor, even though some support for Judge Anderson had developed in the three central counties. Members of the General Assembly were chosen, and they convened in March. After proclaiming "Citizen John Sevier" as the duly and constitutionally elected governor, they selected James Winchester of Sumner County as speaker of the Senate and James Stewart of Washington County as speaker of the House. Blount and William Cocke were chosen as the state's U.S. senators. Concerned that the new state's name was the same as one of the central counties, the General Assembly divided Tennessee County into Robertson and Montgomery counties. The former was named for James Robertson and the latter for Colonel John Montgomery, who had migrated to the territory from Virginia. Grainger County, named for Blount's wife, Mary Grainger, was created at the same time.

In the meantime delegate Joseph McMinn had hurried to the nation's capital with a copy of the constitution and a lengthy communication from Blount petitioning for statehood. McMinn presented the documents to President Washington, who forwarded them to Congress with the message that among the rights that the territory had been given at the time of its formation was that of "forming a permanent constitution and State Government, and of admission as a State . . . when it should have therein 60,000 free inhabitants."

By 1796 two strong political parties had developed in the new United States. The Federalist was the party of Washington, Vice President John Adams, and Secretary of the Treasury Alexander Hamilton. Jefferson, who opposed many of Hamilton's ideas about the powers of the central government, had resigned from Washington's cabinet and become the leader of the new Republican party. (The beliefs of the Republican party were very similar to those of the Democratic party today.) The result was that considerable debate between the two groups developed over the question of Tennessee's admission to the Union.

The Federalist party, which was aware both that the upcoming presidential election would be very close and that Tennessee had strong Republican proclivities, sought to delay the territory's admission until after the election. But, in a close vote strictly along party lines, the Congress voted for admission, and President Washington signed the statehood bill on June 1, 1796. Tennessee became the Union's 16th state.

Congress had insisted that U.S. senators should be chosen by the "State of Tennessee" and not by the "Southwest Territory." Accordingly, Sevier called the legislators into special session on July 30, and they chose Cocke and Blount. The admissions act also had provided that the new state should have one representative in Congress, and Jackson therefore was chosen in the October elections over negligible opposition. When Congress assembled in January 1797, the senators and the congressman proudly took their seats, signaling the end of the eventful struggle of Tennesseans for equal status in the young nation.

The first two decades after statehood were years of growth and development. The population more than tripled, and the people enjoyed considerable economic advancement. Sevier, the hero of King's Mountain and many Indian battles, was elected governor for six

General James Winchester was selected as Tennessee's speaker of the senate in the constitutional convention of 1796, just months before the U.S. Congress voted to admit Tennessee as the Union's 16th state. Courtesy, Tennessee Historical Society Collection

terms, interrupted midway (in 1801) by Archibald Roane's election. Roane's administration was uneventful, and he was overwhelmingly defeated by Sevier when he sought a second term. When Sevier's sixth term was completed, he was elected to the Tennessee Senate and still later to the U.S. Congress, where he remained until his death in 1815.

Although Blount experienced difficulties in the Senate and died in 1800, Jackson rose to national prominence because of his spectacular military victory at New Orleans in the War of 1812. Due to the heroic and unselfish activities of many of its people in the War of 1812, Tennessee became known as the "Volunteer State."

Sevier had been a logical choice for governor. Born in Rockingham County, Virginia, in 1745, he had come with family and friends to take up lands on the Holston and Nolichucky in 1773. He rose rapidly in the civil and military service, claimed thousands of acres of land, operated a country store, fought at King's Mountain, and was governor of Franklin. His main body of political strength lay in the eastern counties, although his contacts in the Nashville area with James Robertson, Andrew Jackson (with whom he later bitterly disagreed), and others gave him adequate political power to remain safely in control throughout his six terms.

Sevier was able to retain the capital in Knoxville throughout his tenure but saw it moved to Nashville soon after his final term expired. The state's western boundary throughout his terms was the Tennessee River. As noted, it was not until 1818 that the area between the Tennessee and the Mississippi rivers was purchased from the Chickasaw Indians and opened for settlement.

Sevier's messages to the legislature, his public speeches, and his communications with constituents generally indicate he was a civic-minded person dedicated not only to the improvement of his own economic and political status but to the development and growth of the state. Throughout his administrations he pressed for improved land and water transportation, a stronger state militia, and better education, "both academic and technical."

The growth of the state's population from about 85,000 in 1796 to 261,727 in 1810 was due in part to the vast migration coming in from Virginia, North Carolina, and other states. As one writer expressed it,

> ... the roads were congested with movers during the summer months—great top-heavy Conestoga wagons drawn by oxen ... befrilled gentlemen astride blooded horses, rawboned farmers on hairy plow-nags, peddlers and merchants with their trains of donkeys, immigrants too poor to afford meager belongings and children on their backs—all moving west toward the promised land in Tennessee.

While many people settled in the eastern counties, the vast majority came to the "western district," as the central settlements were called. Indeed, when Sevier's final term expired, more than 60 percent of all Tennesseans lived in Middle Tennessee as compared to about one-half in 1796. New counties stretched from the Kentucky line on the north to Alabama on the south, and Nashville, with several hundred homes and mercantile establishments, was a thriving frontier town. Two newspapers were published regularly, churches and schools had been built, and a land boom—with land selling as high as two dollars per acre—had developed.

Knoxville, the capital, also exhibited considerable growth during Sevier's term as governor. For several decades it was larger than Nashville, and it developed very early as a commercial and financial frontier center. Other frontier towns that experienced growth were Jonesboro, Greeneville, Kingston, and Rogersville in the eastern settlements, and Clarksville, Lebanon, and Gallatin in the central sector.

Sevier was succeeded as governor in 1809 by Willie Blount, a half-brother of William Blount, who served for three terms. Blount had bought land and settled in Montgomery County before the turn of the century, and thus could claim the political support of the growing central state population.

Soon after Blount assumed office he turned his attention to reapportionment of the legislature, as mandated by Congress. The enormous growth experienced by the central counties meant that the "western district" had gained control of the legislature. Exuberant Middle Tennesseans immediately moved the capital from Knoxville to Nashville and enacted other legislation favorable to the central sector.

As significant as the domestic issues were, foreign problems loomed at the national level, and Tennesseans soon found themselves immersed in a second war with Great Britain.

England, like other major European nations, had become embroiled in war with France soon after the French Revolution had begun in 1789. Both Britain and France regularly interfered with American trade, but American grievances against the British seemed greater. The British had kept troops on American soil long after the United States had won independence, and they had seized merchandise bound for France from American vessels on the high seas. The British also had seized American sailors suspected of being British deserters and forced them to serve in Great Britain's navy. When in 1807 a British ship fired on the American *Chesapeake* because its captain refused to permit a search, Tennessee legislators assured President James Madison that Tennesseans would make any sacrifice necessary to maintain the honor and integrity of the United States.

For years the older generation of Americans had accepted a second-rate position in respect to the major European powers, but the young men who dominated Congress after 1810 would have none of that. Joining other "Warhawks" in Congress were Felix Grundy, John Rhea, John Sevier, and other Tennesseans who proposed to fight England and take Canada in the process. Senator George W. Campbell hoped for war because, as he said, a military victory would lift the United States "from her present degraded position in the eyes of the world."

Also, border warfare between several Indian tribes and American settlers continued to discourage westward expansion. Jackson and other military leaders for years had contended that not only did Great Britain urge the Creeks and other tribes to assault Americans, but actually supplied them with weapons. War was declared in June 1812; Fourth of July celebrations across Tennessee resounded with oratory endorsing war.

Andrew Jackson, who now held the rank of major general in the state militia, was ordered to wage war against the Indians in the south, and he soon earned the sobriquet of "Old Hickory" as he marched his men through the hickory forests of Alabama. Governor Blount's adjutant general, Colonel John Williams, joined Georgia troops in a proposed conquest of Florida. General James Winchester of Sumner County marched north to participate in an invasion of British Canada.

In a reorganization of troops the following year, Jackson was given a federal commission as major general and command of a military district. He again moved south, crushing the Creek Indians in March 1814 at Horseshoe Bend, fighting the British along the Gulf Coast at

Andrew Jackson was elected as the Volunteer State's first representative to the U.S. Congress in October 1796, four months after statehood had been attained. Courtesy, Colonel James S. Corbett

Mobile and Pensacola, and then taking command of American troops at New Orleans. As a diversionary tactic, British troops later in 1814 planned to land a large army at New Orleans, move north up the Mississippi River, and conquer the West. Jackson's troops, which consisted of Tennesseans familiar with frontier warfare, soon engaged a superior military force fighting under Sir Edward Packenham, one of the world's ablest and most recognized soldiers. Fighting much as an earlier generation of frontiersmen had done at King's Mountain, Jackson's men turned them back from the American West. During the spectacular battle General Packenham and more than 2,000 of his men were killed or wounded. Jackson's losses were about a dozen killed and fewer than 50 wounded.

The victory brought Jackson and his fellow Tennesseans international recognition, and it became a major stepping stone in Jackson's ultimate bid for the American presidency. Tennessee's General Assembly, echoing the sentiments of the people generally, urged Congress to give "each officer and soldier" of the victorious army a large land grant from the national lands as a reward for their heroism at New Orleans. Although the War of 1812 was not a major accomplishment for the United States, the victory helped tremendously in establishing respect for the infant nation and especially for the people of Tennessee and the West.

The Battle of Shiloh, April 6-7, 1862, was
the largest land battle ever fought in North
America up to that date. Over 100,000
troops were engaged. It was also the first battle to use field hospitals for the treatment of
the wounded. Courtesy, James A. Hoobler

2

THE GROWING STATE

1815-1870

The War of 1812 was a significant experience for the United States, and especially for Tennessee and the West. Although it resulted in neither equity for commerce nor expansion of the nation's western and northern boundaries, it did increase respect for the United States abroad and established self-confidence in the American people, especially those west of the Appalachians.

If the first quarter-century of the nation's independence established the United States as a boisterous adolescent, the next 50 years brought determined maturation. It was a period of reform and turmoil normally associated with growth and change, but it ended on a sad note. The American people, after disputing slavery and sectional issues for three decades, finally engaged in a suicidal conflict that resulted in the deaths of 600,000 of the nation's youths and inflicted lasting wounds of mental and spiritual anguish.

After 1815 the people west of the Appalachians sought to be heard in Washington—and their sheer numbers deserved an audience. Tennessee and Kentucky became states in the 1790s; Ohio and Louisiana were admitted a few years later; and within the first decade after the War of 1812, Mississippi, Alabama, Indiana, Illinois, and Missouri joined the Union. The Virginia and Massachusetts dynasty was challenged in the presidential contest of 1824, when Andrew Jackson outpolled all others for the presidency but was denied the office because of his failure to gain an electoral majority. Old Hickory's successes in the elections of 1828 and 1832, however, convinced even the most myopically conservative Easterners that Tennessee and the West were to be reckoned with. The subsequent election of James Knox Polk (widely hailed later as "Young Hickory" because of his attachment to Jackson) to the presidency on a westward expansion platform further strengthened Tennessee's place in the Union.

The half-century following the War of 1812 was an era of great expansion. Peaceful means sufficed to establish the northern boundary with English-owned Canada, but negotiations with Spain and a war with Mexico were necessary to adjust the boundaries in the South and West. As the nation grew, so did Tennessee: the Volunteer State was nearly doubled in size by the addition of the Chickasaw Territory between the Tennessee and Mississippi rivers, a vast area that the United States purchased for $300,000. So rapid was the intrusion of the white population immediately after the purchase that within a few weeks John Overton, Jackson, and other speculators had purchased large tracts for resale and then founded Memphis. During the next six years, 16 counties were established. The nation's population increased from 7 million people in 1810 to more than 31 million in 1860; Tennessee's jumped from 261,727 to 1,109,801.

The several decades after the War of 1812 have been described in Tennessee as "the era of Andrew Jackson." Obviously with some exaggeration, one journalist swore that even 10 years after the

Right: *Andrew Jackson was a friend and land speculation partner of John Overton's. In this portrait miniature by John Wood Dodge, painted in April 1842, President Jackson is seen in retirement, three years prior to his death. Courtesy, Tennessee State Museum*

Far right: *Judge John Overton (1766-1833), a friend and advisor to Andrew Jackson, helped to plan Jackson's political campaigns. Along with Jackson and James Winchester, he purchased the land that was to become Memphis, and promoted the settlement of that Mississippi River town. Courtesy, Tennessee Historical Society*

old hero's death in 1845, a few Tennessee backwoodsmen wrote Jackson's name in on their ballots whenever a presidential election rolled around. Actually, Jackson's years as a frontier idol were relatively short, and as a politician he was in some degree of disrepute even by the end of his second presidential term. However, the democratic reforms he initiated and his establishment of the Democratic party were sufficient to ensure that, even today, historians would cast him in heroic terms.

Tennesseans had rallied around John Sevier for a quarter of a century, but after the old Indian fighter's death in 1815, they looked for new leaders. The qualifications for leadership remained the same: candidates not only needed some civil and political experience, but they also must have attained success and recognition on the battlefield—regardless of who the enemy might have been.

Jackson, of course, met these criteria. Far from being the ignorant frontiersman depicted by the Eastern press during later presidential contests, Jackson had attended school in the Waxhaw, South Carolina, area of his birth. Through the years he had absorbed some degree of general knowledge and refinement. He had "read law" in Salisbury, North Carolina, and in 1788 had traveled with Judge John McNairy across the mountains to North Carolina's "western district." There he held an appointment as a prosecutor for the Nashville area.

Not long after reaching Nashville, Jackson met and married Rachel Donelson, daughter of Mrs. John Donelson, widow of one of Nashville's founders. A vivacious young woman, she had returned to her mother's home after an unsuccessful marriage had taken her for a few years to Kentucky. Unbeknown to Jackson, he had married her before her divorce in the Kentucky courts became final, and this misfortune subjected him to ridicule for the rest of his life.

Despite the unfortunate mixup, the Jacksons soon were accepted by Nashville's budding frontier gentry. Most frontier leaders found Jackson politically acceptable and supported him when he ran for Congress in 1796. Two years later he served briefly in the U.S. Senate and then became a member of Tennessee's Superior Court. But it was his military success that brought him to the attention of the nation.

A small group of ambitious local political leaders, led by John Overton and sometimes referred to as the "Nashville Junto," began to groom Jackson for political office soon after his return from New Orleans in 1815. Overton, a lawyer, planter, banker, and land speculator, claimed thousands of acres in and around Nashville, and, after the Chickasaw Purchase of 1818, claimed thousands more in the Memphis area. He had met Jackson as early as 1789 in Nashville, and they had developed a fast friendship. Although he sought no office himself, Overton was a "power behind the throne," and he strengthened his position in the eastern counties through the support of two wealthy and powerful Knoxvillians—Hugh Lawson White (his brother-in-law) and Pleasant Miller, who had married a daughter of William Blount.

Jackson said little after returning to a hero's welcome, and he quietly took up the management of his vast plantation at the Hermitage in 1816. The following year the army put him in charge of the troops assigned to construct a federal road from Nashville to Natchez, and in 1818 he was dispatched with troops to the Georgia-Florida boundary to clear the area of marauders. He soon invaded Spanish Florida, destroyed several military posts, drove the governor and garrison out of Pensacola, and returned to Nashville amid great acclaim. Although his actions brought the Monroe administration considerable embarrassment in its dealings with Spain, Jackson heard Nashville orators describe him as one whose conduct was "marked with energy, valor, skill, and patriotism, not surpassed in the annals of our country." His actions facilitated the purchase of Florida by the United States, and in 1821 he was appointed military governor of the territory. He soon returned, however, to his home in Nashville—to retire, he said, "to the pleasures of domestic felicity." In actuality, it was probably to listen to the wooing of the Overton group and the plans they had developed for him.

Jackson did not have long to wait. The following year, legislators, who convened in Murfreesboro (the new capital), nominated him for president and described him as a person who was "calm in deliberation, cautious in decision, and efficient in action." Although the election was two years away, John C. Calhoun, William C. Crawford, Henry Clay, and John Quincy Adams already had been nominated by people in their respective home states.

In 1823 the Jackson group embraced bold strategy. U.S. Senator John Williams of Knoxville, an enemy of Jackson since the days of their military activity in the Creek War, sought reelection. The Overton crowd had deliberated over whether to offer the "Chief" (Jackson) as a senatorial candidate, run him for governor against William Carroll, or let him appear untested in the presidential campaign a year hence. After consideration they determined upon the Senate race. Accordingly, Jackson appeared before the legislators in October and was chosen by a vote of 35 to 25. He later confided to his friends his deep regret at having to leave Rachel and his business interests in Nashville, but his supporters attached considerable significance to the victory and believed that it unquestion-

Hugh Lawson White (1773-1840) was a leading citizen of Knoxville in the early years of settlement. His father had founded the town. White had a long and eventful life; he served on the state Supreme Court, and was a U.S. district attorney, president of the Bank of Tennessee, a soldier with Andrew Jackson in the Creek War, and a U.S. senator. Courtesy, Tennessee Historical Society

Henry Clay (1777-1852) ran for the presidency three times, and was defeated each time. He was an anti-Jacksonian Whig. Courtesy, Tennessee Historical Society

ably added much to his stature as a presidential possibility.

In the presidential race that followed, Jackson received 99 electoral votes while Adams got 84, Crawford 41, and Clay 57; Calhoun had determined to seek the vice presidential seat. No candidate had a majority of the votes cast, and House members sought Clay's advice. The able Kentuckian, then speaker of the House, urged the congressmen to vote for Adams, and his influence prevailed. When President-elect Adams announced that Clay would be his choice for secretary of state, Jackson exploded. A "corrupt bargain" obviously had been made between the two, he charged, and he promptly vowed to defeat "the New England Puritan" and the "Judas of the West" at the earliest opportunity. He resigned his Senate seat and returned to Nashville determined to devote his waking hours to preparations for the next election.

Jackson opened his 1828 campaign with the "corrupt bargain" theme. Adams' supporters responded by describing Jackson as an illiterate frontiersman unprepared by training or experience to be the nation's chief executive; animadversions ranged from peddling slaves to dueling, and from association with Aaron Burr to misconduct in Florida.

Despite the mudslinging Jackson won handily, and he became the first president from a state west of the Appalachians. He carried the South and West solidly. More than twice the number of Tennesseans who voted in 1824 were counted at the polls in 1828. Sadly, Rachel lived only long enough to see Jackson elected; she died of congestive heart failure shortly before the inauguration.

In the meantime Tennesseans were busy with other political contests and the usual social and economic problems that faced frontier people. Joseph McMinn, at first a very popular governor after his election in 1815, ended his three terms in 1821 in disrepute, largely because of the persistent financial depression in the state and the nation. Many small banks collapsed. The State Bank of Knoxville (with nearly a dozen branches across the state) and the Bank of Nashville were among the urban banks that experienced serious trouble.

William Carroll next became governor. He was in office for 12 years (1821-1827 and 1829-1835), and helped restore prosperity soon after his first inauguration. The "reform governor," as he came to be called, led Tennesseans in the direction of solid and progressive legislation, including constitutional reform. Between Carroll's two six-year stints as governor, Sam Houston was elected governor. He married a young Sumner County woman, but, tiring of the governor's office, he soon left for Texas, where he became involved in the movement for Texas independence. William Hall filled out the few months remaining in Houston's term but exhibited no interest in reelection. Carroll thus returned for six more years.

* * *

Andrew Jackson was a strong-willed individual, and despite the fact that he was "the hero of the common man," he had made enemies through the years among the prominent home folk and other people who knew him best. Therefore, it is of special interest that the southern wing of the Whig party, which developed in

1834-1835 in opposition to Jackson, began in Tennessee.

The Volunteer State had entered the Union as a stronghold of the Republicans (Jeffersonian Republicans, not to be confused with the Republicans of today). Factions developed immediately, and by Jackson's time at least two combinations could be readily discerned. The faction led by John Overton (who died in 1833) traced its origins to the followers of William Blount. The constituency of the other faction, which traced its beginnings to John Sevier, varied from time to time but found its expression until Jackson's second term mainly through Senator John Williams, Andrew Erwin, Newton Cannon, and David Crockett. This group of politicians had to tread softly lest they arouse the animosity of old veterans and other groups who worshipped Jackson. Nevertheless, Jackson did little to placate those who did not like him, and the group grew and attained full flower by 1835.

Two newcomers to the anti-Jackson camp—John Bell and Hugh Lawson White—were leaders of national reputation who had nominally supported Jackson until 1835. Neither had nourished a deep-seated admiration for Jackson, but they had realized the political expediency of nominal support after the Chief's election to the presidency.

Above: Rachel Jackson (1767-1828), the wife of Andrew, was the greatest pleasure in the life of her husband. He defended her honor on several occasions, and even killed one man in a duel. She did not live to see her husband win the presidency. Courtesy, Tennessee Historical Society

Left: Sam Houston (1793-1863) served as governor of Tennessee from 1827-1829. Tiring of the governorship and separated from his wife, he resigned and moved to Texas. He was a friend and ally of Andrew Jackson. Courtesy, Tennessee Historical Society

Far left: William Hall (1775-1856) served out the few remaining months of Sam Houston's term as governor in 1828, after Houston resigned and went to Texas during that state's bid for independence from Mexico. Courtesy, Tennessee Historical Society

John Bell (1796-1869), a lawyer and member of both the Tennessee General Assembly's House and its Senate, ran for president in 1860 on the Constitutional Union ticket. Courtesy, Tennessee Historical Society

Martin Van Buren succeeded Andrew Jackson in the White House in 1837. This portrait was done at the Hermitage by W.B. Cooper in 1842. Courtesy, Tennessee Historical Society

Jackson traditionally had refused to support Bell, a fellow Nashvillian, and actually had used his influence against Bell first when Bell had sought a congressional seat in 1825 and later when he had been elected speaker of the House. In the meantime Governor Carroll and others had left the Jackson camp, but the most significant defection of all was that of Hugh Lawson White—a man to whom Jackson had offered a cabinet post earlier. Jackson's alienation of conservative bankers and businessmen such as White in both Knoxville and Nashville, and his treatment of Clay and Calhoun continued to disturb some who had cherished Clay's leadership and Calhoun's championship of states' rights.

Despite these rumblings of discontent Jackson's national popularity still would have enabled him to remain in control of his home state had he not been resolute in his determination to select Martin Van

Buren for his successor as president. Jackson's affection for Van Buren, a New Yorker who had not supported him until 1828, had been highly disconcerting to many Tennesseans—especially those who hoped to see Hugh Lawson White succeed Jackson as president. These Tennesseans believed White could win if Jackson would support him or at least maintain a hands-off position. A majority of Tennessee congressmen in December 1834 had endorsed the Knoxvillian for president, and early in the following year most of the state newspapers pledged their support. Bell, whom Jackson soon greatly blamed for the formation of the Whig party (as the opponents of Jackson had begun to call themselves), rallied supporters for White. Among other White supporters was Newton Cannon, who as a Whig was elected governor by a sound majority in the fall of 1835; the Bell-White-Cannon party in Tennessee then secured control of the legislature, which promptly nominated White for president.

Unfortunately for White, those who opposed Jackson in the North turned to favorite-son candidates. In the election that followed, the Whig vote was divided, and Van Buren was the victor. Tennesseans, however, voted solidly for White. White won the eastern and western counties by substantial majorities, and these counties became Whig strongholds for the next 20 years. Indeed, the political map jelled for the next two decades; of the 65 counties publishing returns in the presidential elections, 53 continued for 20 years to support the same party they had supported in 1836.

While Tennesseans at home fought political battles, others who had sought their fortunes in Texas fought to cast aside the Mexican yoke. Tennesseans had been among the first Anglo-Americans to migrate to Texas when the territory was opened to settlement—first by Spain and then by Mexico after its independence in 1821. Many Tennesseans joined the colonies of such men as Stephen F. Austin and Sterling C. Robertson; still others trekked across Arkansas and into Texas

on their own. The promise of free or inexpensive land drew hundreds who had suffered financial reverses in the Panic of 1819 or who simply sought a fresh start.

Typical of the latter were Sam Houston and David Crockett. Houston headed for Texas early in 1829. By 1833 he was chairman of a committee that wrote the Texas constitution, and by November 1835 he was commander-in-chief of the Texas military forces. Crockett, a member of Congress from West Tennessee, was defeated for reelection in 1834 by Jackson-backed candidate Adam Huntsman. When he saw the election returns, Crockett reportedly told his constituents that they could "go to hell," but he was going to Texas. He was killed at the Alamo a few months later.

The political revolution of 1835-1836 was a serious blow to the Jackson party and to the spirit and well-being of Andrew Jackson. The Chief had quietly returned to the Hermitage when his term ended—never again to seek office but rather to discuss for the remainder of his life, with the Democrats who visited, the "damnable apostasy" of the home folk who had deserted him in 1836. With Overton dead, Jackson looked to James Knox Polk as his closest friend and one who could restore the Democratic party to power in Tennessee.

Although Polk became governor in 1839, he could not accomplish the impossible, and for two decades the Whig

David Crockett (1786-1836) engaged in hunting, farming, trapping, milling, distilling, politics, and military activities. He served in the Tennessee House, and in the U.S. House of Representatives. When defeated in 1834 for his congressional seat, he told his Tennessee constituents they "could go to Hell, I'm going to Texas." He died there fighting at the Alamo. Courtesy, Tennessee Historical Society

Above: *James K. Polk campaigned for Martin Van Buren in Knoxville in 1840. This painting depicts that event. Courtesy, Tennessee Historical Society*

Right: *James K. Polk, before being elected president, served as congressman for more than a decade, helping to organize Tennessee's Democratic party. Courtesy, Tennessee Historical Society*

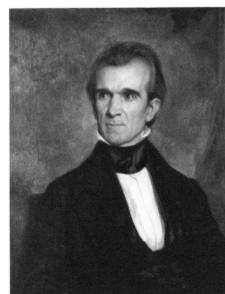

party battled the Democrats on even terms. Perhaps it was the Whig style of campaigning—with brass bands and free barbecues—or perhaps it was just the Tennesseans' love for partisan politics that helped the Whigs remain in power. At any rate the parties alternated in the governor's seat, with elections decided every two years by close margins. The legislative and congressional seats also were about equally divided.

Polk, a well-respected congressman for more than a decade, replaced Jackson as Tennessee's Democratic leader. Although he continued to hold his congressional seat until 1839, he spent a great deal of time during the two years after 1836 reorganizing the party down to the county and precinct levels. He spoke to groups across the state, sometimes taking Jackson with him if the trips were not too long and tiring. He was always careful to extol Jacksonian Democracy and to compare "modern Whiggery" to the Federalist party of Alexander Hamilton. His announcement in 1838 that he would seek the governorship in the following

year was hailed favorably by Jacksonians from Memphis to Bristol. Polk defeated Newton Cannon handily, but his charisma did not hold much beyond that; in the presidential election of 1840, Tennesseans helped elect William Henry Harrison as the nation's first Whig president. The following year young Jimmy Jones, a Lebanon Whig, unseated Polk. Jones then defeated Polk again in 1843 when he tried to return to the statehouse.

Polk, like Jackson, did not take his rejection by the people lightly, and he returned to his home in Columbia determined not to seek high office again. He therefore was probably as surprised as anyone when, on the ninth ballot, national Democrats nominated him for president over Van Buren and others. Henry Clay, who had lost presidential races twice when Andrew Jackson was a candidate, became the Whig nominee. Although Polk lost Tennessee to the Kentuckian by 100 votes, he won the presidency and thus became the second Tennessean in two decades to occupy the White House. Jackson, who died in June 1845, lived long enough to hail Polk's inauguration as a significant return of the Democrats to power.

The chief planks in Polk's presidential platform had concerned the annexation of Texas and the settlement of the Oregon dispute. He was able to accomplish both, although a war with Mexico was

necessary to gain the vast area known as the Mexican Cession. Tennessee, already known over the nation as the Volunteer State, supplied more troops than any other state; initially 2,800 men were called from Tennessee for service, but more than 25,000 volunteered.

Polk, already ill in the final days of his presidency, did not seek reelection. When his term expired in early March, he returned home immediately and died three months later. Zachary Taylor, a Whig, was elected president in 1848, and Franklin Pierce, a Democrat, in 1852; in each case a majority of Tennesseans voted for the Whig candidate.

In the meantime Democrat Aaron Brown succeeded Jones as governor, but he soon was replaced by Neil Brown, a Whig. After the war with Mexico veteran William Trousdale was elected governor. "The Warhorse of Sumner County" had fought as a youth in the Creek War and then with Zachary Taylor in Mexico. Democrats rallied behind him, and he was able to unseat Brown by 1,000 votes. His stay was also short, however, since the Whigs groomed Judge

James C. Jones (1809-1859) was twice elected governor of Tennessee, serving from 1841 to 1845. He instructed the General Assembly to make a final determination of the location for the state capital. Courtesy, Tennessee Historical Society

Part of the war booty brought back to Tennessee following the Mexican War was Mexican President Santa Anna's wine chest. Courtesy, Tennessee Historical Society

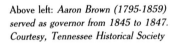

Above left: *Aaron Brown (1795-1859)
served as governor from 1845 to 1847.
Courtesy, Tennessee Historical Society*

Above center: *Neil Brown (1810-1886)
served as governor from 1847 to 1849.
Courtesy, Tennessee Historical Society*

Above right: *William Trousdale (1790-
1872), the "Warhorse of Sumner County"
who served with Zachary Taylor in the Mexican War, was governor from 1849 to 1851.
Courtesy, Tennessee Historical Society*

William B. Campbell, a Whig and war
hero, who won in 1851 by a small majority. This time the jubilant Whigs not
only captured the governor's seat but also
both houses of the legislature—a feat
that enabled them to elect Jimmy Jones,
now a Memphis businessman, to the U.S.
Senate over Trousdale.

The Whigs and Democrats were able
to cooperate in 1843 when they chose
Nashville as the permanent state capital.
Indeed, members of the constitutional
convention of 1834, somewhat wary because the seat of government had already
been at nearly a half-dozen sites, had
commanded the legislature of 1843 to locate the capital permanently. William
Blount had accomplished the territorial
business at Rocky Mount before moving
to Knoxville. Delegates to the first constitutional convention had provided that the
capital should remain there until at least
1802. When the constitutional limit expired, legislators had continued to meet
at the Knoxville courthouse. In 1807
they met in Kingston for a day (to fulfill
the terms of a treaty with the Cherokees)
but promptly returned the next day to
Knoxville, where the Assembly met until
1812. By that time more than 60 percent
of the population resided in the central
counties, and the capital went to Nashville. It was returned to Knoxville for one
year in 1817 and then moved to Murfreesboro. In 1826 it was returned to

Nashville, where it has remained.

The peripatetic nature of the capital
had prevented the building of a statehouse, but plans were soon developed,
with William Strickland as architect. An
out-of-the-way knoll one-half mile west
of the courthouse was chosen as the location. By 1853 the capitol was ready for
limited occupancy, and the legislature
has met there regularly since that time
except for the few years of Federal occupation during the Civil War.

Slavery became a political issue soon
after the development of the Whig party,
and arguments over its expansion ultimately became the major cause of the destruction of the national Whig party.
Blacks had first entered Tennessee with
Robertson, Sevier, and others who had
penetrated the wilderness west of Virginia and North Carolina and established
settlements. According to the census of
1790, about 10 percent of the people in
the new territory were black, the vast majority of them slaves. Soon after the central counties were opened for settlement,
their slave populations grew rapidly. In
the 1820s the opening of the rich West
Tennessee cotton lands drew many
planters with large numbers of slaves,
and more than 50 percent of some of the
southwest counties consisted of blacks.
Throughout the slaveholding period most
lived in West Tennessee, and comparatively few lived in the eastern counties.

Far left: *William Bowen Campbell (1807-1867) served as governor from 1851 to 1853. Courtesy, Tennessee Historical Society*

Left: *William Strickland (1788-1854) was one of the leading architects in America in the early nineteenth century. He designed Tennessee's State Capitol. Courtesy, Tennessee Historical Society*

The Tennessee State Capitol building took 14 years to build and cost nearly $1 million in pre-Civil War currency. It was considered as one of the architectural wonders of America at the time. Courtesy, James A. Hoobler

Tennessee was a state of small land-holdings and small slaveholdings except in a few of the western counties. Men like Montgomery Bell, who had 300 slaves, were rare—in fact, while a half-dozen owners held 200 slaves or more, Bell was the only one in the state with 300 or more slaves in 1850. In 1860 fewer than 40,000 families, out of a white population of more than 825,000, owned one or more slaves. The typical slaveholding family held one or two slaves who worked in the fields along with their owners.

Some Tennesseans were outspoken in their opposition to slavery. In 1819 Thomas Embree and his sons, Elijah and Elihu, had founded in Greeneville the first newspaper in the United States devoted entirely to antislavery agitation. A variety of manumission societies developed in the 1820s and described slavery as "absolutely incompatible with Christianity." Their membership numbered more than 1,000 people.

Colonization also was widely discussed, and in 1820 the Tennessee Colonization Society was formed with the express purpose of placing slaves in Africa or perhaps on uninhabited lands in the West. In 1833 state legislators voted to pay the society for each slave transported safely to Liberia. Earlier, "Nashoba," near Memphis, was begun as a colony designed to prepare slaves for freedom. Operated by Frances Wright, it thrived for a short while under the direction of the Scots reformer, who called upon slaveowners to place slaves in her colony where she would teach them to read and write in preparation for emancipation.

Delegates to the constitutional convention of 1834 vigorously debated slavery and considered a clause that would give legislators the power to emancipate slaves. A majority of the delegates, however, thought that the issue defied solution. If "left alone," delegates concluded, slavery surely would come to an end in "due time," as it had in England.

Widespread rumors and fears of planned insurrections during the 1840s and 1850s caused owners to tighten their grip on slaves. By the late 1850s most Tennesseans regularly defended slavery, although comparatively few of them held slaves. It was the race question, rather than an affection for slavery, that people refused to address properly, but by 1860 Tennesseans had joined the people of the

Bills of sale were issued on slaves bought and sold in Tennessee, just like with any other trade good. This 1829 bill of sale is for a black woman named Anny, aged "about twenty years." Courtesy, Tennessee State Museum

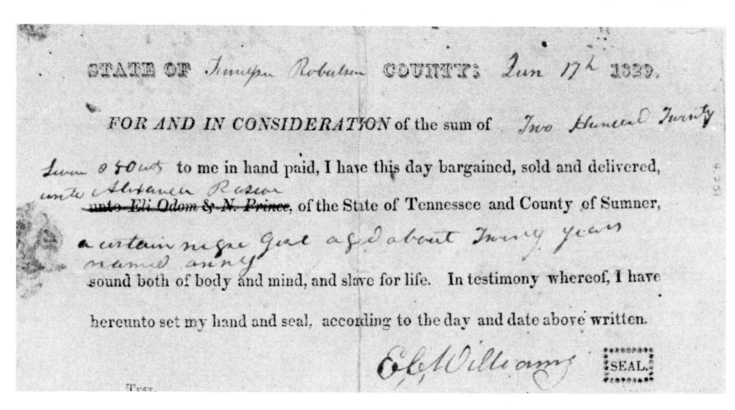

Deep South in defending an institution that most realized was as dehumanizing for whites as it was for blacks.

The election of Andrew Johnson as governor in 1853 brought both slavery and the decline of the Whig party into sharp focus. Johnson was an East Tennessean of humble origins who despised slavery but resented abolitionist and other antislavery agitation out of the North. John Bell, still the leader of the

Whigs in Tennessee, regretted the growing dissension within his party and forecast the Whig decline shortly after the presidential contest of 1852. Congressional arguments over the Kansas-Nebraska Act of 1854 sharpened the dissension when Northern and Southern Whigs could not agree on the question of the extension of slavery into the territories. By late 1854 Whigs were leaving the anti-Jackson party in rising numbers.

Black slaves were advertised in Tennessee newspapers as individual sale items, or as being available through a dealer. This illustration is a particularly telling one regarding the morals of the day. Blacks are being sold in the shadow of the capitol—Tennessee's shrine to democracy. This is from a business envelope. Courtesy, Tennessee State Museum

Johnson's strong appeal lured some into the Democratic party, but most became members of the new American ("Know Nothing") party, formed in 1854. A few East Tennessee Whigs even joined the new Republican party formed the same year.

The gubernatorial election of 1855, when Johnson stood for reelection, was a test of the American party's strength. Whig Congressman Meridith Gentry was among those who already had joined the new party, and he announced for governor early in the year. Many Whigs, including Knoxville newspaper editor

William G. Brownlow, rallied to his side. Although Gentry, as a Know Nothing, carried the old Whig strongholds of East and West Tennessee, Johnson's strength in the central counties, where the Democratic party had traditionally maintained large majorities, was sufficient for him to win a second term. Although his majority was small it sufficed to discourage other former Whigs, who failed to display much enthusiasm in the presidential election of the following year. Although Andrew Jackson Donelson, Jackson's nephew and former personal secretary, led Tennessee Know Nothings to their presidential convention in 1856 and won the party's vice presidential nomination, a majority of Tennesseans still voted for Democrat James Buchanan. They thus brought the state back into the folds of Jacksonian Democracy for the first time since 1832.

Democrats faced the gubernatorial contest of 1857 with a great deal of confidence. Johnson, who chose to await the 1858 senatorial election, did not run again, and the Democrats chose Isham G. Harris, a conservative politician of considerable skill, who already had served in both the state legislature and Congress. Remnants of the Whigs, Know Nothings, and a few anti-administration Democrats joined in what they called the "Opposition party" and chose Robert Hatton of Lebanon. But

Harris' resounding majority of 11,000 votes brought him widespread recognition, and he had no difficulty two years later in defeating his principal challenger, former Whig John Netherland.

By this time some leaders in the states of the Deep South talked of "Southern independence." Many new developments in the 1850s had frightened conservative Southerners—the talk among Northern legislators of stopping the expansion of slavery into the territories, the rapid development of the Republican party with its expressed determination to eradicate slavery, the reaction of the Northern press to the Dred Scott case, and the raid at Harpers Ferry, Virginia. Governor Harris, a slaveholder and a firm sympathizer with the South, told legislators soon after his inauguration of his latent fear of the "reckless fanatics of the North" and his belief that the "right of revolution" might have to be exercised should they persist. He urged Tennesseans to seek "wise, temperate, and calm firm counsel," and hoped that such would enable the country to "avert the impending evils."

Democrats held majorities in both the nation and Tennessee as the time for the 1860 presidential election approached. They were far from united, however, and soon divided into two sectional groups: Northern Democrats nominated Stephen A. Douglas of Illinois while the southern group chose John C. Breckinridge of Kentucky. The old Whig remnants, operating in Tennessee as the "Opposition party" and in other states under other names, organized the Constitutional Union party and nominated John Bell for president. Deploring the agitation the slavery controversy had caused, they believed that a close adherence to the letter and spirit of the Constitution would preserve the Union, and that Bell's "superior qualifications" and "unswerving devotion to the Union and the Constitution" would render him an outstanding leader of the nation in a time of crisis.

The Republican party nominated Abraham Lincoln and won the election, although Lincoln received less than 40 percent of the nation's popular vote. In Tennessee he was the only candidate who received no support. Bell, with the help of the old Whig strongholds in East and West Tennessee, carried the state by 4,000 votes. Democratic Middle Tennessee voted for Breckinridge, and Douglas' support was almost entirely in the Memphis and Shelby County area.

The election of Lincoln—by one section of the country and less than 40 percent of the vote—precipitated immediate secession by the states of the lower South. Two days after the election, leaders in South Carolina convened and enacted an ordinance of secession. In February 1861 six Southern states established a provisional government in Montgomery, Alabama, with Jefferson Davis as president.

Tennesseans and residents of the other border states observed these activities with considerable interest but took no immediate action. The Democratic party, however, under the leadership of Governor Harris, assumed a decidedly pro-Southern stance. Harris called legislators into an extra session, where he urged them to submit to the people the question of whether to call together a convention of delegates to decide if Tennessee should join the seceded states. Accordingly, on February 4, 1861, voters rejected the convention concept by a substantial vote. Only in West Tennes-

Robert Hatton (1826-1862) was an old line Whig. He served in the General Assembly from 1855 to 1857, and then ran unsucessfully for governor. He opposed secession, but once Tennessee seceded, he raised Company H, 7th Tennessee Infantry, C.S.A. He was a brigadier general when he was killed in the Battle of Seven Pines in Northern Virginia. Courtesy, Tennessee Historical Society

see, where agricultural pursuits rendered the economy most like that of the Deep South, did a majority vote for a convention. Press accounts and speeches by legislators reflected what the people had indicated at the ballot box—that something more significant than the secession of a few Southern states would have to transpire before Tennessee would leave the Union.

That "something" was not long in coming. Lincoln was inaugurated early in April and conflict at Fort Sumter erupted a few days later. On April 15 Lincoln issued a call for 75,000 volunteers, and Tennesseans became aware that a peaceful solution to the controversy was no longer possible. Harris answered Lincoln's call with characteristic vigor. "Tennessee will not furnish a single man for purposes of coercion," he telegraphed authorities in Washington, but "50,000 if necessary for the defense of our rights and those of our Southern brothers." Announcing that "in such an unholy crusade no gallant son of Tennessee will ever draw a sword," he called for a second special session of the legislature to convene on April 25, and delegates were promptly chosen and assembled. Expressing strongly pro-Confederate sentiments, the delegates drafted a "Declaration of Independence . . . dissolving the Federal Relations between the State of Tennessee and the United States," but stipulated that to become effective such resolution would have to be endorsed by the people in a referendum set for June 8.

By this time three other border states—Arkansas, North Carolina, and Virginia—had joined the Confederacy, and their actions gave Tennessee Democrats considerable encouragement. The voices of Bell and other Unionists went unheard, and Tennesseans supported secession in the June 8 referendum by more than a two-to-one majority. On July 22, 1861, the Confederate government officially received Tennessee into the provisional government.

The people of most of the counties of East Tennessee stood firm for the Union—as they had in February—but voters in the central and western sections joined overwhelmingly with Harris and the secessionists. Within a few weeks even Bell and other Tennessee Unionists (with the exception of the loyal East Tennesseans) had become disillusioned with Lincoln's leadership and had pledged their support to the South.

Since it had become apparent that the Federal government planned to use force against the seceded states, Governor Harris hastily prepared Tennessee for its own defense. Earlier he had become convinced that Lincoln would send troops across Tennessee into Mississippi, Alabama, and Georgia, and in May he had sought to purchase 10,000 rifles with bayonets from a New Orleans firm. He appointed General Gideon J. Pillow commander of the Tennessee forces, and a

call for volunteers brought enough men to organize 22 regiments of infantry, 2 regiments of cavalry, 10 companies of artillery, an engineering corps, and an ordnance group.

In the meantime Harris' supporters made preparations for the governor's re-election. Opposed by a younger brother of the late James K. Polk, Harris gave little attention to the election and left the campaign to the vast majority of secessionists who supported him. Democrats and former Whigs united to give Harris a tremendous majority, and he became the first three-term governor since Carroll in the 1830s. Secessionists, who were in control of the Tennessee House and Senate, redistricted the state into 11 Confederate congressional districts, and elected two senators to the Confederate Congress along with the congressmen.

General Albert Sidney Johnston had been assigned as commander of the western Confederacy, and he hastily ordered forts built on the Tennessee and Cumberland rivers—rivers that military authorities recognized as veritable highways from Ohio into Tennessee and the lower South. Later in 1861 Harris urged Confederate President Jefferson Davis to return to Tennessee those state troops already fighting in Virginia, and at the same time he begged the governors of Alabama, Mississippi, and Louisiana to send troops to aid in Tennessee's defense.

Battle lines had scarcely been drawn when, in February 1862, General Ulysses S. Grant determined upon a combined land and water assault against the two nearly completed river forts (which had been named for the Donelson

Above: *Albert Sidney Johnston was the Confederate commander for the Western theater, the area between the Appalachians and the Mississippi River, in 1861. He began the construction of fortifications along Tennessee's borders. He died later at Shiloh. Courtesy, Tennessee State Library and Archives*

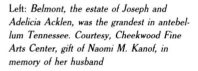

Left: *Belmont, the estate of Joseph and Adelicia Acklen, was the grandest in antebellum Tennessee. Courtesy, Cheekwood Fine Arts Center, gift of Naomi M. Kanof, in memory of her husband*

Union forces attacked Fort Donelson in February 1862 both by land and from the river. In a two-day battle, General U.S. Grant won its unconditional surrender, and earned himself the nickname of Unconditional Surrender Grant. These engravings are based upon sketches by Alexander Simplot. Courtesy, James A. Hoobler

family and for Confederate Senator Gustavus Henry of Clarksville). Fort Henry, on the Tennessee River, was armed with only 12 cannons and was no match for the 65 heavy naval guns with which the Federals bombarded the fort. The Confederates quickly surrendered and moved their troops across the narrow neck of land to Fort Donelson on the Cumberland. Scarcely had the reinforcements arrived when Grant appeared on February 13 with both land and water forces. After two days of battle the Confederates surrendered, and most were marched to prisons in Illinois. Only Nathan Bedford Forrest and his cavalry unit were able to escape. The names of Grant and Forrest, hitherto unknown, now became household words as both men continued to wage war with considerable success during the next few years.

Defenseless and panic-stricken, Nashvillians began to prepare to receive Federal troops, and within a few days General Don Carlos Buell rode triumphantly into the capital. Federal troops then moved hastily southward with plans to invade Mississippi and the lower South.

Johnston, who was not at Donelson when the fort fell, organized a new army to defend northern Mississippi. By April 1862 he had amassed 40,000 soldiers at Corinth. He determined to meet the enemy forces, which, under Grant, were concentrating just south of Savannah, near Pittsburg Landing on the Tennessee River.

Upon hearing that Buell was en route from Nashville to join Grant, Johnston determined to march northward immediately and attack the Federal forces. On April 6 he took the Union commander by surprise, and, in the vicinity of a small Methodist church named Shiloh, one of the bloodiest battles of the war was fought. Although the Confederates prevailed on the first day, they would be weakened following the arrival of Buell in the night with 30,000 fresh troops, which helped turn the tide; the Confederate troops thereupon retreated slowly to Corinth.

As significant as was the loss of the battle, an even greater loss was that of Johnston, who became a battlefield casualty. The Texan had cast his lot with the Confederacy at the beginning of the war, and he had held a command equal to that of Robert E. Lee in the East. Late in the first day of battle he had received a stray shot in the rear of his right thigh; in minutes he was unconscious from loss of blood, and he died before help could be summoned. Governor Harris, who had joined Johnston's new army as an aide, was at his side when he died.

Braxton Bragg soon replaced Johnston, and he determined upon a vigorous campaign designed to drive the enemy from Tennessee. First, however, he invaded Kentucky. He hoped thereby to both win that state to the Confederacy and reprovision his troops with supplies from the rich bluegrass country. After several engagements he established his headquarters at Murfreesboro and in early November made plans to dislodge the Federals from Nashville, now under the command of General W.S. Rosecrans.

Upon learning of the concentration of Confederate troops on Stones River, Rosecrans marched toward Bragg. He arrived on the evening of December 30 and encamped for the night very near the Confederate outposts—so close that the regimental bands competed in their renditions of patriotic tunes, and troops joined in singing songs of home. At daybreak on the following day, the battle began, and by nightfall both sides held their field positions. The troops rested on January 1, 1863, but on the following

day the Federals drove their enemy from the field. The Confederates soon went into winter quarters some 40 miles east of Murfreesboro.

With the advent of good weather in the spring, however, Rosecrans moved toward Bragg's Army of Tennessee and slowly pushed it eastward and southward into Chattanooga and toward Chickamauga. Finally, on September 18, Bragg surprised Rosecrans just north of the Chickamauga River and pushed him back to Chattanooga. Rosecrans soon was replaced by General George H. Thomas, who, with help from Grant and William T. Sherman, drove the Confederates south, where they took up winter quarters at Dalton.

The last of the military activity in Tennessee came at the end of 1864. John Bell Hood, a West Point graduate who had served in Texas under Johnston, replaced Bragg as commander of the Army of Tennessee; he determined upon a bold strategy in his efforts to regain the state. "The Gallant Hood," as a later generation of historians described him, was 31 when he assumed command. His left arm

Below left: *William S. Rosecrans replaced General Don Carlos Buell as the Federal commander in the West after the Kentucky campaign of 1862. Courtesy, Tennessee State Library and Archives*

Below: *The Battle of Stones River took place outside of Murfreesboro on December 31, 1862, and January 2, 1863. Federal general Rosecrans defeated Confederate general Bragg, and drove the Confederates into Tullahoma to the south for the winter. Courtesy, James A. Hoobler*

had been shattered at Gettysburg; at Chickamauga he had undergone a battlefield amputation of his right leg. Although some people questioned Jefferson Davis' judgement in giving the command to a person whose only useful arm carried a crutch, Hood accepted the command with confidence and determination.

Hood's "bold strategy" was to swing northward and regain Nashville and the rest of Tennessee with frontal assaults. More the "dreamer" than the "bold one," he even spoke of moving toward Louisville and Cincinnati after taking Nashville, and of ultimately joining Lee at Richmond. While Sherman wreaked havoc in Georgia as he marched unimpeded toward Atlanta, Hood's barefoot and poorly armed troops moved toward Nashville.

Finally, on November 29, 1864, Hood reached the vicinity of Franklin and engaged the Federals in bloody conflict. After losing some of his best men and officers, Hood, undaunted, moved on to Nashville—a town described by the Federals as the best fortified city in the nation. In a two-day encounter (December 15-16), Hood found his ill-equipped men no match for the larger and well-armed Federal force. Demoralized and thoroughly defeated, the Army of Tennessee retreated southward and fought

no more in the Volunteer State. Four months later Lee surrendered at Appomattox.

Nearly 100,000 Tennesseans fought for the South, and approximately one-half that number for the North. The death toll of Tennesseans in both armies was large. For many who did return home after the war, survival was but a reprieve—weakened and diseased from months of deprivation and suffering, many filled premature graves. Amputation of limbs had been the only defense against gangrene and infection, and most of the maimed men were unfit for the demands of heavy farm labor.

Although more than 50 Tennesseans held the ranks of general or admiral in the Federal or Confederate forces, only Nathan Bedford Forrest became widely known. The Memphis slave dealer possessed great natural ability as a cavalry leader and was active in many battles. But perhaps the most beloved state hero held the rank of private—young Sam Davis. The 21-year-old youth served as a Coleman scout and was captured and hanged as a spy by the Federals near Pulaski in November 1863. "I would die a thousand deaths before I would betray a friend," he exclaimed, when Federal officers at the scaffold offered him his life in exchange for information that would

The Battle of Lookout Mountain was part of the fighting in the campaign for Chattanooga in November 1863. General U.S. Grant was sent to Chattanooga to break the Confederate siege, which he accomplished in battles at Missionary Ridge, Lookout Mountain, and Orchard Knob. Courtesy, James A. Hoobler

enable them to break the spy ring.

While soldiers on the battlefields saw conditions worsen as the war progressed, the folks back home also increasingly felt the cold hand of war as the months passed and the scarcity of food and clothing became more pronounced. When panicked Nashvillians fled upon hearing of the collapse of Fort Donelson, a lawless element remained and looted the city. Legislators hastily adjourned with the expressed intention of reassembling in Memphis, and Governor Harris fled south to the safety of the Confederate lines. The Reverend Collins D. Elliott, president of the Nashville Female Academy, made immediate preparations to remove student boarders from Nashville before the arrival of Grant's troops.

By 1863 shortages of food and manpower had become acute statewide, and deprivation in the cities greatly exceeded that of the rural areas. But farmers also suffered; their fields, once flourishing with corn and cotton, were covered with weeds because of the inadequate labor supply. The fact that military authorities gave furloughs at planting and harvesting times kept many people from starving. Coffee, sugar, and drugs became almost nonexistent, but—thanks to a group of women organized as the "Southern Ladies Aid Society"—quinine and other medicines were smuggled across the lines under women's long, flowing skirts.

After Donelson fell, Federal troops soon occupied most of the state, and Lincoln determined to place it under a

The Battlefield of Franklin, looking north from Winstead Hill. It was from this position that General John Bell Hood sent his men marching in file across these open fields at dusk, in wave after wave, lapping against the entrenchments of the Federals under Schofield. The Army of Tennessee suffered over 6,000 casualties. From Battles And Leaders Of The Civil War, *edited by R.U. Johnson and C.C. Buel*

The impeachment trial of President Andrew Johnson took place in the House of Representatives in Washington. Thaddeus Stevens, one of Johnson's greatest foes, is seated in the right foreground. Courtesy, Tennessee State Museum

military governorship headed by Andrew Johnson. A U.S. senator after 1858, Johnson (a one-time slave-owner) had denounced the secession movement and determined to remain loyal to the Union. Lincoln gave him broad powers as military governor and urged him to remain in office until "the loyal inhabitants" could be returned to power. Johnson was elected vice president on the Lincoln ticket in 1864. Realizing that the war would soon be over, he called together Tennessee Unionists, who, on March 4, elected William G. Brownlow as governor.

Brownlow, Tennessee's Reconstruction governor, served from 1865 to 1869. Born in Virginia, he had grown up in the southern Appalachians. As a young man he had worked as a carpenter and as a circuit-riding Methodist preacher. Already an admirer of Henry Clay and John Bell, he became active in politics with the rise of the Whigs and later edited the Knoxville *Whig*. During the war he was in demand throughout the North as an authority upon the South and Southern conditions.

The new governor, eloquent with tongue and pen, talked of severe retribu-

tion against the former Confederates but actually did little of either a negative or positive nature—other than try to maintain himself and his faction in power. He told one group that prominent Confederates should be rounded up and executed en masse. With no real intent of paying $5,000 for the arrest of former Governor Harris, he proclaimed that such a reward would be paid to anyone who would deliver "this culprit Harris" in chains.

Soon after the war ended the Republican Unionists—firmly entrenched in power—divided into "Radicals" and "Conservatives." The former, led in Tennessee by Brownlow, supported a harsh Reconstruction plan designed to reduce the rebels to a state of poverty. Conservatives, however, followed Lincoln's more lenient plan, which, in his words, would "bind up the nation's wounds, forget the scars of war," and enable the people of both North and South to "again live in peace and harmony." Although Brownlow was seriously challenged by the Conservatives in the election of 1867, his Radical support was sufficient for him to win a second term.

Andrew Johnson became president

with the assassination of Lincoln in April
1865. Although earlier he had talked in
terms pleasing to the Radicals, after his
inauguration he took a Conservative position and vowed to carry out Lincoln's
concept of leniency. He sought to have
Tennessee fully restored to the Union
before 1865 ended, but the Radical Congress refused to seat the Tennessee
congressional delegation until the state
legislature had ratified the 14th Amendment. It was midsummer of the following
year before Congress recognized the government of Tennessee and fully restored
it to its former position in the Union. Tennessee, having been the last of the
southern states to join the Confederacy,
became the first to be restored to the
Union.

President Johnson's inclination toward a lenient plan for Reconstruction
disturbed the national Radicals, and
in 1868 they brought impeachment
charges against him in an effort to remove
him from office. Tennessee's Radical
congressmen played an active role in de-
manding an impeachment trial. Tennessee's two senators, Joseph H. Fowler and
David Patterson (Johnson's son-in-law),
voted for acquittal. One vote spared
Johnson the disgrace of conviction.

A lawless group known as the Ku Klux
Klan was formed in Pulaski shortly after
the war and soon spread throughout the
South. For several years it engaged in
acts of violence, and it soon clashed with
the Freedmen's Bureau. The bureau's
principal duty was to help former slaves
adjust to a free society. Relief funds and
supplies were distributed, contracts with
black workers supervised, and schools
established.

Forty-one schools with 9,000 pupils
were in operation in Tennessee by September 1866, and many teachers came
in from Northern states. Unfortunately,
Klan members undertook to close as
many of the schools as possible and to
encourage Northern teachers to return to
their homes. Finally, the violence became so pronounced that Brownlow declared martial law in several of the
counties. It was largely through the work

of Clinton B. Fisk, who was in charge of
the Freedmen's Bureau in Tennessee,
that the schools functioned at all.

Brownlow was elected to the U.S.
Senate as Patterson's replacement, and
he resigned as governor in February
1869. Speaker of the Senate DeWitt C.
Senter became governor. The Radical
Republicans, aware of the gubernatorial
election to be held later in the year, were
unable to agree upon a single candidate,
and both Senter and Congressman
William B. Stokes were nominees. The
Conservatives determined not to nominate anyone but to support whoever appeared most favorable to their cause.
They initially rejected Senter, who, as a
member of the Senate, had supported
Brownlow. Yet they soon perceived that
his attitude toward Reconstruction fitted
more closely into their concepts and
those of Lincoln than did those of
Brownlow.

The right to vote had been denied
former Confederates after the war, and
enfranchisement became the major issue. Stokes proposed a gradual return
of the rebels to the ballot box which
would require each former Confederate,
through his legislators, to petition the legislature; that body would enfranchise on
an individual basis depending upon the
merits of the case. Senter, however, surprised both Radicals and Conservatives
by promising to remove all restrictions
should he be elected. Fortunately for
him, as governor he could appoint registrars of his own choosing. Consequently,
shortly before the election he removed
many Radical registrars and replaced
them with his friends; they promptly
opened the voting lists to everyone who
wanted to register and vote. Soon thousands of former Confederates were
proudly announcing their intention of
carrying the day for Senter.

Senter won by a majority of more than
65,000 votes. Only five Radicals regained seats in the Tennessee Senate
and only 17 in the House. With the return of the reins of government to the
hands of the majority, Reconstruction
came to an end in Tennessee.

*DeWitt Clinton Senter (1830-1898) served
as governor from 1869 to 1871. He reenfran-
chised former Confederates in Tennessee.
Courtesy, Tennessee Historical Society*

The Nashville Inn was a fine hotel located
on the Public Square in Nashville, on the
northeast side. It was here that the wounded
Andrew Jackson was carried following his
brawl with Jesse and Thomas Benton in
1813. The inn burned down in 1856. Courtesy, Tennessee Historical Society

3

SOCIAL AND CULTURAL DEVELOPMENT

The vast majority of the people who came across the mountains to Tennessee were descendants of those who had emigrated to the New World from the British Isles. Although modern Tennesseans have long emphasized their "Scotch-Irish" heritage, historians have estimated that more than 80 percent of the white population were English. Descendants of the Scotch-Irish folk—Scots, who generations earlier had settled in Ireland, then moved to Pennsylvania, North Carolina, and Virginia, across the mountains to Watauga—easily constituted the second largest ethnic group. Nevertheless, there were others, and national origins on the frontier were diverse. John Carter and Jacob Brown, for example, were English; the Robertsons and Donelsons were Scotch-Irish; the Demonbreuns and Seviers were French Huguenots; Evan and Isaac Shelby were Welsh; William Bean was a Scots Highlander; and Kasper Mansker was German.

Preachers and teachers arrived on the frontier soon after the hunters and herdsmen, and they had an important effect upon the speech patterns and learning habits of the frontiersmen. Although many itinerant ministers rode on horseback from Virginia or North Carolina to preach for a few weeks and then return, Samuel Doak came to Tennessee in October 1777 to stay. The first resident minister in the Tennessee territory, he brought with him impressive credentials: a number of books, a diploma signifying graduation from Princeton University, and a record of two years of successful teaching at Hampden-Sydney. Thomas Craighead, another Princeton graduate, arrived to preach in Nashville early in 1785. Soon came Hezekiah Balch, also a Princeton graduate, and others with sound credentials.

Libraries and good reading habits were by no means confined to the clergy. Many settlers brought copies of the Bible, a dictionary, and probably a volume of Shakespeare and a law book or two. Richard Henderson, for example, a North Carolinian who claimed thousands of acres, brought to the new settlement a 35-volume set of the works of Voltaire—not to mention copies of the *Holy Bible,* Dr. Johnson's *Dictionary,* Blackstone's *Commentaries,* and Smollett's *Letters.* Nashville merchant John Deadrick maintained a library of several hundred works, including six volumes of Shakespeare's plays, works by David Hume and the ever-popular Smollett, and books on geography and poetry. Daniel Smith of Sumner County brought many leather-bound volumes containing some of the best literature of England and France. At the time of the Civil War, when college libraries still were very small, Dr. James G.M. Ramsey, who lived near Knoxville, claimed thousands of volumes and boasted of the best library west of the Appalachians. Not everyone who wanted books, however, could afford them—a five-volume set of Shakespeare sold for five dollars, but that was the equivalent of 10 days of unskilled labor or a cattleman's 200-pound calf.

Not all of the frontiersmen read books or went to church; many sought "the

Right: *James G.M. Ramsey, whose* Annals of Tennessee *was completed shortly after the Civil War, was one of the state's early historians. He served as the president of the Tennessee Historical Society from 1874 to 1884. Courtesy, Tennessee Historical Society*

Far right: *Samuel Doak brought the Presbyterian church across the mountains, and established Washington College in 1780. The school, originally named Martin Academy, is still in existence near Jonesboro. Courtesy, Tennessee Historical Society*

more worldly pleasures." Horse racing was a sport followed by both men and women, and it afforded an opportunity for gambling. Everyone in the Nashville area had seen or heard of Jackson's "Truxton." Thomas Irvin's "Ploughboy" was a competitor of equal standing, and William H. Stokes' "Ariel" was also well-known. Cockfighting was popular among some of the men. Log rolling and house raising were very useful endeavors, and gave men an opportunity to socialize as well as accomplish the necessary construction. Skill with the flintlock rifle gave young men not only status in the community but also the ability to bring home a supply of wild turkeys, squirrels, venison, and bear. Boxing and wrestling matches—or a combination of both—were witnessed and participated in by many and could be expected at almost any kind of gathering. David Crockett told of attending a wedding party at which the bride and groom staged a wrestling match just before the vows were said. To the amusement of the guests, Crockett related, the buxom female threw the nervous groom to the ground "three times in a row."

Fighting sometimes got out of hand, and hundreds would join in a melee resulting in the discomfort and sometimes maiming of the less fortunate. Family feuds were sometimes settled in this way, but they usually were intensified by such

activity. At Elkton in Giles County on a summer day in 1816, for example, the Price family fought the McKinneys in what began as a contest between a youth from each family. Scarcely had the antagonists struck a dozen blows before half the crowd had stripped to fight; for hours the community echoed with the sounds of the free-for-all.

Frontier duels and tavern brawls were common, even though dueling was illegal after 1796. The law did not prevent upper-class men of high political position from "defending their honor" when affronted by other "gentlemen." Sam Houston, William Carroll, and Thomas Hart Benton were among those who fought. Before he became president, Andrew Jackson set an example for all: the doughty warrior was a key figure in more than a dozen episodes involving gunplay, horsewhipping, and caning.

Jackson fought only "gentlemen," and one encounter in 1803 involved Governor Sevier. Although ostensibly a friend of the governor, Jackson for several years had secretly gathered information that indicated Sevier had sought to defraud North Carolina of public lands equivalent in size to one-fifth of Tennessee. When Sevier campaigned successfully against Archibald Roane for governor in 1803, Jackson made his information public. But few people believed Jackson, and the allegations did little but raise the ire of the old Indian fighter. When in October, shortly after the election, the two encountered each other on the streets of Knoxville, neither was in a peacemaking mood. When Jackson boasted of his services to the state, Sevier touched a tender chord with his retort. "Services," Nollichucky Jack thundered as a crowd gathered, "I know of no services you have rendered the country except taking a trip to Natchez with another man's wife."

"An unearthly light invaded the blue eyes of Andrew Jackson," a Jackson biographer wrote, and both men displayed weapons. Friends separated them, however, and Jackson returned to his hotel to pen a challenge. The governor did not respond, and Jackson called him "a base coward and poltroon" in the Knoxville and Nashville newspapers. Although there was an exchange of letters and a chance meeting outside of Knoxville, they did not engage in a formal duel.

The next few years were a distressing time for Jackson. Debts and probably deep depression worried him, and he exhibited recklessness and a lack of respect for his own life and the lives of others. In the fall of 1804 he inserted in the Nashville *Gazette* his infamous "runaway slave ad," in which he offered not only a standard reward for the return of his slave but "ten dollars extra for every hundred lashes any person will give him, to the amount of three hundred." Following his altercation with Sevier, he engaged Secretary of State William Maclin in a dispute and fight. It ended when Jackson drew his sword, and Maclin, after throwing a brick at his antagonist, ran for his life. Soon Jackson resigned as judge and experienced such financial distress that he was forced to sell his home and a portion of his plantation. He applied for the position of governor of the Louisiana Territory in the belief that the salary would enable him to escape from financial distress, but his application was rejected by President Jefferson.

Not long thereafter Jackson risked his life in a duel with the best marksman in the West. Jackson had become engaged in se-

rious disputes with Captain Thomas Irwin and his son-in-law, Charles Dickinson, over trivia involving horse racing. Soon Jackson and Dickinson were publicly labeling each other as being "worthless," a "drunkard," a "poltroon," and a "coward." Jackson issued a challenge, and the two met on the Red River in Kentucky at daybreak on June 30.

At the appointed time and place, the two assembled with their entourages. Quick on the trigger, Dickinson fired; his bullet struck Jackson's breastbone, breaking two ribs but not otherwise seriously injuring him. Jackson took aim and squeezed the trigger, but his gun misfired. Then, he deliberately recocked the weapon and fired again—this time striking his adversary in the abdomen, mor-

David Crockett's Almanac *was full of fanciful tales of frontier life and of the exploits of David Crockett. This illustration depicts the table manners of a frontiersman. Courtesy, Tennessee State Library and Archives*

tally wounding him.

Jackson's wounds healed, but not his reputation. A large number of Nashville professionals and businessmen signed a petition of condolence as the word of Dickinson's death got around. The following year the Davidson County grand jury indicted Jackson for an assault upon one Samuel Jackson, but the attorney general did not prosecute.

During the next several years Jackson's financial position improved. He bought several hundred acres of land, purchased stock in a Nashville bank, and unsuccessfully sought a judgeship in the Mississippi Territory. Soon, however, he was engaged in another affair of violence—this time a tavern brawl—which again almost cost him his life.

Thomas Hart Benton and Jesse Benton, brothers who had moved from North Carolina to Franklin, were considered friends of Jackson. But in June 1813 Jesse, the younger of the two, fought William Carroll in a duel in which neither was seriously injured. Jackson served as Carroll's second. Thomas Benton was in Washington at the time, and, upon his return, he accused Jackson of encouraging the fight and upbraided him for doing nothing to prevent it. Talebearers and gossips magnified the quarrel.

Soon the Bentons were in Nashville

Thomas Hart Benton moved to Missouri after his fight with Andrew Jackson on the public square in Nashville. From the distance of an adjoining state, Jackson and Benton became political allies, while Benton served Missouri in the U.S. Senate. Courtesy, Tennessee State Library and Archives

on business, and Jackson, in the company of John Coffee, decided to face and perhaps horsewhip both of them. Learning that they were regaling themselves at the Talbot Hotel on the public square, Jackson burst into the bar and, with upraised whip, approached Thomas Benton with the words, "Now defend yourself, you damned rascal." Both pulled guns, and soon a half-dozen men were engaged in a brawl featuring gunplay, stabbing, wrestling, kicking, and shoving. Jesse finally fired in the direction of Jackson; he struck the general in the left shoulder just as Jackson got off a shot which went through Thomas Benton's coat sleeve. After Jackson fell to the floor, bleeding profusely, he was carried across the street to the Nashville Inn, where a team of doctors was summoned to repair a severed artery, and soon the general was on the road to recovery. The country already was at war with Great Britain, and Jackson, despite his wound, in a few weeks led troops to the Gulf Coast.

Whiskey drinking was common on the frontier and may have been a cause of the excessive violence and mayhem. Most farmers maintained a still, which they used to render up surplus grain into a supply of "red-eye" sufficient to keep off winter chills. Peter Cartwright, a Methodist circuit rider, testified that he had known many ministers and thousands of laymen who drank whiskey regularly; they gave many reasons, he said, such as alleviating the pains of rheumatism, keeping warm in cold weather, or simply celebrating an event such as a wedding or the birth of a baby. Bishop Francis Asbury had seen men drink moderately in Virginia taverns but was astounded at the bibulous habits of the Tennessee frontiersmen.

Excessive use of alcohol was condemned by both physicians and preachers, but nothing was said about the use of tobacco. Practically all men smoked, and many chewed—whether they were at home, in the fields, on the streets, in courthouses, or in church. Dr. Phillip Lindsley, president of the University of

Nashville, once told of standing for prayer in Thomas Craighead's Presbyterian congregation, and just behind him, a tobacco-chewing parishioner let loose such a salvo of tobacco juice onto Lindsley's pew that the professor was unable to find a dry spot to sit after prayer was concluded. Rachel Jackson, who smoked a corncob pipe, and her mother-in-law, Mrs. Robards, who dipped snuff profusely, were by no means unique among frontier women.

Most of the very early Presbyterian preachers were Princeton or other university graduates who also organized and taught schools. After the Great Revival of 1800, however, the number of ministers and congregations increased at such a rapid pace that some of the denominations licensed preachers who had acquired only the rudiments of an education. Many were "preacher-farmers" (a term used by Baptist leaders), who cultivated crops during the week and preached on Sundays. Abounding in grace and dedication if not literary attainment, some nevertheless became confused when they tried to read and explain passages from the Bible or preach from commentaries which might have come to their attention. One had read a description of John the Baptist calling him an "austere man," but he read "austere man" as "oysterman." He compared him to Peter and other disciples who were fishermen but who specialized in oysters.

Another, preaching on the topic "This Untoward Generation," read "untoward" as "untowered" and urged his congregation to "seek a tower of refuge." Still another, after hearing a contemporary preach on the text "The Lord is no Respecter of Persons," spoke the following Sunday on "The Lord is no Respectable Person." Peter Cartwright, a veteran frontier circuit rider, resented the presence of preachers of educational attainment and believed that some were sent by the devil and not by God. He wrote of one "fresh, green, young preacher" from the East, who thought that all Methodist preachers "were a poor, illiterate set

of ignoramuses . . . almost cannibals," who did more harm than good. Much more pleasing to him were ministers who, like himself, could motivate most congregations into "the jerking exercise" within minutes.

Presbyterians had arrived soon after the first permanent settlers, and had organized congregations and built log churches. Presbyterian ministers, who were plentiful in the Abingdon district of western Virginia, were the first to arrive, and by statehood in 1796 they could count at least 27 organized congregations between Bristol and Nashville. Probably the first church was one built near Blountville as early as 1773, although the Salem congregation, organized two years later in Washington County near Jonesboro by Samuel Doak, often is de-

Bishop Francis Asbury helped to establish Methodism in Tennessee. Courtesy, Tennessee State Museum

Dr. Phillip Lindsley, president of the University of Nashville, was a Princeton-trained Presbyterian. He built the University into one of the finest schools in the state, and was succeeded upon his retirement by his son John Berrien Lindsley. Courtesy, Tennessee Historical Society

scribed as the first. The Abingdon Presbytery had been expanded to include the western churches in both Virginia and North Carolina, but in 1785 it was divided. The new presbytery, Transylvania, had jurisdiction over the Kentucky and Cumberland Valley congregations. As the preachers organized churches they also established schools, and they soon were training other ministers for work on the frontier. At the beginning they were the state's most powerful religious influence due not only to their training and education but also to their zeal and energy.

On the scene almost simultaneously with the Presbyterians were preachers of the Baptist faith. After encountering opposition from leaders of the Church of England in the seaboard states, pioneer Baptist preachers and congregations crossed the mountains in search of religious freedom. The first Baptist preachers to settle in Tennessee were Matthew Talbot and Jonathan Mulkey, who arrived in Watauga and Carter's Valley, respectively, in 1775. The Buffalo Ridge Church in Washington County was established soon thereafter by Tidence Lane. By the time of statehood more than 20 churches had been organized in both the state's pockets of settlement.

Methodist groups had formed among members of the Church of England who desired a more personal religious experience than that afforded by the ritualistic Anglican Church. Methodists did not separate from the mother church until after the Revolution, but once Methodism became Americanized, leaders gained a strong foothold both on the seaboard and west of the mountains.

While Bishop Francis Asbury kept a watchful eye on the progress of the Methodist congregations and carefully recorded in his journal details of his 62 trips across the mountains into Tennessee, other pastors came to live among the parishioners. Jeremiah Lambert, the first resident pastor, was assigned to all of the Holston Conference soon after its formation in 1783. Four years later Benjamin Ogden arrived on the Cumberland. He

soon pastored a small church near the river in Nashville and organized other churches in the area.

Scholars have characterized the two decades after the Revolution as a time of moral laxity on the frontier. A European traveler visiting the West in 1798 was so astonished at the lack of morality among Knoxvillians that he wrote of his belief that "the Devil" probably had taken up residence in Knoxville. That same year the Presbyterian General Assembly noted "with pain and fearful apprehension" a "general dereliction of religious principles and practices among our fellow citizens" to the extent that "profaneness, pride . . . intemperance, lewdness, and every species of debauchery and loose indulgence greatly abound."

Perhaps it was a coalition of moral dereliction and ministerial zeal that brought about the Great Revival of 1800. Beginning in Kentucky in 1799 the movement soon spread to Tennessee with significant results. Both Methodist and Presbyterian preachers conducted services, and thousands gathered for camp meetings and protracted revivals.

Thousands of people who had not professed any faith joined one of the churches during this period. Methodist preachers were the most enthusiastic participants in the revivals, and they reaped the most new members as people responded to the lack of ritualistic demands and the Arminian views of John Wesley, who had placed emphasis upon freedom of will. The organized system of circuits, in which some ministers zealously traveled as many as 500 miles during a year, added to the Methodists' success. By 1808 five Methodist districts claimed several thousand members in the western area. At mid-century the Methodists boasted of more than 1,000 churches scattered from Memphis to Bristol, with at least one in every county.

Most Presbyterian ministers became appalled at the physical extravagances of the revival and withdrew support, but a few preachers in the Cumberland area wanted to continue. In 1810 they orga-

Far left: *Barton W. Stone, a founder of the Disciples of Christ and the Church of Christ, was an active frontier preacher in Tennessee during the "Great Revival." Courtesy, Tennessee State Library and Archives*

Left: *Alexander Campbell was the person chiefly responsible for the successful creation of what would ultimately become the Disciples of Christ and the Church of Christ. Through his dynamic public speaking he built up the new church on the western frontier. Courtesy, Tennessee State Library and Archives*

nized the Cumberland Presbyterian Church, which was designed to doctrinally and spiritually accommodate the frontier mind. Claiming a "medium theology"—between Calvinism and Arminianism—the Cumberland Presbyterians grew rapidly, and their membership at mid-century was just behind the Tennessee Methodists and Baptists.

A second new group, the Disciples of Christ, was also an outgrowth of the religious instability of the time. Barton W. Stone, a Presbyterian minister, repudiated the rigidity of Calvinism and also adopted the baptismal methods of the Baptists. Alexander Campbell deprecated all "human creeds," urged unity among all Christians, emphasized an interpretation of the Scriptures as he saw them, and proclaimed baptism by immersion a necessity for salvation. The eloquent and able Campbell preached in Nashville and the surrounding area many times and was primarily responsible for the success of the group—variously called Disciples of Christ, Christians, and Churches of Christ. The denomination ranked fifth in size among the Tennessee Protestants by 1860.

Stephen Theodore Badin, who arrived in Knoxville in 1808, was the first Catholic priest to settle in Tennessee. His acquaintance with Governor Sevier may have been why he came to Tennessee and why he preached in the Knox County

courthouse in Knoxville upon his arrival. In 1819, when the Nashville Bridge Company brought 30 skilled Irish bridge builders and their families from Pittsburgh to construct a span across the Cumberland, the shocked Irish workers threatened to leave upon learning that Nashville did not have a priest who regularly celebrated mass. Father Robert A. Abell was dispatched to Nashville the following year; he helped the Irish workers build a small frame church near the present location of the capitol, and he became the first resident priest in Nashville. Abell was transferred to Louisville in

Left: *Father Stephen Theodore Badin was the first Roman Catholic priest to settle in Tennessee. Other priests had passed through the area with Spanish and French explorers, but Father Badin, who arrived in 1808, was the first to stay. Courtesy, Diocese of Nashville*

Above: *Father Robert A. Abell was the first Catholic priest to serve in Nashville. Following his arrival in 1820, he built Holy Rosary Church on Campbell's Hill, near the site of the State Capitol. Courtesy, Diocese of Nashville*

Right: *Eugene Magevney was one of the first members of the Catholic Church in Memphis; he lived next door to St. Peter's Church. He established an academy in Memphis on the public square. Courtesy, Memphis Parks Commission and Museum System*

1824, but he was soon replaced by Richard Pius Miles, Tennessee's first resident bishop. Railroad construction in the 1840s and 1850s brought more Irish workers, and in 1839 the first mass in Memphis was celebrated. By 1843 St. Peter's Church was in use, with Father Michael McAleer as priest, and Irish pride in a permanent place of worship brought recognition to the Irish community—generally looked down upon by many Memphians of that time. With a population of nearly 1,000 in Memphis in 1850, the Irish, by the time of the Civil War, constituted about one-fifth of the city's population.

The clergy of many of the rural churches exercised very close oversight over the conduct and moral life of their parishioners. Public drunkenness, lying, use of profanity, and selling cattle on Sunday were offenses for which men were tried and excommunicated; "speaking harsh words," "taking up with a married man," and "not being obedient to

her husband as commanded by St. Paul" were offenses which subjected women to church trials. Even the conduct of the preachers was not immune from close scrutiny. When a pastor of the Turnbull Baptist Church sold a parishioner sick farm animals, he was brought before the church session for an explanation and given the opportunity to make restitution.

Many early preachers organized schools. Samuel Doak, the first resident pastor, became the first academician. After building a church at Salem, he established Martin Academy (named for a North Carolina governor) in 1783 at Jonesboro. Davidson Academy (later the University of Nashville) was opened in Nashville by Thomas Craighead two years later, and John W. Doak, Samuel Doak's son, founded Tusculum Academy a few years after that at Greeneville. Blount College, claimed today by the University of Tennessee as its antecedent, was begun by the Reverend Samuel C. Carrick at his home in Knoxville in 1793. Scarcely was Memphis well settled when Eugene Magevney, an Irishman, opened a one-room log cabin academy on the public square.

Scores of private academies were chartered in all sections of the state during the several decades following the War of 1812. The Compact of 1806—an agreement among officials of Tennessee, North Carolina, and the federal gover-

ment concerning their public land claims in the state—provided that 100,000 acres were to be sold and the proceeds used to establish an academy in each county. Most of the counties immediately applied for charters but, regrettably, realized very little from the land sales. Tracy Academy at Charlotte, for example, was chartered in 1806 but did not open until the mid-1830s, with funds supplied largely by local patrons.

Tuition costs and curricula varied with each academy. Tracy, for $30 per year, offered studies in mathematics, science, Latin, Greek, and French. Students at the Male Academy in Bolivar paid $51.50 per year and studied the classical languages, mathematics, astronomy, rhetoric, logic, and history. Trustees at the Nashville Female Academy charged $75 for a five-month session; the fee covered not only tuition but also rooming facilities complete with firewood, candles, and servants.

Established in 1816, the academy

was considered one of the most outstanding female institutions in the country. When President James Monroe visited Nashville in 1819, Nashville officials included the academy on the tour; the president probably evoked twitters of laughter and perhaps applause when he told the young women that, in his opinion, "the female presents capacities for improvement" and therefore, like the male, should have opportunities for education. The Reverend Collins D. Elliott, academy president for two decades, assured women of a broad education and their parents of close and careful care and concern. He offered a program of studies that included the classical and Romance languages, vocal and instrumental music, art, and "fancy needle work." Strongly disapproving of young men who might venture upon the campus, Elliott assured parents that their daughters saw no "company," read no novels, and did not "leave the . . . [campus] but in company with a teacher."

Federal troops used the Nashville Female Academy during the Civil War. Prior to the war it was one of the leading girls' schools in Tennessee. Courtesy, Tennessee State Museum

The University of Nashville merged with the Western Military Institute in 1855. From 1824 until his death in 1855, Dr. Phillip Lindsley headed the university; he had been the acting president of Princeton when he was recruited to lead this school. Moving to Nashville, he built the University of Nashville into a leading center of learning in the South. Courtesy, Tennessee State Library and Archives

Legislators tried from time to time to establish a workable public school system, but with little success. Delegates to the state constitutional convention of 1834 had written into the fundamental law that because "knowledge, learning, and virtue" were essential to the preservation of democratic government, it was incumbent upon the General Assembly "in all future periods" to "cherish literature and science." But legislators failed to carry out the mandate when they refused to appropriate the necessary funds. Governor Andrew Johnson noted in 1853 that of 316,409 people over 20 years of age, more than 25 percent could neither read nor write. He urged legislators to "give life and energy to our dying or dead system of common school education." Legislators did levy a poll tax for a public school system, and Memphis and Nashville during the 1850s operated workable public school systems, but the paralysis of civil action caused by the Civil War brought efforts to a halt.

Also taking a toll were negative attitudes toward schools taken by some legislators, preachers, lawyers, and the public in general. Typical were the words

of one bombastic legislator, who, after observing that many of the people of the state were illiterate, exclaimed on the House floor that "book learning" was "cramping and stupefying." One frontier preacher, shocked at the "sinfulness" of female education, urged his parishioners to carry St. Paul's gospel to its logical conclusion by silencing women in all public places. Venerable old Peter Cartwright would have denied formal education to all preachers. To him they were "dull manuscript readers" who reminded him of "lettuce growing in the shade of a peachtree."

Despite discouragements educational leaders in 1807 established East Tennessee College in Knoxville by expanding Blount Academy. For several decades, East Tennessee College and Cumberland College of Nashville were the state's only significant institutions of higher education. In the 1820s, Cumberland became the University of Nashville, with Princeton graduate Phillip Lindsley as its president. The school at Knoxville became East Tennessee University in 1840, and, after a shaky start, found an able leader in Dartmouth graduate

This memorial marble panel commemorated Jenny Lind's visit to America in 1851, when she toured with P.T. Barnum. Courtesy, Tennessee State Museum

Joseph Estabrook. For two decades he helped advance the institution "from almost total prostration to a respectable rank." A dozen other colleges, including Cumberland University at Lebanon, flourished in the decades before the Civil War.

European visitors during the first few decades of settlement found the frontier culturally deprived. But it was the table manners of the frontiersmen that worried the Northern and European traveler-journalists most. Englishwoman Frances Trollope, for example, was nauseated at the eating habits of early Memphians. On one occasion while dining in a Memphis hotel, she watched horror-stricken when, at the sound of a dinner bell, 50 diners rushed in from off the streets and took their places at the table. Not a word was spoken; she heard only sounds of smacking, chomping, and an "unceasing chorus of coughing." Englishman James Alexander was equally repulsed in Nashville when men, spitting tobacco in one direction and blowing their noses in the other, devoured chunks of roast beef and loaves of bread as though they were party sandwiches.

Written with considerable exaggeration and designed chiefly to attract readers back home, the reports may have had a small degree of truth in them. But by the 1850s upper-class city dwellers displayed an appreciation of art, music, and theater comparable to that of people in the eastern cities, and Tennessee was attracting quality lectures and concerts. Jenny Lind performed in Nashville and Memphis to capacity crowds, and Edwin Booth, cast in those cities as Hamlet and Macbeth, was billed as "the distinguished young tragedian." Lind introduced her audiences to the Italian composer Gaetano Donizetti, and in 1854 a group called the Italian Opera Company performed Donizetti's *Lucia di Lammermoor* and selections from other operas in Nashville. Christy's Minstrels were well received in the major cities.

The United States, especially in its early period, was characterized by an effervescent society with a variety of ever-developing reforms, and Tennessee had its share. A revision of the harsh penal codes, the building of a state penitentiary and a state hospital for the mentally ill, and attempts to curtail the widespread consumption of alcohol were among them.

The penal codes of North Carolina and Virginia had been written with a view to deterring crime, and Tennessee's early statutes were based upon those of the other two states. The whipping post, pillory, stocks, and branding iron were in wide use in 1800, and horse thieves and counterfeiters might be subjected to all of them.

Sevier had called for a "revisal" of the "sanguinary laws" as early as 1807, but officials did not find legislators responsive until the 1820s. During the next two decades, however, most of the harsh laws were revised or repealed, and in 1831 a state penitentiary was opened. The commodious prison not only alleviated crowded conditions in scores of small jails across the state but enabled willing convicts to learn trades, including carpentry, hat making, tailoring, and blacksmithing. Efforts to abolish capital punishment were not successful, but reformers did succeed in getting authorities to conduct executions only inside prison grounds.

Dorothea Dix, the Boston social reformer, visited Tennessee on several occasions in the 1840s. Finding the penitentiary satisfactorily maintained and the penal laws revised, she turned to the need for an adequate state hospital for the insane. She addressed legislators and convened with influential citizens, and

soon convinced Tennesseans that better facilities were necessary. A small hospital had been opened in 1839, and a decade later larger facilities became available. Schools for the deaf and blind were in operation by mid-century.

The 1831 legislation legalizing saloons aroused temperance and governmental leaders alike. Governor Carroll was unable to understand why legislators could enact laws condemned by "the wise and virtuous everywhere," and cited a recent study which showed that three-fourths of the convicts incarcerated in the new state penitentiary attributed their problems to alcohol. Terming the use of intoxicants a "blighting curse," 374 women presented a petition to the General Assembly asking that the legislation be repealed, and at least two temperance journals—one in Maryville and one in Nashville—pointed to the "ignominy and horror" of the "drunkard's grave" for which such legislation could be responsible. By 1838 Tennessee had returned to the quart law, but a year later people complained that it was not being enforced and saloons were still operating.

After the Civil War reformers again took up the struggle, and in 1877 they enacted the Four Mile Law, which for-

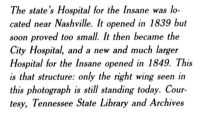

The state's Hospital for the Insane was located near Nashville. It opened in 1839 but soon proved too small. It then became the City Hospital, and a new and much larger Hospital for the Insane opened in 1849. This is that structure: only the right wing seen in this photograph is still standing today. Courtesy, Tennessee State Library and Archives

bade retail liquor sales within four miles of any school outside an incorporated town. At first the law received only limited attention, but soon towns controlled by reformers surrendered their charters, and in that way whiskey sales ended. Activists founded the Prohibition party in 1880, but its candidates received very little support. Most leaders found their efforts to be more effective when they worked within the two major political parties.

The liquor traffic was the principal political issue of the first decade of the twentieth century, and, after frequent street fights, legislators made whiskey manufacture and sale illegal throughout the entire state in 1909. The law was difficult to enforce, however, and in some cities— notably Memphis—whiskey was sold in defiance of the law.

By the end of the nineteenth century, Tennessee had repeatedly served as a place of refuge for people who were interested in social and economic experiments or were seeking opportunities for economic advancement. Before the Civil War Frances Wright had established a short-lived colony near Memphis designed to prepare slaves for freedom. Another colony, Gruetli, was settled in 1869 by Swiss colonists who marketed produce cooperatively. Eugen Plumacher, an agent for the Swiss Emigration Society, purchased 15,000 acres of land in Grundy County and settled 100 families there. A group principally composed of "wood carvers, farmers, and makers of fine wine," they soon abandoned the cooperative aspect of their colony; most of the families purchased land and continued as independent farmers. Plumacher later became the U.S. ambassador to Venezuela.

Rugby, in Morgan County, was begun in 1880 by an Englishman named Thomas Hughes, who envisioned his experiment as a haven for young British aristocrats who would live "by labour of their hands." Designed for young men from the English gentry who were barred by the law of primogeniture from inheriting family titles and estates, the colony

afforded them a chance to work cooperatively in carving out for themselves an estate in the new world. From royalties paid on his book *Tom Brown's School Days,* Hughes bought more than 75,000 acres. However, an unfavorable climate, famine, and disease caused the colony to fail within one year. Most of the men remained in the state, married, and established homes and families.

The Ruskin Cooperative Association was formed in Dickson County in 1893 by a self-styled "grass roots socialist" named Charles Augustus Wayland. Wayland had published an internationally circulated newspaper called *The Coming Nation* in Indiana, and he brought the paper to Tennessee and continued publication. Several hundred colonists industriously manufactured a variety of items and sold them over a wide area. They also sold farm produce locally. Internal dissension, however, doomed the colony within a few years of its founding. Accusations and counter-accusations of mismanagement soon had the colony in chancery court, where lawyers' fees and court costs consumed much of the association's property. Some of the colonists moved to Georgia in an effort to continue serving the ideals of John Ruskin, but many of them bought

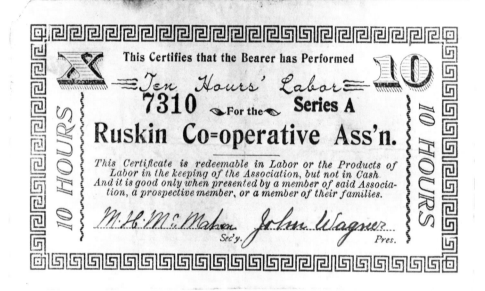

Top: *This 1896 photograph of the Ruskin Cooperative Association's cannery shows some of the settlers at work. They used the large cave on their Dickson County commune as their canning facility due to its coolness. Courtesy, Tennessee Historical Society*

Bottom: *Ruskin was a utopian socialist commune where money was not used. This labor coupon was "redeemable in Labor or the Products of Labor" by the members, prospective members, or the families of members. Courtesy, Tennessee Historical Society*

quicentennial celebration, and Tennesseans, perhaps weary from the war, did not manifest the interest in the activities of 1946 that they had in 1897. The state's celebration of the U.S. bicentennial, well organized and orchestrated by members of the Tennessee American Revolution Bicentennial Commission, captured the attention and imagination of the people. When the celebration ended, national authorities said that the efforts of Tennesseans to commemorate the nation's birth ranked among the best in the nation.

Although even in 1989 interested educators and political leaders worried about the large number of illiterate Tennesseans, considerable progress had been made in improving the educational system that, prior to Reconstruction, consisted mainly of church-related private academies. Governor John C. Brown told legislators in 1873 that the high illiteracy rate ranked Tennessee near the top among other states "in ignorance," which led to the establishment of a public school system. County reports submitted to the state superintendent in the 1870s and 1880s outlined many problems—inadequate funds, little or no interest among parents and students, impudence among the pupils, and poor facilities—but the system survived.

A lack of adequate teachers was addressed by legislators in 1909, when four normal schools were established to train teachers. East Tennessee State at Johnson City and Middle Tennessee State at Murfreesboro opened in 1911, while schools at Memphis and Nashville opened the following year. Blacks attended the Tennessee Agricultural and Industrial State Normal School (now Tennessee State University) at Nashville. A state-sponsored school for Negroes had been mandated by the Second Morrill Act of 1890, but state officials had largely ignored it. After Chattanooga leaders made a serious attempt to have the institution located in their city, officials decided upon Nashville. The Tennessee Polytechnic Institute (now Tennessee Technological University)

small farms and remained in Tennessee.

Tennesseans celebrated the state's centennial and sesquicentennial and the nation's bicentennial with considerable interest and fervor. Preparations were not complete in 1896, the proper time for the state's centennial celebration, but on May 1, 1897, President William McKinley opened an exposition in Nashville, where thousands of celebrants heard the usual bursts of oratory and cannon and then viewed the extravaganza. Just after World War II came the ses-

was authorized in 1915, and Austin Peay Normal School (now Austin Peay State University) was established in 1927. Authority was later given to expand the University of Tennessee into campuses in Memphis, Martin, and Chattanooga.

Not long after World War II ended, many southern states made educational opportunities more available to the people by developing two-year "community" colleges. Tennessee's legislature authorized three such schools in 1965, with one in each grand division of the state—at Cleveland, Columbia, and Jackson. Motlow (near Tullahoma) and Dyersburg State were opened in 1969, and others in the 1970s.

Governance of the public system was changed at about the same time. The Higher Education Commission, formed in 1967, analyzed the programmatic funding needs of all public institutions of higher education. In 1972 two boards replaced the State Board of Education, which for years had governed at all levels. A board of regents controlled institutions of higher learning (except for the University of Tennessee, which had its own governing board), and another board of education controlled public institutions below the higher education level.

In 1985 legislators enacted the Comprehensive Education Reform Act to improve education at the elementary and secondary levels. Governor Lamar Alexander's Better Schools Program produced a variety of improvements, including rewarding "Master Teachers," and provided funding through a one-cent sales tax increase.

Several private colleges and universities established before the Civil War were reopened after hostilities ended, and some new ones were established. The University of Nashville, well known before the war for its schools of liberal arts and medicine, took the lead in teacher training after the war with funds supplied by Boston philanthropist George Peabody. After the initial grant, Peabody money continued to flow into the Nashville school, and trustees in 1880 changed the name to Peabody Normal

College. In 1914 the school was moved to Hillsboro Road across from the Vanderbilt University campus, and it became the George Peabody College for Teachers. Absorbed by Vanderbilt in 1979, Peabody continues to place an emphasis upon teacher training.

Vanderbilt University was chartered in 1873, and before the turn of the century it was recognized as an outstanding Southern school. The generosity of the Vanderbilt family and the untiring efforts of leaders of the Southern Methodist Episcopal Church, particularly those of Bishop Holland N. McTyeire and Landon C. Garland, made the institution's existence possible. By 1900 academic, theological, pharmaceutical, and engineering departments were maintained on the main campus, while departments for medicine, law, and dentistry were located in other parts of town. Dentistry and pharmacy soon were phased out, and law and medicine moved to the main campus.

Fisk School was founded in Nashville in 1866 through the joint efforts of the American Missionary Association and the Western Freedmen's Aid Commission of Cincinnati. It soon became a well-known institution under the name of Fisk University. Central Tennessee College,

President William McKinley visited the Tennessee Centennial Exposition in 1897. He is visible here at the left side of the entrance holding a white hat, seated to the right of a white-haired man standing in front of the column. To McKinley's left sits Major John W. Thomas, one of the organizers of the exposition. The crowd is listening to Ohio's Governor Bushnell deliver a speech. Courtesy, Tennessee State Library and Archives

Tennessee Agricultural and Industrial State Normal School opened in Nashville in 1912. This is a view of the campus in about 1940. It was part of the state's segregated educational system that at the same time had established Memphis State, Middle Tennessee State, and East Tennessee State universities. Today the school is known as Tennessee State University, and it is still primarily black in its enrollment. Courtesy, Tennessee State Library and Archives

founded in the same year by the Southern Methodist Episcopal Church, was home to the Meharry Medical Department, named for the Meharry family of Ohio, who donated funds for medical education among blacks. In 1915 Meharry became a separate medical school, and the George W. Hubbard Hospital was located there in 1910.

A pundit has referred to Tennessee as "the buckle of the Bible Belt"—a term that, if it implies that interest in public worship continues unabated in the state, is accurate. More Tennesseans are members of Baptist churches than of any other Protestant denomination, but Methodists, Presbyterians, and the Church of Christ are not far behind.

Baptist, Methodist, and Presbyterian bodies divided sectionally as a result of strife before and during the Civil War. Preachers across the state perhaps subscribed to Parson Brownlow's motto that "neutral is nothing." When Andrew Johnson came to Nashville in 1862 as military governor, he called together the city's preachers and ordered them to stop preaching "Confederate sermons." After the war the country reunited—except for the major Protestant denominations. It was 1939 before members of the South-

ern Methodist Episcopal Church rejoined their Northern brethren, and in 1985 the Presbyterians reunited. The Baptists have not reunited to this day, and the Southern Baptist Convention includes more members than all the other Baptist groups.

The Fundamentalist-Modernist controversy occupied center stage for a decade after World War I. It paved the way for the enactment of an anti-evolution law in 1925 and the resulting Scopes trial in Dayton that same year. Liberal religious thought, widespread in Europe and some Northern universities decades earlier, centered in Tennessee at the School of Religion of Vanderbilt. Dean E.O. Brown took the lead among faculty members in "higher criticism" and questioning such "fundamentals" as the Virgin Birth of Christ, the alleged inerrancy of the Bible, and creationism. He was strongly supported by Vanderbilt Chancellor J.H. Kirkland, and soon fundamentalists, defending what they considered to be the basic tenets of the faith, charged that Vanderbilt had become a "hotbed of modernism." Although fundamentalists brought to the state such evangelists as T. Dewitt Talmadge, Billy Sunday, and William Riley (the president of the World's Christian Fundamental Association), their knight in shining armor was three-time presidential candidate William Jennings Bryan, who addressed an enthusiastic Nashville audience in 1924 on the subject, "Is the Bible True?"

As a result of Bryan's speech, legislators were urged to enact an anti-evolution law. On January 21, 1925, Representative John W. Butler, a Primitive Baptist from Macon County, introduced a bill that prohibited any public school teacher from teaching "anything that denies the story of the Divine Creation of man as taught in the Bible, and [teaches] instead that man descended from a lower order of animals." Chancellor Kirkland, Peabody President Bruce Payne, and others criticized the bill, but hundreds of fundamentalist leaders across the state urged legislators to "do their duty" and pass it.

In signing the measure into law, Governor Peay stated his belief that among the things "wrong in the nation" was the "abandonment of the old fashioned faith and belief in the Bible," and thousands cheered him for his words and deed.

Governor Peay's signature was scarcely dry when John T. Scopes, a teacher in the Rhea County High School of Dayton, was indicted for violating the law. Interest multiplied when the announcement came that Bryan would assist in the prosecution, and that Clarence Darrow, Dudley Field Malone, and Arthur Garfield Hayes would aid with the defense. In many respects the trial took on the air of a revival meeting.

The main issue in the case—obscured by the dominance of the counsels' personalities—was whether the legislature had the right to specify by statute what could be taught in the public schools, and, in particular, whether it could prevent the teaching of a theory that was contrary to the cherished religious beliefs of many people. Bryan prevailed, and Scopes was found guilty by a Rhea County jury and fined $100.

A week after the trial, Bryan, who was still in Tennessee, died, a victim of the stress of his Dayton experience. Admirers soon contributed funds sufficient to establish the William Jennings Bryan University, dedicated to the preservation and teaching of "Christian fundamentals."

After World War II members of the Tennessee Academy of Science quietly sought to repeal the law. For several years fundamentalists vigorously opposed repeal, and a commissioner of education as late as 1959 suggested to a college biology professor that he must abide by the law or seek a position elsewhere. It was 1967 before the law was quietly removed from the statute books.

In 1986 the Hawkins County Textbook Case (*Mozert v. Hawkins County Public Schools*), which bore some resemblance to the Scopes trial, was heard in Greeneville. Several fundamentalist families jointly sued public school officials because their children were required to read and study "offensive" textbooks in grades one through eight. Claiming First Amendment rights guaranteeing freedom of religion, they successfully persuaded U.S. District Court Judge Thomas Hull to rule that their children could not be required to study books that offended their sense of religious propriety. Hull's decision was ultimately reversed by the U.S. Supreme Court.

* * *

Not only was educational development slowed by the onset of the Civil War, but the conflict tragically interrupted the older Southern civilization, and several decades elapsed before literature, art, music, and drama again were well received in the state. The Fisk Jubilee Singers, a student chorus at Fisk University that performed under the direction of Professor George L. White, was probably the first musical group to bring recognition to Tennessee after the war. They performed in the nation's major cities and before the crowned heads of Europe. When state legislators heard them in 1879, they wrote a resolution of commendation and described the performance as "truly remarkable." A few years later the music departments at George Peabody College and Ward Belmont College enjoyed considerable suc-

The Fisk Jubilee Singers have entertained the world for more than 125 years. This group toured in 1873. Courtesy, Tennessee State Library and Archives

Mary Noailles Murfree, whose pen name was
Charles Egbert Craddock, won a national
readership for her novels set in Tennessee's
Cumberland Mountains. Courtesy, Tennessee
Historical Society

Seeking to return to an agriculturist and
preindustrial past, the 1930s group of writers
known as the Agrarians are seen battling the
forces that they abhorred in this December
1933 Masquerader cartoon. Courtesy, Vanderbilt University, Special Collections

Here we have three little Agrarians in their chosen element. By the happiest
accident, the tree of Civilization grows in their orchard; but alas! it is vermicu-
lated. D. D. has been puffing away like the very dickens with his little flit-gun
to remedy this. One of these little pests which looks like the sort of thing one
finds beneath the hood of an auto—but which the eccentric Dr. Werm intended to
represent one of the curses of the machine age—growing weary of it all, has
accommodatingly bitten the dust. In D. D.'s eyes may be seen the dawn of a
new day. A. T. has allowed himself to become slightly choleric over the derisive
behavior of an even less tidy assemblage of spare parts; while J. C. R.—as bonny
and blithe as ever you please—thrills to the feel of the good earth beneath his
unshod feet. In the background may be seen this and that. In the upper left
corner is a bush around which other embattled Agrarians are beating.

cess. Arthur Henkel, a member of the
Ward Belmont faculty, organized and directed the Nashville Symphony in the
1920s and did much to establish Nashville as a cultural center.

Cultural leaders in the major cities organized clubs and literary societies, and
Nashville and Knoxville town-and-gown
clubs fostered intellectual development.
Nashvillians, conscious of the scholarly
achievements at Vanderbilt, George
Peabody, and Fisk, revived their claim
to the title of "Athens of the South."

By the beginning of the twentieth century, Southern writers were achieving
recognition. Mary Noailles Murfree
(Charles Egbert Craddock) was Tennessee's contribution—her collection of
short stories published under the title In
the Tennessee Mountains (1884) established her reputation. By the time of her
death, she had published more than a
dozen novels and scores of short stories,
each with a Tennessee or Southern
setting.

The year of Murfree's death (1922),
a group of Nashvillians published the first
issue of The Fugitive, a small magazine
of poetry with a Southern flavor, and
thus announced what modern scholar
George B. Tindall has described as "the
existence of the most influential group in
American letters since the New England
Transcendentalists." These inaugurators
of a Southern renaissance, most of whom
were Vanderbilt professors, published 19
issues before disbanding in 1925. Seeking to preserve a Southern heritage with
traditional spiritual values, they revolted
against both "sentimental tradition" and
the materialism of the "New South" philosophy. Of the 16 scholars, four—John
Crowe Ransom, Donald Davidson, Allen
Tate, and Robert Penn Warren—devoted their careers to literature as a profession.

These four also formed the nucleus of
the "Agrarians"—a group of 12 writers
associated mainly with Vanderbilt University who published a variety of tran-
scendental essays, articles, and books,
the best known of which was an anthology titled I'll Take My Stand: the South

and the *Agrarian Tradition* (1930). Like the works of the Fugitives, their essays were both praised and condemned, but scarcely ignored. Attacking the "cultural imperialism found in the North," they sought to turn society from the monotony of conformity and secular progress that nurtured pragmatism and relativism, and point it in the direction of the significant traditional spiritual values of an agrarian economy. More specifically, they posited that only in an agrarian economy could people achieve a proper relationship with nature and cultivate the traditional ame-

nities of culture and spiritual values. The Agrarians were hailed in the South but generally dismissed by Eastern critics as harmless visionaries and social planners, whose societal plans, if adopted, would turn the country back to horse-and-buggy days.

The most successful work ever penned by a Tennessean was Alex Haley's *Roots* (1976). Haley, a native of Henning, spent 12 years preparing the monumental work, which was first published by the *Reader's Digest* in 1974. When it was telecast in 1977, it was acclaimed as television's most popular program to date. The novel was translated into 12 languages and televised in 28 countries. A Pulitzer Prize jury, unable to agree upon whether the work was history or fiction, presented Haley with a "special award."

Haley's story of Kunta Kinte's faith in his noble African heritage and the

Above: *Moving out of the State Capitol in 1952 and into its own building, the Tennessee State Library and Archives is the premier repository for materials relating to the history of Tennessee. As a result of the U.S. Bicentennial and the publication of* Roots, *with a subsequent increase in interest in genealogy, the library is today a very busy place, where the whirring of the microfilm readers and excited sounds of researchers finding an important lead can be heard seven days a week. Courtesy, Tennessee State Library and Archives*

Above left: *Alex Haley first won widespread public notice when he penned* The Autobiography of Malcolm X. *In 1976 he won international recognition for his novel* Roots. *Courtesy, Alex Haley*

Left: *In 1932, Clifton, Tennessee, native T.S. Stribling won the Pulitzer Prize for* The Store, *the second volume in his trilogy on southern Middle Tennessee and Northern Alabama from the Civil War to the Great Depression. He was the first Tennessean to win the Pulitzer. Courtesy, Tennessee Historical Society*

World-famous recording star and actor Elvis Presley called Memphis, Tennessee, home. Courtesy, Tennessee State Museum

strength he drew from it inspired confidence and hope in blacks and whites alike. Older generations of whites—who had admired Longfellow's masculine and gentle Hiawatha and his tender grandmother, Nakomis, along with James Fenimore Cooper's Chingachgook— were unfamiliar with a noble African in either English or American literature. Their literary and entertainment pablum, when it referenced blacks at all, consisted more of Uncle Tom, Uncle Remus, and such television and radio shows as "Amos'n Andy" and "Step'n Fetch It." More recent generations had experienced the violence and trauma of the civil rights movements of the 1960s and 1970s. But with Haley's epic they could warmly embrace a superior black of Africa's golden age, peaceful and gentle, who

drew pride, strength, and spiritual stamina from his roots. Some whites, who before had had difficulty remembering or even caring who their great-grandfathers were, now stepped forth with blacks to trace their roots in an unprecedented boom in genealogical research.

Besides Haley, other Tennessee scholars in a variety of fields have received awards in recent years. Sidney Cohen of Nashville and John Buchanan, a Murfreesboro native, were winners of Nobel Prizes in 1987 for their work in biochemistry and economics, respectively. Peter Taylor was the recipient of a Pulitzer Prize for his novel, *A Summons to Memphis* (1987).

Nashville, the home of the "Grand Ole Opry," in recent years has been called by some the "Music Center of the

World" because of the city's plethora of country music artists and publishers. But it was Memphis that gave the world Elvis Presley, vocalist Bessie Smith, and composer W.C. Handy—who was known as the "Father of the Blues" for his "St. Louis Blues" and "Memphis Blues." But Memphis has produced much more. A concert at Washington's Kennedy Center in 1977, for example, featured the voices of three outstanding opera performers—Ruth Weltin, Nancy Tatum, and Magnon Dunn.

Radio stations began to broadcast in Tennessee in the early 1920s—stations in Lawrenceburg, Memphis, Chattanooga, and Knoxville developed in 1922—and the appreciation of Tennesseans for music soon made itself known through the volume of requests from listeners for "more music." WSM in Nashville began operation in 1925, and late in that year announcer and programmer George D. Hay (the "Solemn Old Judge") began the "Grand Ole Opry." Many rural folk as far as the signals would reach tuned in on Saturday nights. City dwellers with more delicate tastes sometimes became annoyed with such performers and renditions as Uncle Dave Macon and his "Keep My Skillet Good and Greasy," but Uncle Dave and his "Moonshiners" were among the more popular of the artists for decades and indeed until his death in 1952.

By the 1980s Nashville studios were the scene of such nationally known productions as "Hee Haw" and programs syndicated by Johnny Cash, Porter Waggoner, and others. Indeed, more than 250 recording studios sustained a thriving business as the 1980s drew to a close. While the "Nashville Sound" was not exactly what earlier cultural leaders had had in mind when they spoke of the "Athens of the South," the sound did attract many listeners, chiefly rural folk and first generation urban dwellers.

Rutherford County natives Uncle Dave Macon and his son Dorris are seen here in the WSM studios. Courtesy, Tennessee State Museum

The Tennessee Centennial Exposition was
held in 1897, one year late, in Nashville. An
artificial lake was created at the fair site and
named Lake Watauga in honor of the first
area of settlement in Tennessee. Seen across
that lake is the fair's art exhibition space, a
copy of the Parthenon. To its right is the
Memphis/Shelby County exhibition building,
an Egyptian pyramid. Enid Yandell's statue of
Pallas Athena stands to the left of the Parthenon. Courtesy, Tennessee State Library
and Archives

4

ECONOMIC DEVELOPMENT

Transient hunters and herdsmen arrived in the Tennessee territory in the mid-eighteenth century, but farmers who wanted to build homes and cultivate the soil were not far behind. The permanent settlers gave their attention first to shelter—usually a one-room log cabin, with earthen or puncheon floors and roofs of thatch or long oak clapboards held in place by ridgepoles or wooden pegs. While not fancy, such a structure provided protection from the elements and could be built quickly. Inside, the very necessary fireplace, for cooking the year round and heating in the winter, took up much of one side. Primitive furniture was placed about the room. On the bed was a mattress—a bed tick filled with corn husks, pine needles, or straw—and a stack of quilts. A supply of dinner plates made of wood or pewter was on the table, along with a few spoons cut from horn or wood. Articles of clothing, made from deer skin and linen, hung from deer antlers attached to the wall. A hunting knife or two lay on the table or in a corner near a rifle and several powder horns.

By 1800 living conditions had much improved, and the homes of affluent people were larger and better furnished than most. By that date some of the residences in Knoxville, Nashville, and Jonesboro were two-story structures of brick, stone, or clapboard. The two-story home of Francis Ramsey, for example, built near Knoxville in 1797, was designed in the Gothic style by an English architect and constructed of marble and fieldstone. General James Winchester's Cragfont, built near Gallatin in 1803 by stonema-

sons from Baltimore, was about as commodious. A decade earlier Daniel Smith, an official in the territorial government, had completed a less elegant home of stone in Sumner County—a structure that probably was the first stone home on the Cumberland. A few residences at the turn of the century were being furnished with pieces made by experienced craftsmen from the East.

To make their livings, the first settlers turned to the soil for food and clothing. Everyone able to work raised gardens and field crops of varying sizes, and even those primarily concerned with iron or whiskey manufacture had crops and livestock. No simple patch with a half-dozen tomato plants and a squash vine or two, a pioneer garden consisted of at least a half-acre on which was grown enough to feed the family during summer and fall and to put up a food supply for the winter. Irish potatoes, planted before the last frost, were harvested in July in time to sow another crop—perhaps corn or turnips—to be harvested just before the first frost of that fall. Beans of several varieties, onions, pumpkins, sweet potatoes, and corn were grown in abundance and processed for winter use. Walnuts, hickory nuts, and chestnuts were gathered in late summer and early fall.

Clearing a place in the forest for planting was a tremendous task, and farmers were unable to prepare more than a few acres each year. The Robertson family on the Cumberland, for example, was especially industrious, but the family cleared only about 30 acres during its first 10 years there. Most farmers began by just cutting the underbrush and gird-ling the trees. Farmers with proper equip-ment and adequate labor felled the trees—but they still had to contend with the protruding stumps. This meant that, despite ownership of a team of oxen and a bull-tongue plow, much of the cultiva-tion was done by hand with hoes. Indian marauders added to the problems, and planters had to protect not only them-selves and their families but their crops as well.

The farmer who had a growing house-hold of a half-dozen or more children considered himself indeed fortunate, because children supplied much of the necessary help on the farm. Ben and Margaret Corlew in Montgomery County had reared 18 children before mid-century; four were born before Margaret had reached the age of 20. John Sevier, married when barely 16, also boasted of 18 children (by two wives). In 1820 Green and Mary Hatton, at ages 40 and 39, respectively, had 11 children ranging in age from three months to 20 years. The Willie Balthrops had 14 and the John Sowells 18 when the census of 1820 was taken.

The close spirit of community life en-abled people to "swap work" to do things that otherwise would have been impossi-ble. House and barn raisings and land clearings could be accomplished quickly when neighbors with children and a few slaves helped a nearby planter.

Slaves, although never as numerous in Tennessee as in the Deep South, were a very important source of labor. At mid-century about 8 percent of the East Ten-nessee population was black—considera-bly less than the 25 percent in Middle Tennessee and the 33 percent in the western counties. Robertson had brought one or more slaves on his first trip to the Cumberland, but the population grew slowly until after 1800, when the cotton gin came into widespread use. Blacks were productive workers in the cotton fields, and after the Chickasaw lands of West Tennessee were opened for settle-ment, the black population increased tremendously. Nashville and Memphis became well-known centers for buying and selling slaves, and men like Isaac Bolton, John Armfield, Isaac Franklin, and Nathan Bedford Forrest did well in the trade. As the price of cotton fluctu-ated, so did the price of slaves. Toward the end of the prosperous 1850s, able-bodied men brought $1,000 each. A few years earlier—especially just after the Panic of 1837—they had sold for less than half of that.

Corn was the universal crop, and ev-ery agricultural census from the earliest to the most recent has shown an abun-dance in every county. Corn did not re-quire the detailed physical labor and cultivation that many of the other crops did; indeed, after corn was planted, it re-quired very little labor until the harvest. By 1840 Tennessee produced more corn than any other state in the Union. Al-though it soon lost this distinction to states in the Midwest, farmers like Mark Cockrill and William H. Neal produced crops that won prizes at various fairs.

The most important money crop in the central and western counties was cotton. John Donelson had grown a small crop near Nashville as early as 1780, but it was after 1800—with the development of the gins—that cotton became an im-portant crop. In the early 1820s, with the settlement of the Chickasaw territory, the state's production began to rank with that of other states in the Deep South. Al-though Tennessee produced only 2,500 bales in 1810, the crop of nearly 200,000 bales 40 years later was ex-ceeded only by those in the states of Ala-bama, Georgia, Mississippi, and South Carolina. At mid-century the western counties produced 90 percent of the state's crop, and in 1851 Colonel John Pope of Shelby County grew "the best cotton known to the world," as attested by his gold medal from the World's Fair in London. By 1860 production had in-creased 50 percent over that of 1850.

Tobacco became an important money crop, which was grown mainly in the northern counties from Weakley in the western sector to Greene in East Tennes-see. During the several decades before the Civil War, Tennessee's production was exceeded only by that of Kentucky and Virginia. It was not until after the war that production in North Carolina began to exceed that of Tennessee.

Farmers in all sections of the state raised livestock and poultry. Turkeys and chickens were produced not only for home consumption but for the markets as well. Middle Tennesseans often drove flocks of 750 or more turkeys overland to Nashville and put them on steamboats for New Orleans. Before the Civil War Mark Cockrill bred choice Merino sheep and other animals on his 5,000-acre farm near Nashville, and in 1854 he won first prize at the World's Fair in London for the best wool in the world. Legislators placed his bust in a position of honor in the capitol and cited his "devotion of a long life to the advancement and development of . . . [Tennessee's] agricultural resources."

Among the other crops in which antebellum Tennesseans displayed a warm interest was silk. Captain James Miller of Knox County told of owning 5 million silkworms at one time, and Samuel Martin, also of Knox County, asked legislators to fund annually the purchase of worms and eggs to be distributed among the state's interested farmers. Governor Jones appeared for his second inauguration (1843) clad in a suit made of Tennessee silk, but people generally were not as bold as the governor, and the crop was not a money maker. By 1860 silk was produced only in Humphreys, Sevier, and Lincoln counties, and only in very limited quantities.

Flax and hemp also were grown as money crops, although not as widely as cotton, corn, and tobacco. In East Tennessee, where the growing season was too short for cotton, flax cultivation was very popular for several decades. The plant yielded linseed oil and fine linen, both of which brought good prices on the open market. Hemp, used chiefly for rope, was also a material used for clothing for field hands and working folk in general. Like cotton, tobacco, and flax, hemp production required much more labor than corn but brought better prices. Flax and hemp, like silk, were replaced by other crops during and after the Civil War.

Agricultural reformers in the 1840s and 1850s urged Tennessee farmers to practice crop rotation and recommended other changes in their methods of production. Tolbert Fanning, editor of *The Agriculturalist,* met with farmers at county fairs and elsewhere to explain the advantages of proper fertilization, crop rotation, and of the selection of appropriate livestock breeding methods. Others emphasized the need to grow less cotton and more grain and livestock. A State Agricultural Bureau, established in 1854, organized state, county, and regional fairs at which farmers displayed their produce and competed for prizes. Fairs offered incentives for better production and opportunities for learning more effective farming methods.

Industry as we know it today scarcely existed on the frontier. Instead, home industries developed, and frontier wives and daughters manufactured a variety of items for family use, including candles, soap, and clothing. Many families had spinning wheels, and they spun wool, flax, and cotton into thread and then wove it into cloth. Colors were as varied as the available dyes. Flax did not take well to dyeing, and linen therefore was usually white. But cotton and wool dyed well, and colors from the bark of black walnut, hickory, and maple were used in addition to indigo cakes when available on the market.

Men were primarily farmers but by necessity became involved where "heavy" industry was concerned. The "shelter industry" was in the hands of men, and most built their own houses, with occasional help from neighbors or such skilled labor as one could afford. Primitive furniture also was built by the owners, although some pieces were made by skilled carpenters or ordered from the East or even Europe. But farming and manufacturing were so closely intertwined that it is difficult to say where one ended and the other began.

Stills were found on most farms and

made enough whiskey for home consumption. Indeed, one observer in 1800 counted at least 60 stills among a population of 4,000 in Davidson County, but John Overton a few years earlier had estimated there were 500 in all of the Cumberland settlements. Some men manufactured it in much greater quantities and sold it to tavern owners in Knoxville, Jonesboro, and Nashville, or stored it in hogsheads and shipped it to Philadelphia or New Orleans. Johnnie Boyd, for example, was an expert distiller who came with the Donelson party to the Cumberland. As the Cumberland's first commercial distiller, he not only manufactured whiskey whenever he could procure the required raw materials, but he also instructed others on the finer points of booze-making for a small fee. Whiskey usually meant corn, but Boyd and some others were equally adept at making it from rye.

Tennessee has produced some rather distinctive pieces of furniture. This is a Jackson Press, or a bookcase on top of a cabinet. Courtesy, Tennessee State Museum

Iron manufacture began in East Tennessee at an early date and was being developed on the Cumberland by the end of the eighteenth century. David Ross established the first iron works in Tennessee near present-day Kingsport; one of his employees, James King, learned furnace operation so well that he established another works nearby, largely with financial support from William Blount. James Robertson, who was well situated in Nashboro, had been granted 640 acres on Barton's Creek 40 miles west of Nashville, and in 1795 he built a small furnace there. He apparently developed a fair trade. In 1804 he sold his holdings to a young Scotch-Irish trader from Pennsylvania named Montgomery Bell, who had arrived in Cumberland County in 1802 or earlier, probably as a worker or manager for Robertson. Within a decade Bell was well on his way toward becoming the foremost industrialist in antebellum Tennessee.

For 50 years Bell dug the brown hematite ore from a hard cherty soil in the Western Iron Belt. Not only did he develop a lucrative trade in Nashville and throughout the Cumberland area, but he shipped both pig iron and finished iron products to New Orleans and other points chiefly in the South and Southwest. Since he needed vast stands of timber for charcoal, Bell bought thousands of acres of land in the vicinity of the Cumberland Iron Works (a name Robertson had given the Barton's Creek property) and then built other forges and furnaces nearby. The size of his operations can be estimated by his repeated advertisements in Nashville newspapers for wood and slaves. In 1805, for example, he advertised for 5,000 cords of wood and 8 or 10 slaves, for which he promised "a generous price"; later in the same year he would buy 7,500 cords at "any fair price." In 1820 he owned 83 slaves; in the 1840s he owned 300 slaves. In busy seasons he called upon neighborhood owners to hire out their slaves to him.

The mining of ore was a comparatively simple operation for muscular men with picks and shovels. They scratched the ore from the surface, hauled it to washers where it was cleansed of as much soil as possible, and then placed it in the furnace after adding a charge of charcoal and lime. Temperatures rose to 3,500 degrees Fahrenheit. Under the intense heat the lime would coalesce with the impurities and form a fusible glass, which, being lighter than the molten ore, would float to the top and be taken off as slag. Workers then drew off the molten iron from underneath into "pig banks"—small gutters of sand. After the iron had cooled, it was broken into pieces about 18 inches long and cast into cannon, cannon balls, kettles, and kitchen utensils.

As the United States moved closer toward a second war with Great Britain, furnace men considered the market in munitions. As early as 1809 Bell offered to ship cannonballs manufactured at his Cumberland Iron Works to federal depots in New Orleans. He could cast 18-, 24-, and 32-pound balls, he informed the Secretary of War, and ship them to "any port south of the mouth of the Cumberland." Two years later he signed a contract with federal authorities and shipped munitions ranging from very small canister to 32-pound balls.

As the effects of the Panic of 1819 deepened, Bell raised money by selling some of his iron works, including the massive Cumberland Iron Works on Barton's Creek, to Pennsylvania industrialist Anthony Vanleer, who operated it until the Civil War. After the war it was reopened by Vanleer's son-in-law and continued to operate until the 1930s. It was finally dismantled in the early 1940s and sold as scrap metal. Bell remained active in his other operations until his death in 1855.

Copper, coal, and other minerals were being mined in several of the eastern counties at mid-century. Copper mines in Polk County were especially productive. Efforts by enterprisers to arouse interest in textile manufacture, however, met with little success. Advice from Mack Cockrill and other reformers to establish cotton and woolen mills—which "would render the South magnificently

rich and gloriously independent"—fell on deaf ears. In 1860 the state reported less than $700,000 worth of manufactured cotton goods, while nearby Georgia produced goods valued at $2.4 million.

In addition to farmers, businessmen, and industrialists, there were of course professional people who practiced law or medicine, taught school, preached, and surveyed, and who contributed to the economic well-being of the time.

Every county seat had a large supply of lawyers who handled a variety of litigation. It was not the litigation, however, but the lack of formal requirements that drew many to the bar, coupled with the prestige that supposedly accompanied working in the legal profession. There were no formal academic requirements for practicing law. The state issued a license upon affirmation by a judge or peers that the applicant had "read law." Not until the mid-nineteenth century (by which time Cumberland University had opened at Lebanon) did most prospective young lawyers even have an opportunity for formal study. At Cumberland, one year was required, but "well prepared" young men could finish in less time. Cordell Hull, for example, graduated in 1891 at age 19 after one semester.

Those attorneys who practiced regularly handled a variety of cases such as horse thievery, manslaughter, and mayhem. Crimes that fill today's docket— child abuse, sex perversion, and drug addiction, for example—were unknown. Most lawyers wanted to become judges, but judges, as today, were poorly paid. John McNairy was compensated only on a per court session basis, and Jackson, as a member of the Supreme Court of Law and Equity, earned only $50 per month.

Physicians also generally were unschooled. They "read" medicine under the tutelage of a practicing physician and helped with rounds and medicinal preparation. No small task for the student was that of digging and preparing the proper roots, teas, and other concoctions that served medicinal purposes. Most doctors prepared their own medicines; for

those who did not, most crossroad stores stocked a variety of patent remedies. Quinine, opium, camphor, laudanum, and a variety of other painkillers could be had without a thought of a prescription. All doctors made home visits, but seldom for obstetrics because every community had a midwife or two.

In 1830 the health of Tennesseans—and indeed of many people in surrounding states—received a boost when John C. Gunn's *Domestic Medicine* appeared. It was "the poor man's friend," the Knoxville physician said, "in the hour of affliction, pain, and sickness." Gunn had come to Knoxville from Virginia in 1827, and within a decade his book had become a reference volume for physicians as well as people looking for home remedies. (Frequently reissued, as late as 1920 it circulated in its 243rd edition.) Gunn was straightforward in style and wrote on syphilis as well as snakebites, and bloodletting as well as bathing and loose bowels. He urged the consumption of seafoods instead of pork, favored frequent exercise and baths, and abhorred drugs, especially opium. His commonsense approach may have been the reason some Tennesseans were especially long-lived.

Opportunities for medical education improved considerably in 1851, when the University of Nashville opened a medical school with John Berrien

Lindsley as dean and Paul Fitzsimmons Eve as chief surgeon. Lindsley was the son of the university's first president, and Eve, who performed surgery only after anesthetizing patients with sulphuric ether or chloroform, was widely recognized in his field. By 1860 Lindsley had 456 students and required two years of attendance at professional lectures, three years of service in the office of a practicing physician, and the composition of a thesis for graduation.

Daniel Smith, John Sevier, James Robertson, and several of the Donelson men were among those who worked part time as surveyors. Andrew Jackson apparently could also run a line, as evidenced by his letter to Smith requesting the loan of the surveyor's compass. On the frontier close accuracy was not always required, and neighbors simply would agree upon a line without a formal survey.

Only after the War of 1812 did banking as an economic stimulus and convenience to investment became very widespread. By 1815 banks had become established in most towns, but poor banking practices caused their collapse during the Panic of 1819. A system of barter was widespread on the frontier, and prices often were quoted in salt or some other commodity. The United States had adopted the dollar as the monetary unit soon after independence, and Tennessee, two years after statehood, had de-

clared that dollars and cents should be used in all matters of record. But for at least two decades, rural merchants quoted prices in pounds and shillings, and in salt.

A good transportation system was necessary for proper economic development, and pioneer Tennessee had a good system of rivers flowing in and out of much of the state. Naturally, most of the early settlements were along the banks of the rivers. Land transportation also was necessary, and the first roads were the Indian trails and buffalo paths that followed the ridges and valleys. As the population increased, these trails were widened into wagon roads (and eventually into today's highways). At first, virtually no grading was done on these trails; stumps were cut as near surface level as possible, and trees and brush were chopped away to widen pathways. Seldom graveled, in the best of weather trails were dusty and often deeply rutted. In the winter and rainy season these routes became rivers of mud. Nevertheless, some roads tying Knoxville and Jonesboro to both the East and West had been cut by the time of statehood, enabling people to supplement the water routes with land traffic. Andre Michaux, who traveled through Jonesboro in 1796, noted in his journal that many merchants obtained "their goods from Philadelphia by land."

Perhaps the first road of significance

in Tennessee was the Wilderness Trail, which was marked in 1775 by Daniel Boone from the Long Island of the Holston through Cumberland Gap into Kentucky. It was the road that Robertson and thousands of others traveled as they headed toward Nashborough. More than a decade later a road was cut from Knoxville across the Cumberland Mountains to the Middle Tennessee settlements, and it was this road that Jackson and Judge McNairy took on their way to Nashville in 1788 to assume their new judicial duties. As settlements grew the county courts built pikes and bridges and established ferries. All able-bodied white adult males aged 50 and under were required to keep the roads in passable shape or pay a fine.

During the 1830s Tennessee experienced a road-building boom, and by 1840 more than 400 miles of stage roads stretched across the state. Also, several hundred miles of "second class wagon roads" were built; these roads were "improved" but were inferior to the stage roads. Nashville became a hub of transportation, with more than a half-dozen routes stretched like spokes in all directions. One of the best known roads leading south from Nashville was the Natchez Trace, built by the federal government in 1802.

Steamboats came into Nashville from Cincinnati and New Orleans as early as 1819. Because of the shoals on the Tennessee, the boats were unable to serve Knoxville until some years later, but East Tennessee merchants frequently ordered goods shipped by steamboat into Nashville and then transported them eastward by land.

Interest in railroads developed in the 1820s, but it was 30 years later before lines were functioning in Tennessee—although the 10-mile Memphis-to-LaGrange road operated for a few months in the early 1840s. The first completed railroad was the Nashville and Chattanooga, which reached Chattanooga in 1854 and was built at a cost of about $1.5 million. The Louisville and Nashville tied the state's capital to Louisville,

Dr. Paul Fitzsimmons Eve was the first chief surgeon at the Medical School of the University of Nashville. He served on the street barricades of Paris while studying medicine there in 1830, as well as being a Confederate surgeon, and a volunteer surgeon in Warsaw during a Polish revolt against Russia in 1831. Courtesy, Tennessee Historical Society

and the Nashville, Chattanooga and St. Louis to points in the West. The Memphis and Charleston was completed in 1858; the East Tennessee and Virginia and East Tennessee and Georgia also were completed that year, and tied the Eastern markets to points both north and south.

The railroads fared poorly during the Civil War, but they later became an important link between Tennessee and Eastern markets as industry expanded from the 1870s onward.

Scarcely were guns stacked after the Civil War when the urban press, supported by men of enterprise and business, vigorously sought capital and industry in an effort to build a New South—no longer of slavery and secession but of business and industry. The editors of both the Chattanooga *Daily Republican* and the *Daily Times,* for example, urged Northern "carpetbaggers" with money to consider the vast resources of their town for development. Chattanooga, readily admitted one editor in 1871, "no longer wished to stay in the background," and he urged Northern men of capital to "leave the bleak winds of the north" and settle in their growing city, where no questions of sectional sympathies would be asked. By that date Chattanooga industrial establishments already had increased fourfold, and "the greatest of the carpetbaggers," J.T. Wilder, had established the Roane Iron Works in nearby Roane County and revived several industrial establishments in Chattanooga. By the late 1870s Wilder had made steel using the first open-hearth furnace south of the Ohio River. Colonel S.B. Lowe, who had been in Chattanooga before the war, had returned by 1871 and established the Vulcan Iron Works. Furniture factories and a variety of mills were established, but iron and steel works predominated to such an extent that the press predicted Chattanooga would eclipse Birmingham, Alabama, as an iron and steel center.

Knoxville, a financial and banking center before the war, also attracted Northern capital and expanded as a commercial and industrial center. Even before the war Knoxville had full rail connections as far north as New York City and had established commercial ties in Virginia and North Carolina. By 1885 Knoxville was the fourth-largest wholesaling center in the South, and its trade in dry goods, hardware, shoes, furniture, and saddlery had an annual business volume three times that of manufacturing. Its population of nearly 10,000 in 1880 was three times what it had been during the war.

Memphis and Nashville also sought Northern capital, and some predicted that Memphis might surpass St. Louis as a commercial and manufacturing center. As the city climbed toward becoming the world's greatest processor of cottonseed, the editor of the *Appeal* questioned why businesses should close on Sundays and thus lose "one seventh of the week." Cholera was rampant during the late 1860s, and yellow fever threatened to decimate the population in the 1870s, but by the 1880s Memphians again moved forward. With the cotton business as the mainstay, the value of annual trade increased from an estimated $72 million in 1880 to $200 million 10 years later. Nashville had to recover from three years of military occupation, but by 1870 economic recovery was complete, and the city boasted several new establishments in milling and cotton processing. Woolen mills were opened not only in Nashville but in Tullahoma, Jackson, and other towns.

Both farmers and industrialists complained of a short labor supply, and the urban press joined state officials in seeking to interest European and Asian workers in coming to Tennessee. State officials commissioned a Knoxvillian named Hermann Bokum to publish a "handbook" in both English and German that advertised the opportunities for success. Both laborers and entrepreneurs were welcomed. Encouraged by reports of Chinese labor in California, the Memphis *Appeal* suggested that such workers would be superior to Europeans. In the summer of 1869 Memphians welcomed

500 delegates to a convention to consider the importation of several thousand Chinese laborers. The list of those attending the convention read like a Confederate *Who's Who*: Isham G. Harris, home from a self-imposed exile in Mexico and England, was named chairman, and Gideon J. Pillow and Nathan Bedford Forrest played active roles. Forrest, for example, had become associated with a Southern railroad. He pledged to employ 1,000 Chinese workers and pay them their wages in cash.

Tennesseans entered the twentieth century on an optimistic note. The timber and lumber business ranked just behind grist and flour milling, and Memphis had become the largest inland hardwood lumber market in the world. Hundreds of farmers and other laborers cut timber over a wide area of virgin forest, and either floated the logs down the river to Nashville or Memphis, or hauled them in horse-drawn wagons. Iron and steel manufacture continued to employ thousands of people, especially in East Tennessee, as did other industries such as textile manufacturing and tobacco processing. By 1920 the value of manufactured goods was twice that of agricultural products. Considerable diversification developed during the first few decades of the new century, and by 1930 knit goods ranked first, with lumber second and milling third. Chattanooga, with a population of less than 60,000, was the state's center of the knit goods industry.

World War I served as a stimulus to industrial and financial growth, and the 12 years before the Depression comprised an era of urban and industrial growth unprecedented in the state's history. The single most significant development brought on by the war was the powder plant built by E.I. du Pont de Nemours and Company on 5,000 acres 10 miles northeast of Nashville. At its peak, 50,000 people were employed, more than one-half of whom were housed in the company town soon to be called Old Hickory. After the war the Du Ponts converted to peacetime pursuits and manufactured rayon and cellophane. In

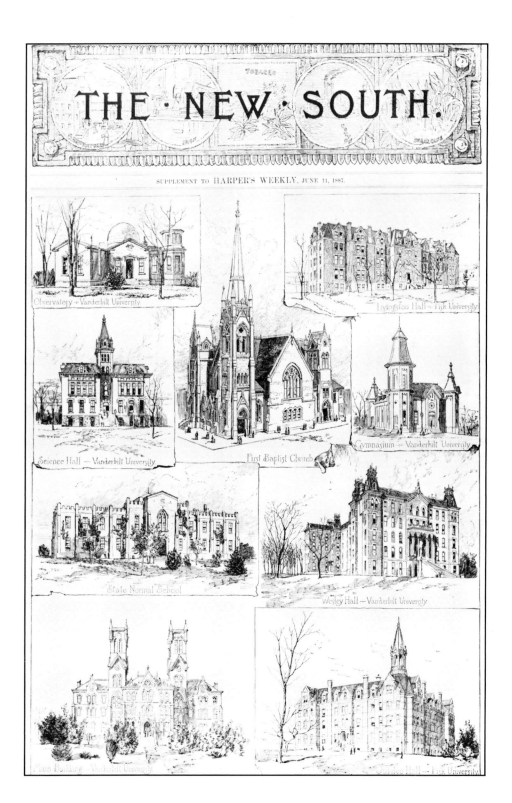

Louis Joutel made the sketches for these engravings of educational and religious buildings in Nashville for an 1887 Harper's Weekly.
Courtesy, James A. Hoobler

Above: *Following the Civil War,* Harper's Weekly *hired the famous wartime field artist Alfred R. Waud to tour the South and draw sketches of the rebuilding. Here is his 1866 view of Memphis from the Arkansas shore of the Mississippi River. Courtesy, James A. Hoobler*

Right: *In 1877* Frank Leslie's Illustrated Newspaper *sent an artist to Memphis to record that year's Mardi Gras parade. Memphis no longer celebrates Mardi Gras, probably because the weather is too cold in February. Now Memphians instead celebrate what they call "Memphis in May." Courtesy, James A. Hoobler*

later years other "miracle fabrics" were developed.

Both Nashville and Memphis exhibited growth, but East Tennessee surprised everyone with its phenomenal development. Chattanooga, for example, in 1910 had 192 factories that produced $26.7 million in goods. Ten years later it held 332 factories that produced goods worth more than $135 million. Knoxville grew even more rapidly—its population doubled in the 10-year period, and its 350 factories manufactured textiles, furniture, and other products. Kingsport, a small town in Sullivan County, by the 1920s had a variety of plants that manufactured hosiery, paper, textiles, glass, and cellulose. The Kingsport Press claimed to be the largest press in the nation devoted exclusively to book manufacture.

Nashville developed into a major financial center, with an emphasis on insurance, banking, and securities. Few insurance groups could match the pace of the National Life and Accident Insurance Company, a newcomer to Nashville in 1900 whose assets grew to $2.3 million in 1916 and to an astounding $29.6 million in 1930. Life and Casualty, a smaller group, grew at an even faster pace; with only $300,000 in assets in 1914, the company boasted of $12.2 million in 1930. Both exploited the black and poor-white markets by selling "industrial life" policies.

National Life had its beginning in 1897 in Huntsville, Alabama, as a company that sold industrial insurance solely to blacks. When it was moved to Nashville and reorganized a few years later, a group of "first generation" Nashvillians—young men mainly from the "country," including C. Runcie Clements, Cornelius and Edward Craig, Rufus E. Fort, Thomas J. Tyne, and William Ridley Wills—bought it and launched a business that soon attained gargantuan proportions. When some of the old business heads of Nashville poked fun at a company that sold only "Negro insurance," these young men laughed with them—all the way to the bank as they deposited huge profits.

The banking business also prospered. Annual clearings of Nashville banks rose from $232 million in 1915 to $1.24 billion in 1929. In 1915 Nashville had five national banks and five state banks, but new ones appeared frequently. One, chartered in 1916, was organized by 19-year-old Ed Potter, Jr., whose father managed the Broadway National Bank. Potter's bank, which ultimately merged in 1987 with Sovran Financial Corporation of Virginia, first was organized as the German American Bank. It soon changed its name, however, to Commerce Union—a name it retained for 60 years. Potter dominated much of the banking business in the Nashville area, and by 1924 had expanded to Camden, Springfield, Lawrenceburg, Sparta, Lebanon, and Murfreesboro.

Most of the highly successful men in banking and insurance came from country towns within a radius of 100 miles from Nashville. American National's P.D. Houston and Paul M. Davis hailed from rural Marshall and Coffee counties, respectively. The Potters were from Smithville, the Craigs from Giles County, Andrew M. Burton (of Life and Casualty) from Sumner County, and a half-dozen leaders at Third National and American National from nearby White Bluff.

Rogers Caldwell, the founder in 1917 of Caldwell and Company, was more responsible than any other single individual for Nashville's rise as an investment and financial center. Within a decade he made Caldwell and Company one of the biggest conglomerates in the South. Observing that no Nashville agency handled bonds exclusively, Caldwell began with a small local bond market but soon branched into every state of the old Confederacy. So profitable did this become that in 1919 he established the Bank of Tennessee solely to receive deposits from bond sales. After getting firm control of the bond market, he began a broad expansion. He bought a controlling interest in numerous department stores, textile and clothing companies, an oil company,

Ed Potter, Jr., founded the German-American Bank in 1916. Soon finding the name unacceptable due to war hysteria, he changed it to Commerce Union Bank. In 1987 it merged with the Sovran Financial Corporation of Norfolk and Richmond, Virginia. Courtesy, Sovran Financial Corporation

and even the Nashville baseball team. With Luke Lea he purchased a controlling interest in the Holston National Bank of Knoxville, and two banks in Memphis. Soon his holdings spilled over into North Carolina, Arkansas, and Kentucky. By 1919 Caldwell and Company controlled about 75 banks, numerous other business enterprises, and (with Lea) newspapers in Knoxville, Memphis, and Nashville.

Greed and mistakes in judgment spelled the doom of Caldwell. When the Depression came Caldwell's lavish lifestyle far exceeded his annual salary of $95,000. Bad judgment in buying and selling reduced his holdings to such an extent that within a month after Black Thursday (October 24, 1929), the House of Caldwell had collapsed. The state lost nearly $7 million when the Bank of Tennessee failed, and demands were made for the prosecution of both Lea and Caldwell. Lea ultimately served two years in prison, but Caldwell escaped conviction.

The state's economy was, of course, depressed during the 1930s, and many manufacturing establishments closed. World War II provided a stimulus to the economy, however, and by 1947 the manufacture of chemicals and allied

products had become a leading industry. It was closely followed by foods and kindred products and textile manufacture. Six counties accounted for 50 percent of the total value of manufactured goods produced in the state.

The progress of agriculture in the twentieth century was marked by considerable change. The tractor, electric power, and a variety of chemicals and fertilizers changed the lives of row-crop farmers as well as those of dairy and beef producers. County agents from Mountain City to Memphis introduced farmers and beef producers to a variety of improved methods as well as to federal subsidy programs.

The number of farms, which increased steadily until the 1920s, decreased substantially following the Depression, as more land was absorbed by urban and industrial development. In 1935 there were 273,783 farms, but by the mid-1980s there were only about one-third that number. The average value, however, had increased from less than $30 per acre to more than $1,000. The average value of land and buildings had increased from $2,000 in 1935 to $139,141 in 1982. Cash receipts from the marketing of farm produce also had increased substantially.

The production of soybeans and other grains became increasingly profitable in the 1970s and 1980s, while cotton production declined. From less than 4 million bushels in 1950, the annual soybean crop increased to a high of 48.1 million bushels in 1984. Corn gave way to beans, but by 1985 the crop of 79.5 million bushels exceeded that of all previous years. Wheat production also increased from 3 million bushels in 1950 to 21.5 million in 1984. Despite the warnings from the surgeon general's office about the dangers of tobacco usage, the tobacco crop volume changed very little after 1950. Cotton production in 1983, however, was less than one-third that of 1960.

Farmers hailed the introduction of burley tobacco during the 1920s, which, unlike the East and West Dark Fired, did not require firing. Since the plant was superior in quality to the other leaves yet easier to produce, nearly 90 percent of all tobacco grown in the state by 1984 was burley. Greene, Macon, and Sumner counties are the leading producers, while the Dark Fired variety still is a favorite in Montgomery and some of the other nearby counties of the Highland Rim.

The dairy industry also has declined in recent years, while beef cattle production has increased. The number of cattle milked in 1986 was less than one-third the number milked in 1950. The number of hogs grown remained constant, but the sheep and wool industry—where labor costs were again a factor—declined.

The New Deal had a profound effect upon agriculture and rural life in general. Congressman Joseph W. Byrns, a tobacco farmer from Robertson County who later became speaker of the House, was among those who drafted Roosevelt's Agricultural Adjustment Act, under which farmers were paid to reduce output in such basic commodities as cotton, corn, wheat, and tobacco—all significant farm produce in Tennessee.

But of all the New Deal legislation, the most significant for Tennessee agriculture was the development of the Tennessee Valley Authority. Broad in scope, it provided not only for electric power production, but also for flood con-

Dark fire tobacco production in Robertson County in the 1930s had not changed much since it had begun there prior to the Civil War. A wagon, a team of mules, and hand picking for many backbreaking hours was still the time-honored way to bring in a crop. Courtesy, Tennessee State Library and Archives

Soil erosion severely damaged much of America's agricultural lands in the 1930s. Tennessee was no exception, as seen on this Fayette County farm. Courtesy, Tennessee State Library and Archives

trol, improvement of navigation on the Tennessee River, fertilizer production, reforestation, retirement of worn-out farmland, and "the development of the natural resources of the Tennessee River drainage basin and its adjoining territory for the general social and economic welfare of the Nation." The Tennessee River was a natural choice for such a project. The western slope of the Unakas, where the rivers that feed the Tennessee rise, enjoy the highest annual rainfall in the eastern United States, and the hilly countryside makes flood control easier.

Electric power production, however, helped Tennesseans most. The Rural Electrification Act brought power to small towns and rural areas throughout most of the state. In 1933 the people in the valley had consumed 1.5 billion kilowatts of power and had paid 10 cents or more per kilowatt hour. By 1960 consumption had reached 57.2 billion kilowatts, and high-volume users paid less than one cent per kilowatt. By 1975 usage was at 113 billion, and 10 years later it had risen to nearly twice that figure.

Today, 54 percent of the power generated is used for commercial and industrial pursuits. Less than half is generated by hydroelectric power; coal accounts for 34 percent and nuclear power for 10 percent.

One reason for the location of the atomic fission plant at Oak Ridge during World War II was the proximity of the facilities provided by the TVA. After the war the facility at Oak Ridge was converted to peacetime pursuits, which included space exploration, agricultural and biological research, metallurgy, and electric power generation.

By the 1980s the influx of Japanese industrialists and capitalists exceeded the dreams of those post-Civil War leaders who sought captains of industry to develop the state's natural resources. The Japanese have taught Tennesseans exactly what Arthur Colyar, Joseph E. Killebrew, and other exponents of the New South longed for: quality control, efficient management, and how to make money. By 1988, 31 Japanese companies with investments of more than $1 billion and over 8,000 employees were located in plants from Memphis to Greeneville.

The largest automotive plant in the world outside of Japan, and the largest investment by a foreign company in U.S. history, is the Nissan Motor Manufacturing Company plant at Smyrna. This $848-million facility manufactures passenger cars and light body trucks, and it employs over 3,500 people. Japanese industrialists have mentioned geographic and climatic similarities between Japan and Tennessee as reasons for locating in the Volunteer State, along with favorable tax structures and land costs, a plentiful supply of moderately priced labor, and a vigorous recruiting effort by state leaders and officials.

Tennessee's population, estimated at 4,717,000 in 1985, has grown at a rapidly accelerating rate since 1950, but it now appears to be leveling off. People tend to be concentrated in and near the four largest cities. Nashville—sometimes called "the South's newest Cinderella

The Tennessee Valley Authority, born during the New Deal era, created an enormous series of dams in the Tennessee River Valley to prevent flooding and to generate electricity. Courtesy, Tennessee State Museum

The first Nissan Sentra automobile rolled off the assembly line on March 26, 1985. Marvin Runyon, head of the Tennessee plant, and Governor Lamar Alexander congratulated each other for bringing Japanese investment and entrepreneurial skills to Smyrna. Courtesy, State Photo Services

City"—has has a highly diversified economy and therefore a variety of jobs to offer. While Nashville's population showed little increase in recent years, the surrounding counties of Williamson, Rutherford, Sumner, and Cheatham grew as much as 12.6 percent during the five-year period after 1980. Nashville has much to offer: not only is it the seat of state government, but it also is the center of the country music industry, the home of profitable financial institutions, a transportation and commercial hub, and a city of many tourist attractions and spectacular entrepreneurial successes. The acquisition of manufacturing establishments such as Nissan at Smyrna and the proposed $3.5-billion General Motors Saturn plant, which is to be located in nearby Williamson and Maury counties, points to continued economic and population growth in the Middle Tennessee area.

Most of the eastern counties also have shown substantial population growth in recent years, with increases in Jefferson and Sevier counties of 10 percent or more between 1980 and 1985. The World's Fair exhibition of 1982 may not have met expectations, but it did bolster Knoxville's economy, as has the continued development of the state's largest university. Knoxville continues to be a significant financial center, although the collapse of Jake Butcher's financial empire and the United American Bank, which by 1982 accounted for more than one-half the business loans of the city, had a negative impact. Chattanooga, which depends largely upon industrial-type businesses like iron and steel, also has experienced significant growth, although, like Knoxville, the city recently experienced a major bank failure when the Hamilton Bank collapsed.

During the past few years West Tennessee has registered a growth rate significantly below state and national averages, although Memphis has shown modest and expected growth. Much of the western section is rural and lies outside the predominant rail and highway transportation routes.

Experts predict that the state's population will rise by nearly 700,000 by the year 2000, which presents many opportunities for significant advancement in all phases of the economy.

Tennessee troops paraded up Capitol Boulevard to the statehouse through a temporary arch after the Armistice ended World War I. Tennessee, upholding its "volunteer" tradition, provided more than 75,000 men and women for the effort; more than 1,800 Tennesseans lost their lives. Courtesy, Tennessee State Library and Archives

5

TENNESSEE IN PEACE AND WAR

1870-1920

Tennesseans have not cherished fond memories of Governor William Brownlow. Those living in the late 1860s, happy that the Brownlow era had ended, then turned to other matters. Constitutional reform, settlement of the state debt, and prison reform were among the matters addressed during the first three decades after the Civil War, and new problems arose as the twentieth century dawned.

Soon after Dewitt Senter's inauguration in 1869, Tennesseans made plans for a revision of the state constitution, and early in January 1870 delegates assembled for the first such meeting since 1834. John C. Brown, a pre-war Whig and former Confederate general, was chosen convention chairman, although most of the other members also were men of experience and ability. More than one-half had been legislators, most had fought in the Federal or Confederate armies, and four—including Brown—had held the rank of general.

Several matters drew their attention. After lengthy debates on the question of suffrage, delegates enfranchised black men but also included a clause that all voters must pay a poll tax—a provision which naturally curtailed voting among poor blacks and whites. Aware that Governor Brownlow had loaned state funds to bankrupt railroads, they prohibited future legislators from lending money to "any person . . . or corporation." Lawmaking sessions were limited to 75 days, and the complicated amending process was retained. The Supreme Court henceforth was to consist of five members, not more than two of whom could reside in any one grand division of the state. Although the Radical element opposed most of the revisions, Tennesseans ratified the "new" constitution by a three-to-one majority. Basically, the document of the past 75 years remained in place. It was, indeed, to continue to be the basic law, although several "limited" conventions have made revisions since 1952.

The Democratic party regained control after the Brownlow era and has continued to dominate state politics to the present. Its leaders in the late 1860s consisted in large measure of pre-war Whigs who were more interested in business and industrial development than they were in expanding the principles of Jacksonian Democracy. John C. Brown had captured the attention of voters during the constitutional convention, and he had little difficulty in winning the governor's seat in the November 1871 elections. Preferring the party label of "Conservative" to that of "Democrat," he was interested primarily in the expansion of the railroads and industry. Soon after his two terms as governor had expired, he became president of the Tennessee Coal, Iron, and Railroad Company. His successor, James D. Porter, another former Whig, also pursued business interests. Soon after his gubernatorial term ended, he became president of the Nashville, Chattanooga, and St. Louis Railroad. The elections of both Brown and his successor were accompanied by election to the legislature of a predominance of Conservative Democrats and former Whigs.

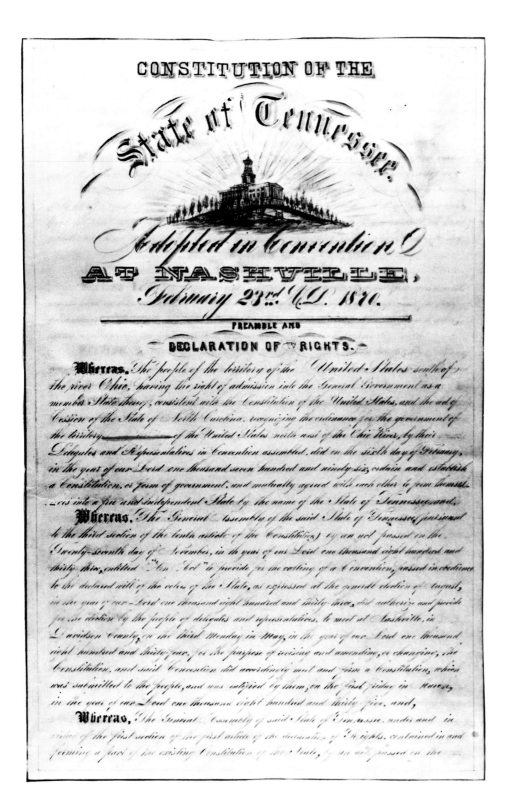

The 1870 Constitution effectively ended Reconstruction in Tennessee. It also instituted a poll tax, which in effect disenfranchised poor black and white Tennesseans. That Constitution remains in effect today, but since 1952 a number of amendments have been adopted, including the repeal of the poll tax. Courtesy, Tennessee State Library and Archives

The inherently divisive nature of the Democratic party—which consisted not only of Whigs, but also of former plantation owners, yeoman farmers, and men of such diverse antecedents as Isham G. Harris, Andrew Johnson, Nathan Bedford Forrest, and Thomas A.R. Nelson —meant that dissent rather than strong party allegiance characterized the group. But the unifying bond among Democrats always was a determination that Radical extremists such as those who had prevailed during the Brownlow era would never again gain control of the state government. Writers sometimes have characterized the Democrats as "redeemers," because they "redeemed" the state from the Radicals.

The Republicans, who sought to divorce themselves from the extremes of Radicalism, constituted the minority party, but they occasionally won state control when dissent hopelessly split the Democrats. Their strength came mainly from the East Tennessee counties which had opposed secession and fought for the Union, but they also boasted of strong support in a narrow band of counties along the Tennessee River, which separated West Tennessee from the central section where people had opposed secession. Aided by federal patronage because of party control in Washington, Republican leaders such as Leonidas C. Houk of Knoxville were able to maintain a tightly knit political machine which could challenge the Democratic majority effectively. Tennessee consisted of 10 congressional districts, and the minority party usually could count on winning three or four of them.

Brown and Porter each served two terms as governor; Porter was succeeded by Albert S. Marks of Winchester, who, unlike his two predecessors, had voted for the Southern Democratic candidate in the presidential election of 1860 and considered himself a lifelong Democrat. He was strongly aligned, however, with the Whig faction, which was led by his kinsman, Arthur S. Colyar, the chief of the dominant industrial wing of the party. That naturally affected his political and

Far left: *John C. Brown (1827-1889) served as governor from 1871 to 1875. He encouraged the expansion of railroads and industry in the state. Courtesy, Tennessee State Museum*

Left: *James D. Porter (1838-1912) served as governor from 1875 to 1879. Courtesy, Tennessee State Museum*

economic proclivities, as Colyar quietly exerted effective control of the party from behind the scenes through his Nashville *American* and his widespread railroad and business interests.

During the 10 years of Brown, Porter, and Marks, the question of the state debt constantly defied legislative settlement, as the state obligation continued to grow by alarming increments. For decades before the Civil War, Tennessee had issued bonds from time to time—to purchase the Hermitage property, complete the capitol, and buy stock in railroad and turnpike companies—but only during the Brownlow years did officials recklessly lend money to railroads, some of which were already bankrupt and in the

hands of unscrupulous people. Leaders divided the indebtedness into the "state debt proper"—which most believed should be paid in full—and the "railroad debt." As the decade continued and the effects of the Panic of 1873 became keenly felt in the state, Democrats divided bitterly over how and whether the railroad debt should be paid at all. The "State Credit Wing," principally former Whigs and businessmen, argued that defaulting or scaling down would frighten away Northern and foreign capital at a time when the state needed it most. Conversely, others argued that the debt incurred by the Brownlow government— "a revolutionary enterprise"—should be repudiated. The "Low Tax Demo-

Far left: *Albert S. Marks (1836-1891) served as governor from 1879 to 1881. Courtesy, Tennessee State Museum*

Left: *Arthur St. Clair Colyar controlled the Democratic party in Tennessee through his newspaper the Nashville* American. *Courtesy, Tennessee State Library and Archives*

Right: *Alvin J. Hawkins (1821-1905) served as governor from 1881 to 1882. His legislation to solve the state's nagging debt was declared unconstitutional by the U.S. Supreme Court, and he was defeated by Democrat William Bate in 1882. Courtesy, Tennessee State Museum*

Far right: *William Brimage Bate (1826-1905) served as governor from 1883 to 1887. He succeeded in solving the indebtedness problem that had plagued the state since before the Civil War. Courtesy, Tennessee State Museum*

crats"—mainly small farmers in predominantly rural counties, led by Warren County legislator John H. Savage—argued for a scaling down of the debt after careful negotiation with the bondholders.

The failure of Brown, Porter, and Marks to solve the debt problem gave considerable strength to the Republican party, whose leaders continually cast aspersions upon the Democratic leadership. Consequently, in 1880 when the bolting Low Tax wing nominated its own candidate and the Democrats were hopelessly split, Republican Alvin J. Hawkins from Carroll County won the governorship by 25,000 votes. Hawkins immediately turned his attention to the debt problem, but his efforts resulted in legislation which the Supreme Court ultimately declared unconstitutional. His work discredited, Hawkins was defeated in 1882 by Sumner County Democrat and Civil War leader William B. Bate, after the Democrats through compromise modified the demand for repudiation sufficiently to win back voters who had balloted for Hawkins two years earlier.

Bate's success with the debt question was an important factor in bringing prosperity in the 1880s and winning for him a second term as governor. His proposal—to pay most of the "proper" debt at par and most of the remainder at 50 cents on the dollar—was satisfactory to most creditors and taxpayers, both weary

of years of debate and indecision.

In the meantime other state business had continued, with various attending problems. Men of such varied Civil War propensities as Andrew Johnson and Isham G. Harris had quietly taken seats in the U.S. Senate. Johnson's indomitable ambition had remained undimmed after his return from Washington in 1869, and he had immediately sought rehabilitation in the Democratic party, although Old South leaders dubbed him a party and sectional traitor. By 1875, however, he had established himself sufficiently with farmers, debtors, and Low Taxers to win a Senate seat. Although President Grant sent word to Tennessee legislators that he would consider Johnson's return to the Senate "a personal insult," lawmakers chose him on the 55th ballot over former governors Bate and Brown. He took his seat on March 4, 1875, promptly denounced Grant as a charlatan, and sought immediately to assume leadership within the minority Democratic party. The strain was too much for him, however, and he died a few weeks after taking the oath of office. David M. Key of Chattanooga succeeded him. Two years later Key was appointed to a cabinet position in the administration of President Rutherford B. Hayes.

That same year Harris was elected to the U.S. Senate, and he served there until his death in 1898. As mentioned earlier, he had led Tennessee into the Confederacy, and after the war he had lived in Mexico and England for two years before returning to Tennessee to his law practice and business interests. He had immediately become a leader of the Bourbon wing of the party—conservative men of Old South orientation who reluctantly admitted a "new order" after Appomattox.

Tennesseans were shocked when in January 1883 Marshall T. Polk—state treasurer, avid Democrat, and strong defender of the State Credit position—disappeared after his defalcation of approximately $400,000 from the treasury became known. A nephew and adopted son of the former president and a Confederate officer on the staff of General Leonidas Polk during the Civil War, Polk had been the trusted state treasurer since 1877. Investigations revealed that his books had not been audited in several years and that he apparently had siphoned off substantial amounts to invest in a variety of enterprises, including Mexican silver mines, Alabama iron mines, and the Louisville and Nashville Railroad. Captured near the Mexican border and returned to Nashville for trial, he was convicted of embezzlement, fined $366,540 (the amount of the deficit in the Treasury after the bonding company had paid its obligation), and sentenced to 20 years in prison, where he died a few months after his incarceration.

Memphis, in the meantime, had suffered devastation much worse than that of the Civil War. Yellow fever epidemics in 1873, 1878, and 1879 actually reduced the official population of Memphis from 40,200 in 1870 to 33,600 10 years later, as people died or fled the city. Only with aid from the state government was the city able to rebuild after sanitation and public health improvements convinced people that they could survive in the river town.

One bright spot in the 1870s and 1880s was that more than a dozen black men of ability became active in state politics. Sampson W. Keeble, a Nashville businessman, was elected to the Tennes-

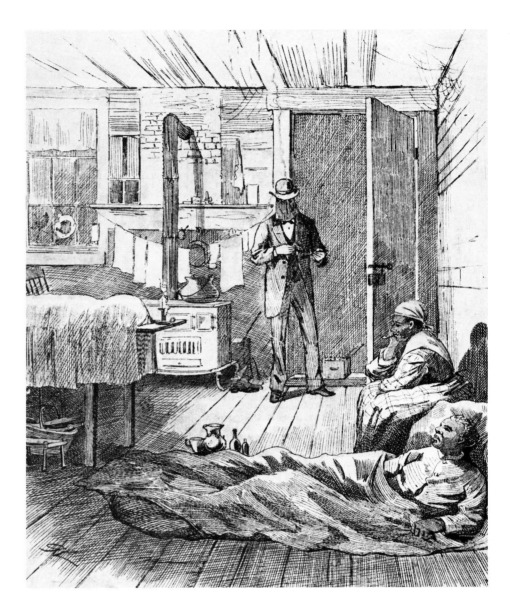

see House in 1872 and became the first black to serve in the General Assembly. Other black politicians included Thomas A. Sykes of Nashville and Samuel A. McElwee of Haywood County, both of whom worked actively to repeal a law passed in 1875 requiring segregation in railroad cars. These men of the 1880s were the last blacks to serve in the legislature until 1965. By the late 1880s Democrats, who were unhappy with the consistency with which Negroes voted for Republican candidates, had sought effectively to curtail their voting and office holding, especially in the cities. Inasmuch as many were illiterate, black participation was curtailed by the Dortch Law (1889), which prescribed a secret ballot. By 1890 Jim Crow was obviously

Yellow fever decimated the city of Memphis in the 1870s. As a result of the business disruptions and the loss of population through death and relocation, the city went bankrupt and lost its charter. The 1880s saw renewal, however, with many civic improvements and an overall boost to the quality of life in the Bluff City. Courtesy, Tennessee State Library and Archives

present in Tennessee, six years before the Supreme Court officially placed a stamp of approval upon the separate but equal doctrine.

New party alignments brought an East Tennessean to the governor's chair in 1886, and he soon became one of the state's most beloved chief executives. Although Bate had solved the debt question, he had been unable to weld a strong bond between factions within the Democratic party. The rural farmers and urban laborers, although actually in the majority, were known for their political lethargy in the absence of strong leadership. Therefore, the voice of 36-year-old Robert Love Taylor from Carter County was heard and given attention when he mounted the platform at the Democratic Convention early in 1886. "We have been . . . discordant, belligerent, and rent with feuds," he told fellow Democrats, and he despaired of continued party growth unless attention was given to de-

mands for recognition of the young and rising leaders. The selection of a candidate not wedded to any particular faction, Taylor said, would interest the young and woo the rural folk, whose attention already was being turned to the developing agrarian movement in nearby states. When Taylor spoke, people listened, and Democrats nominated him on the 15th ballot.

Interestingly, a few weeks earlier Republicans had nominated Bob's older brother, Alfred A. Taylor. An able debater—although lacking his brother's charisma—Alf, strongly backed by the minority party, accepted the challenge to meet in debate. Both already had had some political experience; Alf had served in the state legislature while Bob had spent two years in Congress. Their family had for years played prominent roles in public affairs.

Enormous crowds turned out to hear the candidates on the hustings. Although both were able orators, each brought along his "fiddle" to entertain the crowds should the issues prove dull. Usually they traveled, slept, and ate together, but on the platform each vigorously defended the issues supported by his party.

Bob's popularity with the rural masses was an important factor in his victory, although Alf surprised many observers by winning a respectable vote in predominantly Democratic counties. Despite his victory, Bob Taylor was unable to capture the wholehearted support of the Bourbon wing. Two years later he was able to secure renomination only after 40 ballots and some "trading" with the

Bourbon leaders. The Republicans offered little in the way of opposition, and in the fall Taylor won a second term. His four years in office are not remembered particularly for profundity of legislation or leadership, but for the stability he gave to his party and for his ability to interest the rural people in politics. His popularity continued throughout his lifetime, and 10 years later he was returned to the governor's chair. In 1906 he was elected to the U.S. Senate.

Although Bob Taylor helped awaken rural voters, organizations among farmers actually had been in existence for more than a decade before he became governor. The farmers' groups were not politically oriented at first; operating principally in the South and West, they sought chiefly to address the worsening economic conditions attendant upon farm life. The Grange was organized in Washington early in the 1870s. Its primary object was not only to achieve "the general improvement of husbandry" but also to increase the "general happiness . . . and prosperity of the country." By 1875 Tennessee's interest was such that the state ranked third in membership among the states of the South and West.

Other agricultural groups followed. In contrast to the Grange the Greenback group had strong political interests and nominated candidates for governor during the 1870s and 1880s. By 1880 a national group called the Agricultural Wheel had more members in Tennessee than in any other state, while a new orga-

Tennessee's colorful "War of the Roses" gubernatorial election pitted brothers Bob and Alf Taylor against each other in 1886. After making their speeches they would tell stories and jokes and play their fiddles to entertain the crowds. From Frank Leslie's Illustrated Newspaper, *1886. Courtesy, Tennessee State Museum*

nization known as the Farmers' Alliance boasted of more than 20,000 members. Finally, by 1890, the Wheel and other groups merged into the Alliance, and its leaders, now boasting a Tennessee membership of more than 100,000, openly sought control of the Democratic party. John Buchanan, a Rutherford County farmer and landowner who had been president of the Wheel, immediately gained control of the Alliance.

When the Democrats met in Nashville in July 1890, farm leaders already had announced their support of Buchanan for governor. Although the Bourbon wing supported Josiah Patterson of Memphis and the industrial wing backed Jere Baxter of Nashville, the jubilant rural faction carried the day and nominated Buchanan after three days of disputing and voting. Seeking to bind up the party's wounds by pledging to maintain "the great principles of Democracy as enunciated by Jackson, Polk, and Johnson," Buchanan helped to draft a platform which he hoped would be suitable to all the factions.

Buchanan won by a majority of nearly 40,000 votes, but, lacking the charisma of Bob Taylor, he was unable to unite the dissenting Democratic factions. He was blamed for giving too many state jobs to Alliance men, using state troops for pacification of a miners' insurrection in East Tennessee, and being a tool of national

agrarian leaders, particularly among members of the new Populist party. Consequently, when two major factions of the party announced a determination to nominate Supreme Court Chief Justice Peter Turney for governor, Buchanan refused even to attend the Democrat nominating convention. He still had a respectable following among rural Democrats, however, and he was drafted by them to run as an independent with the support of Alliance men, Populists, and "Buchanan Democrats." But when rumors began to spread—hotly denied by Buchanan—of "deals with Republicans and Populist-Republican coalitions," enough Democrats returned to party regularity to win the election for Turney. As governor the former judge followed a conservative course and was acceptable enough to party members to win renomination in 1894.

The election of 1894 became a major catastrophe for Democrats even though, amid cries of fraud and deception, they were able to return Turney to a second term. The aging governor, plagued by recurring illnesses, was unable to enter actively into his own campaign and had to depend largely upon others, including Edward Ward Carmack, vigorous editor of the Memphis *Commercial Appeal* and champion of the free coinage of silver, to carry it across the state. Republicans had chosen a Pennsylvania-born businessman and politician—Chattanooga industrialist H. Clay Evans—as their candidate after he had served two terms in Congress. For two months the industrialist-politician talked his way across the state in a way which reminded some people of Bob Taylor. When his campaign had ended the Republican chances of victory appeared to be the best since Hawkins had been elected more than a decade earlier.

The official count gave Evans a plurality of less than a thousand votes, but the Democrats alleged fraudulent voting in some of the counties where Evans' majority had been large, and they announced their intention of contesting the results. When the Democratic-dominated legislature assembled in January 1895, a commission, consisting of seven Democrats and five Republicans, examined the charges of fraud. Needless to say, the Democratic majority prevailed, and Turney finally was inaugurated for a second term on May 5.

The industrial wing of the party had opposed the contest from the beginning, and Turney's victory was won at the expense of whatever good will he had earned during his first term. The Democrats, as they had done 10 years earlier, in 1896 again called upon Bob Taylor to repair the raveled sleeve of party harmony. In a closely fought contest Taylor's charm and charisma won the election for him by 7,000 votes. The thunder of the Populist party had become little more than an echo, and Taylor's vote came largely from the rural voters.

In the meantime Tennesseans addressed prison reform and convict leasing—two matters long overdue for attention and remedy. Built in the early 1830s, the state penitentiary had been used as a military prison throughout most of the Civil War, and after decades without repairs it was in a dilapidated condition. The prison population had increased considerably since Appomattox; freed blacks—many hungry and ignorant of societal rules—and displaced whites had caused the prison population to increase to such an extent that incarceration within any parameters of decency was impossible. Blacks, who before the war had composed only about 5 percent of the prison population, by 1866 made up more than one-half of the inmates.

Tennesseans were not slow in observing the success with convict leasing that other states, both North and South, appeared to have. Consequently, as early as 1866, convicts were leased to a Nashville furniture manufacturer who built shops on the prison grounds and agreed to pay the state 43 cents per day for each convict. By the early 1870s articulate industrialists, maintaining that felons could best be employed in coal mines, had convinced legislators that branch prisons should be established at Tracy City and

other East Tennessee localities where convicts would be leased to mine owners.

The contracts before 1883 were small when compared with one signed that year with the Tennessee Coal, Iron, and Railroad Company in which the company leased the entire state penitentiary, containing more than 1,300 convicts, for $101,000 per year. Not only would such a deal be profitable for all concerned, said the company's general counsel, Arthur Colyar, but "free laborers would be loath to enter upon strikes when they saw that the company was amply provided with convict labor."

Criticisms of the lease system were made by humanitarians from Memphis to Bristol, but to little avail. Press representatives occasionally entered into investigations among the prisoners and told of "cruelty, rage, vice and despair." A Chattanooga *Times* reporter wrote early in 1885 of convicts being forced to mine coal "in water a foot deep" and of being struck with a lash of "3-ply sole leather braid." While legislators admitted to unsafe and unsanitary conditions, they also pointed in 1890 to a net profit of $771,400, which was only a little short of the total prison costs during the past half-century.

The most effective criticisms of the lease system came not from humanitarians but from free laborers who wanted to mine coal for a living at a decent wage. By the 1890s the coal mining industry had grown to a respectable size in Tennessee, but miners were dissatisfied: not only did they receive only bare subsistence wages, but most were paid in "company scrip" (which could be spent only at the company store, or, if used elsewhere, usually was discounted), and most had to pledge not to strike as a condition of employment. Usage of convict labor only added to the insecurity of their opportunities to earn a livelihood.

Uprisings and violence in Anderson, Roane, and Grundy counties brought on Governor Buchanan and units of the state militia, but they did little to pacify disgruntled miners. Hundreds were arrested on charges of insurrection and

Above: *In 1898 the state opened the present Tennessee State Prison at Cockrill Bend, west of Nashville. Today it looks much as it did in this photograph taken when it was new, except that the tower's bell chamber and top two floors were removed, and the old roof placed back on top of the truncated tower. Courtesy, Tennessee State Library and Archives*

Above right: *Benton McMillin (1845-1933) served as governor from 1899 to 1903. Courtesy, Tennessee State Museum*

other crimes, but few were convicted when tried before sympathetic local juries.

Candidates in the gubernatorial campaign of 1892 promised to abolish the lease system, and in the following spring legislators complied. Two new prisons were planned immediately, to be "managed and conducted upon just, humane, and civilized principles." For the main prison the state purchased the Mark Cockrill farm—1,128 acres located 6 miles west of Nashville on the south bank of the Cumberland River. Modern in every respect, the prison was completed and occupied by 1898. Officials also bought 9,000 acres in Morgan

County, where they quickly built and made ready the Brushy Mountain Prison. There the grounds included rich veins of coal that by 1895 prisoners mined for the state. A few years later the state bought the "Herbert Domain," which consisted of 11,000 acres in Bledsoe, Van Buren, and White counties. Tennessee thus became the first state in the South to abolish the convict lease system.

A few years earlier Colonel Edmond W. Cole had provided funds for the establishment of a reformatory for youthful offenders. By 1897 the Tennessee Industrial School had been established to house both youthful offenders and "abandoned children."

Bob Taylor did not seek reelection in 1898. His name was often mentioned when politicians talked of a U.S. Senate race, and in 1906 he defeated incumbent Senator Edward Ward Carmack. Taylor remained in the Senate until his death in 1912. Benton McMillin, an eight-term congressman from Celina, was elected governor without serious opposition. A man of considerable charm and "common sense," McMillin was acceptable to the people generally, and he easily won a second term in 1900.

Several months before McMillin's election, four Tennessee regiments were mustered into service after the United States declared war on Spain. Tennesseans, like people in other states, had

viewed with disdain reports of Spanish cruelty and abuse in Cuba; they then were aroused when early in 1898 the American battleship *Maine* was destroyed, with the loss of nearly 300 American lives. Although Congressman Carmack and some other Democrats suspected that the Republican administration's policy was directed toward imperialism and territorial expansion in the Pacific, Congress declared war after agreeing to oppose any efforts to add Cuba to the United States. Some Tennesseans fought in Cuba and others in Manila, while Tennesseans in the navy and marines saw service in the Pacific. The war lasted for only a few months, and late in 1899 Governor McMillin welcomed the veterans home with a florid speech before a large throng of soldiers and citizens.

Prohibition was a recurring theme in Tennessee politics during most of the next two decades, as "wets" and "drys" struggled to control the political turf. Attempts had been made before the Civil War to regulate the liquor traffic, and in 1877 legislators had adopted the Four Mile Law, which forbade the sale of intoxicants within four miles of chartered schools outside of incorporated towns. The law was extended from time to time, and by McMillin's term only the metropolitan areas were legally wet. The Prohibition party had been highly vocal (if

not effective in winning votes) for several decades, and groups such as the Woman's Christian Temperance Union, Order of Good Templars, Anti-Saloon League, Temperance Alliance, and Protestant evangelical denominations openly sought to end the whiskey traffic.

Shortly after Taylor's first inauguration, prohibition had been soundly defeated when legislators submitted the question to a referendum. East Tennesseans approved the measure by a vote of 42,000 to 31,000, while people west of the Tennessee River rejected it by approximately the same vote. It was the Democratic voters of Middle Tennessee who gave prohibition the most resounding defeat—by a two-to-one majority. Prohibitionists, however, rather than being discouraged by the results of the referendum, actually became more active as new temperance organizations boasting large memberships made their appearance.

When McMillin refused a third term, Democrats elected James B. Frazier, a Chattanooga lawyer, for two terms. Although he was not considered a prohibitionist, Frazier was friendly with many of the temperance leaders and actually agreed to a prohibition plank in the party platform. He supported the Adams Law of 1903, which extended the Four Mile Law, but, reluctant to alienate liquor interests in the cities, he opposed its application in urban areas. Shortly after his second inauguration as governor, Frazier was elected to the U.S. Senate when 77-year-old William B. Bate died less than two months after being reelected. Frazier's term was completed by Senate Speaker John I. Cox. Tennesseans looked to 1906 as a major election year because both a governor and a U.S. senator were to be chosen.

The senatorial race pitted two old pros against each other in the Democratic primary. Incumbent Edward Ward Carmack, who had edited newspapers in Nashville and Memphis, had been elected to the Senate in 1900 after two terms in Congress. Although Carmack had retained a highly spirited following throughout his political career, he also had made enemies who now sought a candidate who could defeat him. Bob Taylor was widely considered to be a logical candidate, and his aggressive announcement to challenge Carmack won wide acclaim. Taylor and Carmack then agreed to a direct primary (which meant that the question of their election would be referred to the people), the results of which would be binding upon the Democratic Executive Committee. As the Republicans did not plan to nominate a strong candidate, victory in the primary was tantamount to election.

The various issues which were widely debated seem minuscule from today's perspective, but the two gifted orators drew crowds wherever they spoke, and they reminded old timers of the gubernatorial race of two decades earlier when the Taylor brothers were candidates. Taylor won the closely contested primary, thanks to support evenly distributed across the state. Carmack, who some had thought would win large majorities in Nashville and Memphis, actually ran poorly in those areas because he had made enemies with his journalistic style as an editor.

The gubernatorial race of the same year generated equal enthusiasm after the Democrats chose Malcolm R. "Ham" Patterson instead of John Cox. In a close contest the Memphis Democrat

won and served for two terms.

Progressive legislation was enacted during Patterson's first term, including laws that prohibited the sale of falsely branded foods or drugs (the Pure Food and Drug Act), banned gambling at horse races, purchased a mansion for the governor, and extended the concept of the Four Mile Law to the cities (the Pendleton Act). But Patterson's successful bid for reelection resulted in irreconcilable differences within the Democratic party when Carmack, still smarting from his defeat in the 1906 Senate race, was persuaded by prohibitionists to run for governor. As late as February 1908 Carmack had expressed a preference for local option, but now he endorsed statewide prohibition. Although Patterson boasted that he had "closed 400 saloons" when he signed the Pendleton Bill, he continued to reject state-imposed prohibition in favor of local option because he believed it to be the only "safe, fair, and democratic" method of handling the inflammatory matter.

Patterson's nomination by 7,000 votes was due principally to urban voters; Carmack carried most of the East Tennessee counties and much of the rural area west of the Tennessee River. In the general election Republican George N. Tillman declared for state-imposed prohibition, but his failure to unite his own party on the issue became a cause for his defeat. Patterson was drawn off the hustings for most of the month of October to deal with pressing state business—especially violence in the Reelfoot Lake region which required him to mobilize part of the state militia. Difficulties had developed when landowners, announcing plans to drain the lake and develop real estate operations, had encountered the wrath of natives who had fished and otherwise enjoyed the lake for generations. Before Patterson could send troops angry people had hung and shot one lawyer representing the owners, had tried to kill another before he miraculously escaped, and had otherwise taken the law into their own hands.

Whatever plans Patterson may have

had for uniting his party were soon dashed when Carmack was killed on the Nashville streets by Robin and Duncan Cooper, prominent Democrats close to Patterson. Luke Lea, a flamboyant and rising power in the Democratic party, recently had established the Nashville *Tennessean* and employed Carmack as editor. Bitter over his two recent political defeats, Carmack had resorted to a strident, personal journalistic style—the one he knew best—and he had soon encountered problems with some of those he had denounced, including Duncan Cooper.

Carmack had begun his journalistic career years earlier on the staff of Cooper's Nashville *American,* but the two had parted company later, when Cooper had supported Bob Taylor in the senate race against Carmack, and Patterson in the governor's race. An elderly Confederate veteran of prominent lineage who enjoyed the respect of party leaders, Cooper had been outraged when Carmack poked fun at him by referring to him as "Major," "Old Baldheaded Dunc," and "a little baldheaded Angel, Dunc Cooper." Carmack also had insinuated that Cooper was associated with the Nashville underworld and steeped in "perfidy and dishonor." Although members of his family tried to dissuade Cooper, he soon procured a pistol and sent so many threats to Carmack that Carmack also began going about the streets armed.

Finally, one late afternoon in early November 1908, Cooper, accompanied by his son, Robin, and by former Davidson County Sheriff J.A. Sharp, walked along Union Street en route to the governor's new mansion across from the capitol. Entirely by chance Carmack, walking up Seventh Avenue en route to his nearby home, happened to meet the three at the corner of Seventh and Union. Apparently taken by complete surprise, Carmack, seeing Cooper with his hand upraised and hearing him bark, "we've got the drop on you . . . you dastardly coward," believed his life to be in danger. At any rate he quickly withdrew his pistol, fired in the Coopers' direction, and sought shelter

behind a nearby lamp post and a chance passerby. Duncan Cooper tried to draw his weapon at the same time, but he found that it was hopelessly wedged deep within his pocket. Robin Cooper, simultaneously with Carmack's gunfire, stepped between the editor and his father. He received one of Carmack's bullets in his right shoulder and another through his coat sleeve. He then fired three times in rapid succession, each bullet striking Carmack; each, according to an autopsy, could have been fatal. Carmack fell dead in the street.

Led by the drumbeat of Lea's *Tennessean,* public opinion immediately turned against the Coopers. Both were indicted and placed in jail to await trial. Interestingly, old Sheriff Sharp, who had walked a half block by the time the shooting be-

Edward Ward Carmack, a newspaper editor and U.S. senator, was shot on Seventh Avenue North by Robin and Duncan Cooper. His career had ended but his influence, and "martyrdom," ensured that prohibition would become the law in Tennessee in 1909. Courtesy, Tennessee State Library and Archives

In death, Edward Ward Carmack was a much more heroic figure than he ever had been in life. The year after his demise prohibition became the law in Tennessee, and in the 1920s the grateful Woman's Christian Temperance Union erected this monument to their hero at the south entrance to the Capitol. With great irony, that statue now presides over the Motlow Tunnel entrance to the Capitol complex. The tunnel is named in honor of the late state Senator Regor Motlow, one of the Jack Daniel's Distillery Motlows. Courtesy, Tennessee State Library and Archives

gan, also was indicted and placed in jail, but the suit against him was dismissed when the trial began.

After a 16-day trial the Coopers were convicted of second degree murder and sentenced to 20 years in prison. Upon appeal to the Supreme Court, the conviction of Duncan Cooper—who had not fired a shot—was upheld by a three-to-two majority, while the case of Robin Cooper was remanded for retrial. Governor Patterson then incensed prohibitionists and Carmack supporters by pardoning Duncan Cooper. Robin Cooper was acquitted a few months later when a Davidson County criminal court jury returned a verdict of not guilty.

Carmack—like Abraham Lincoln two score years before—was much more beloved and politically influential in death than he had been in life. While memorial services were held for him at the place of the shooting and elsewhere across the state, prohibition leaders made preparations to outlaw whiskey. When legislators gathered in January 1909, the prohibitionists controlled the assembly through a coalition of Republicans and "Independent" Democrats, and they soon enacted legislation making the sale, manufacture, and consumption of alcohol illegal. This action presaged the advent of a fusion between "dry" Democrats and Republicans, which in 1910 brought the second Republican governor since Reconstruction to the capitol.

In May 1910, 5,000 enthusiastic Independent Democrats convening in Nashville repudiated the "Regular" Democrats and described Patterson's announcement for a third term as "brazen effrontery." Accusing the governor of trying to influence even members of the Supreme Court in the Cooper case, they nominated and elected in the primary an "Independent" slate of Supreme Court candidates. Republicans, who hoped to win Independent support in the forthcoming gubernatorial election, endorsed the Independent court slate and refused to enter candidates of their own in the general election. For governor they nominated a self-proclaimed "avowed friend

of total abstinence," 39-year-old Newport attorney Ben Hooper, and, openly soliciting Independent support, announced that his campaign would not be a partisan race but rather a crusade against "the hideous political monster" which Patterson and the Democratic Regulars had created.

Patterson withdrew from the gubernatorial contest early in September, and the Regulars attempted to woo the Independents by doing that which past generations of Democrats had found effective: they nominated Bob Taylor, now 60 years of age and a member of the U.S. Senate. But this time even Taylor's magnetism did not prevail. The Independents refused to cooperate with the Regulars and voted with the Republicans for Hooper, who won by 12,000 votes.

Hooper proved to be a popular governor, and in 1912 he won a second term by defeating former governor Benton McMillin. Regular Democrats controlled the Tennessee Senate, but the Independent-Republican coalition held the House. After the Regulars abandoned plans to unseat Hooper, some degree of harmony prevailed on Capitol Hill, but little was accomplished. Hooper tried to enforce the prohibition laws, but he was not successful in the cities; in Memphis he angered Mayor E.H. Crump, who had supported the Independents and was rapidly emerging as a polit-

ical boss to be reckoned with. Newspaper publisher Luke Lea and Supreme Court Justice John K. Shields—both Carmack men and Independent Democrats—were elected to the U.S. Senate.

The Democrats settled their disputes sufficiently by 1914 to regain the governor's seat. One factor was undoubtedly the Democratic enthusiasm for Woodrow Wilson, who, in 1913, became the first "Southern" president in nearly 50 years.

When Hooper announced for a third term, he found that many of the Independents had returned to the party. Democrat Thomas C. Rye, a Memphis lawyer and prohibitionist acceptable to party leaders in both factions, defeated Hooper by more than 20,000 votes. Determined to enforce the anti-liquor laws, he ousted Memphis Mayor Crump, who openly had boasted that he would not even try to enforce the laws in Memphis, and soon filed successful suits against Mayor Hilary E. Howse of Nashville and other city officials. Kenneth D. McKellar began the first of his six terms in the U.S. Senate by defeating Lea in the primary and Hooper in the general election. Rye had no difficulty in winning a second term in 1916 because of the developing Democratic harmony and because the attention of most Tennesseans was upon the war in Europe and the presidential race, in which Wilson narrowly won a second term.

Alvin Cullom York, born in the Valley of the Three Forks of the Wolf River, was 31 years old when he was drafted for the First World War. He sought conscientious objector status, was refused, and agreed to serve. He became the most decorated common soldier to have served in the war, due to his single-handed capture of 132 German soldiers. Courtesy, Tennessee State Museum

In the meantime Europe was at war, and Americans watched developments there with considerable interest. Early in the conflict a few state newspapers had tried to heed Wilson's advice regarding neutrality, but most Tennesseans sympathized with the British and the French, and a few men even went to Canada to join the Allied forces. After the British liner *Lusitania* was destroyed in 1915 and several American ships (including the *City of Memphis*) were sunk early in 1917, the Tennessee congressional delegation gave Wilson unanimous support in his call for a declaration of war.

Upholding the "volunteer" tradition, more than 75,000 Tennesseans were mustered into service. They soon arrived in France to relieve the war-weary Allied troops fighting to withstand the Ger-

man attack on Paris. The 30th ("Old Hickory") Division of Infantry became the first unit to experience major action when, after a brief period of training, they relieved British troops in France. They were in almost continuous action until the war ended. More than 1,800 Tennesseans lost their lives in the conflict, and six—including Alvin C. York—received the Congressional Medal of Honor.

York, a "country boy" from Fentress County, won wide acclaim when he staged a one-man assault on the enemy, after becoming separated from his own troops, and captured 132 German soldiers. Tennesseans always have gratefully received war heroes, and York was no exception. They purchased a farm for him in his home area, established an agricultural institute in his honor, and placed a bronze statue of him in the state capitol. In the year of his 100th birthday (1987), they placed a memorial for him in France near the town where he had fought and named him "Tennessee's Historical Personality of the Year."

Interestingly, Luke Lea, defeated for reelection to the Senate in 1916, had joined the army and risen to the rank of colonel. After the armistice he became a laughingstock when he almost succeeded in capturing the German Kaiser, Wilhelm II, after Lea had gathered a few troops together and approached the chateau in Holland where the old man had fled and then been granted asylum.

By the time the war ended, Tennesseans had held their biennial gubernatorial election and had chosen Albert H. Roberts of Livingston. The Democratic party unity which the genial Rye had achieved was strained by the active primary race between Roberts and Clarksville lawyer Austin Peay. Rye, who sought election to the Senate instead of reelection as governor, joined with Roberts in urging unity.

Legislators had no difficulty in ratifying the Eighteenth Amendment, which prohibited the sale, manufacture, and consumption of liquor nationwide. The recent war had added considerable impetus to the move to ratify, and the Memphis *Commercial Appeal* had suggested during the conflict that anyone supplying whiskey to soldiers should be put to death. The state's legislators voted 28 to 2 in the senate and 82 to 2 in the house. Tennessee became the 23rd state to ratify; soon others followed suit, and early in January 1920 the amendment went into effect.

Albert H. Roberts (1868-1946) served as governor from 1919 to 1921. Courtesy, Tennessee State Library and Archives

The Vultee P-38 assembly line in Nashville produced aircraft for World War II. About one-third of the work force consisted of women. Courtesy, Tennessee State Library and Archives

6

TENNESSEE IN MODERN TIMES

By 1920 whatever unity the Democrats had developed during the preceding six years had been shattered, as party leaders argued over tax reform, prohibition, labor unions, and other matters which traditionally had plagued the party. Governor Roberts, seeking a second term, found that the Democrats were especially disgruntled with his efforts to extend to the Railroad Commission the power to oversee the work of county tax assessors, presumably so that tax rates could be equalized. His efforts to collect taxes on personal property alarmed wealthy businessmen, and his plan to reassess property values disturbed farmers and landowners. Although prohibition still was the law, "wets" remained powerful. Roberts had used troops to break strikes called by street and railway workers in Nashville; for this and other anti-labor activities the Tennessee Federation of Labor denounced him, pledging his defeat in the November election. Serious personality clashes had developed among Lea, Crump, Nashville *Banner* publisher E.B. Stahlman, Chattanooga Mayor William R. Crabtree, and others. In the August primary Roberts again was nominated, but he faced serious opposition when the Republicans chose Alf Taylor, who had not sought statewide office since 1886.

Roberts had enough problems within his own party, but Taylor's popularity gave him little hope for reelection. Launching his campaign on a high and jovial plane, Taylor, the 72-year-old scion of a prominent East Tennessee family, was accompanied by members of his family as he toured the state. Especially appealing to the crowds was a vocal quartet of family members, who delighted voters with country ballads while Alf played his fiddle. The middle-aged and "old" men of the state remembered Taylor from his campaign for governor in 1886, and even Democrats admitted that he was "qualified" and "eminently respectable." He thus had no trouble in defeating Roberts, polling about 55 percent of the vote.

In the same election Republican presidential candidate Warren G. Harding won Tennessee's electoral votes, and the Volunteer State became the first state of the old Confederacy to return a Republican majority since Reconstruction. Economic discontent and dissatisfaction with the Democratic administrations of both the state and the nation were important factors in Harding's victory.

Even before the autumn elections national interest had shifted to Tennessee as legislators considered the Susan B. Anthony (Nineteenth) Amendment. Thirty-six states were required for ratification at that time; already, by the summer of 1920, 35 had accepted it and 8 had rejected it. Of the remaining five, only Tennessee, Vermont, and Connecticut were considered to be states where ratification was possible. Since the two New England states refused to address the matter until after the November elections, suffrage leaders sought a summer ratification in Nashville.

Feminist leaders had been more active in Tennessee than in the other former Confederate states, and as early

Alfred E. Taylor (1848-1931) served as governor from 1921 to 1923. Courtesy, Tennessee State Museum

as 1883 legislators had talked of limited suffrage for women. Shortly after the turn of the century, the Tennessee Equal Suffrage Association had been formed, with Sue Shelton White of Henderson in the forefront of this and other feminist organizations. White frequented the legislative and congressional halls alike, was instrumental in the enactment of a law passed in 1919 which gave women the right to vote in municipal elections and for presidential electors, and called frequently upon President Wilson. She ultimately was arrested for demonstrating and starting a fire on the White House lawn, where she burned Wilson in effigy.

Four days after the Democratic Primary was over, Governor Roberts called a special session of the state legislature to consider ratification. After a heated struggle in both houses, ratification was accomplished. A tie vote in the House was broken only when Representative Harry T. Burn of McMinn County, who earlier had been outspoken against ratification, changed his vote. Some disgruntled House members even fled to Alabama in an effort to prevent the formation of a quorum. But ratification, once accomplished, brought Tennessee continued recognition as a progressive state.

Taylor's affable manner soon turned to frustration as he faced not only a predominantly Democratic legislature but also strife within his own party. Although he approached his job with vision and dedication—seeking better schools, new highways, economy in government, and a revision of the tax laws—he could not persuade legislators to pass vital measures. In 1922 he again campaigned with enthusiasm—playing his fiddle to the accompaniment of the male quartet made up of family members who sang mountain ballads, and telling tall tales about his dog, "Old Limber"—but he lost to Austin Peay, whose more formal approach included appearing on the hustings wearing a Prince Albert coat and stiff white collar. Actually, their platform differences were few, and Peay argued for the very things Taylor had unsuccessfully sought, such as better schools and highways.

Austin Peay became one of the most successful governors of the twentieth century; despite continued conflict and division within his party, he was the first chief executive in 100 years to win three successive terms. Taking a "business-progressive" approach, he accomplished a number of much-needed reforms. His first major achievement was a law to "promote economy and efficiency" by reorganizing the state government into eight major departments, each headed by a commissioner who reported directly to the governor. His supporters claimed that this alone saved the state millions of dollars.

Although Peay guarded state revenues carefully, he did not hesitate to spend for needed improvements. With the advent of the automobile, people demanded better roads, and the construction of primary and farm-to-market roads became Peay's next major priority. Although road builders and cement manufacturers—the people who would profit the most—supported a massive bond issue, Peay insisted that those who used the roads should pay for them. Soon, therefore, Tennessee had a high automobile registration fee and a gas tax which exceeded the cost of the gasoline. The road system, probably more than anything else, endeared Peay to the rural

folk, who soon saw their profits increase and their land values climb because of better roads. Before Peay's first year had ended, highway costs ranked first among state expenditures.

Vast improvements in education, the establishment of the Great Smoky Mountains National Park, and the building of Reelfoot Lake State Park were among Peay's other major accomplishments.

Peay won a second term by a landslide but experienced difficulty in his primary bid for a third term because his independence had alienated the city bosses. Nevertheless, Peay won the contest by a bare 8,000 votes. He carried East and Middle Tennessee and won more than 60 percent of the rural vote. Having been elected in 1922 by voters of the large cities, Peay by 1926 had become the choice of the farmers and voters in the small communities.

Peay died in October 1927, early in his third term. His death brought to the governor's mansion a 61-year-old Marshall County farmer and lawyer, Henry H. Horton. The new governor was politically unknown before his election to the Senate in 1926, and he had been a compromise choice for speaker only after senators could not break a deadlock among a half-dozen better known lawmakers. Since he knew little about politics, Horton soon came under the influence of Lea, who by this time

owned newspapers in Knoxville, Nashville, and Memphis, and was associated in various business operations with Rogers Caldwell. Lea was instrumental in getting Horton elected in 1928 and reelected in 1930—although Republican presidential candidate Herbert Hoover won Tennessee's electoral votes thanks to Tennesseans' fear of Democrat Al

Above: *The Commonwealth Fund sent Dr. Fred S. Mustard to Rutherford County in 1926 to work on the establishment of a model health-care program in the county. Frequently, following a rain storm, the roads washed out, making the doctor's work more difficult. Courtesy, Tennessee Historical Society Collection*

Above left: *Following the Tennessee legislature's ratification of the Nineteenth Amendment to the Constitution, cartoonists frequently depicted Tennessee as an antebellum gentleman, presenting women with the right to vote. Courtesy, Tennessee State Library and Archives*

Left: *Austin Peay (1876-1927) served as governor from 1923 to 1927. He reorganized state government and worked toward the improvement of education and highways in the state. Courtesy, Tennessee State Library and Archives*

Above: *These ragged, yet proud, children caught the sympathetic eye of Dr. Mustard in his health tour of Rutherford County. Courtesy, Tennessee Historical Society Collection*

Right: *At least poverty knew no color line in rural Tennessee. This white family in Rutherford County was living in squalor just as grim as their black neighbors. Courtesy, Tennessee Historical Society Collection*

Below: *The former Lowe School in Rutherford County was no longer in use when Dr. Fred Mustard worked on public health in the county, but it shows the primitive state of education in the area in the early twentieth century. Courtesy, Tennessee Historical Society Collection*

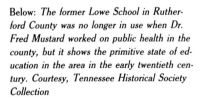

Above: *This typical country schoolhouse in Rutherford County was visited by Dr. Fred Mustard in 1926 as he toured the county to set up a health-care program. Courtesy, Tennessee Historical Society Collection*

Left: *At Lavergne in 1926, a health fair was held at the schoolhouse in order to encourage the children to improve their health. Courtesy, Tennessee Historical Society Collection*

Below: *Tennessee's black Republican leader Robert Church is seen in the front of his Beale Street office with the elite of black Republicanism in the 1920s. Left to right they are: Church, Henry Lincoln Johnson of Georgia, Roscoe Conkling Simmons of Chicago, Walter Cohen of Louisiana, John T. Risher of Washington, D.C., and Percy W. Howard of Mississippi. Courtesy, Roger Biles*

Smith's Catholicism and proclivity toward a repeal of the Eighteenth Amendment.

Unlike Peay, Horton resorted to bond issues to build the necessary roads, bridges, and schools. Money received from the sale of bonds was deposited in the Bank of Tennessee and other banks owned and controlled by Caldwell and Lea. Indeed, when the stock market crashed in October 1929, Caldwell and Lea, aided by a friendly state administration, owned banks and business interests in Tennessee from Bristol to Memphis, and in several nearby states.

A few days after the elections of November 1930, the Bank of Tennessee was declared insolvent. By November 14 Caldwell and Company had been placed in the hands of receivers. Gone were the millions of dollars of state money deposited in Caldwell banks; Crump, who had delivered a 21,000 majority vote to Horton in 1928, now led the pack in calling for the governor's impeachment, and he was widely quoted when he expressed a belief that Lea, Caldwell, and Horton should "go to [the federal penitentiary in] Atlanta." Although the impeachment move failed, mainly due to a coalition of Republicans and rural and small-town Democrats who opposed Crump's influence, Crump became the dominant figure in the Democratic party. Horton served out his term unheralded, and Lea went to federal prison for bank fraud. As one editor wrote, Crump now "became boss of Tennessee politics, succeeding Col. Luke Lea."

Crump was able to exercise control

The Bicentennial Capitol Mall State Park in downtown Nashville commemorates the state's 200th birthday. It covers 19 acres and preserves the northern view of the Capitol. Courtesy, Bicentennial State Park.

Above: *The most visited national park in the United States, the Great Smoky Mountains National Park was dedicated by President Franklin Roosevelt in 1940. The park preserves numerous species of plants, insects, and animals that live nowhere else. Courtesy, State of Tennessee Photographic Services*

Right: *Built in 1826 by former Nashville mayor Randal McGavock, Carnton Plantation is one of Tennessee's best examples of an antebellum plantation house. Near here on November 30, 1864 the Battle of Franklin, one of the bloodiest of the Civil War, was fought and the house served as a field hospital. Courtesy, Williamson County Convention & Visitors Bureau.*

Nashville on the Fourth of July. Tennesseans celebrate just about everything with fireworks. Courtesy, State of Tennessee Photographic Services

Left: The Hunter Museum of American Art in Chattanooga opened in 1952. Housed in a 1904 classical revival mansion and an adjoining contemporary building, the museum sits on an 80-foot bluff overlooking the Tennessee River. Courtesy, Tennessee Department of Tourist Development.

Built in 1991, the Memphis Pyramid is located on the banks of the Mississippi River. The structure is taller than the Statue of Liberty and is the home of the Memphis Grizzlies of the National Basketball Association. Courtesy, State of Tennessee Photographic Services

Alex Haley Monument, in Haley Park, Knoxville. Haley (1921–1992) was the Pulitzer Prize winning author of Roots, *which was the story of his family from West Africa to Henning, Tennessee. Courtesy, State of Tennessee Photographic Services.*

Rhea County Courthouse in Dayton was built in 1891 and was the site of the famous trial of Tennessee v. John Thomas Scopes *of 1925, familiarly referred to as the "Scopes Monkey Trial." The event is reenacted in the restored courtroom on certain summer evenings. Courtesy, Tennessee Department of Tourist Development.*

One of Memphis's most popular attractions, Beale Street is best known for its live blues and jazz music and its distinctive cuisine. Some claim that it was the "home of the blues." Courtesy, State of Tennessee Photographic Services

Opened in 1961 and expanded in 2000 to hold 147,000 fans, the Bristol Motor Speedway remains one of the most popular tracks on the NASCAR circuit, attracting visitors from all over the world. NASCAR is the fastest-growing sport in the United States. Courtesy, Bristol Motor Speedway Public Affairs Office.

Above: *Jubilee Hall at Fisk University was the first permanent building erected at the school. It was built with funds raised by the singing tours of the Jubilee Singers. One of the first institutions of higher learning for blacks in this country, Fisk continues to educate future generations of black leaders. Photo by James A. Hoobler*

Left: *St. Peter's Church in 1843 became the first Catholic church formed in Memphis. The present building dates from 1855. Photo by James A. Hoobler*

Above: *Nashville's Grand Ole Opry, which began hosting its country music shows 64 years ago, remains an attraction for visitors from around the world and for Tennessee residents as well. Photo by Dan Dry*

Right: *The stage microphone stands ready for another show at Nashville's famous Grand Ole Opry. Photo by Dan Dry*

The Civil Rights Museum in Memphis preserves the history and legacy of the Civil Rights Movement in America. The museum is located on the site where Dr. Martin Luther King, Jr. was assassinated in 1968. Courtesy, State of Tennessee Photographic Services.

The "Dickens of a Christmas," held in Franklin on the second full weekend in December. In this Victorian holiday street festival there are carriage rides, carolers, period foods, and costumed characters from A Christmas Carol. *Courtesy, Williamson County Convention & Visitors Bureau.*

Playing host to approximately 1 million visitors each year, Dollywood Amusement Park in Pigeon Forge is partly owned by Sevier County native and international music legend Dolly Parton. It is a long-standing tradition that Dollywood's season opens with a parade led by Ms. Parton herself. Courtesy, Dollywood Publicity

The Memphis home of Elvis Presley, Graceland is a classical revival mansion on 13.8 acres. Now a museum housing Presley material, on March 27, 2006 it was declared a National Historic Landmark. Courtesy, Tennessee Department of Tourist Development.

Nashville is the home of country music in America, and at the Country Music Hall of Fame in downtown Nashville, country music fans can find memorabilia from their favorite entertainers. Courtesy, State of Tennessee Photographic Services

Jonesborough was founded in 1779 and is Tennessee's oldest town. Now a town of approximately 4,200, it is the home of the International Storytelling Center and October's National Storytelling Festival. Courtesy, Town of Jonesborough Department of Tourism

Opposite page, top: *Built on the site of the former Opryland Amusement Park, Opry Mills in Nashville is one of the largest malls in the state. Courtesy, Opry Mills Director of Tourism*

Opposite page, bottom: *The Ocoee River in southeastern Tennessee has long been a favorite of kayakers, rafters, and whitewater enthusiasts. It was the site of the 1996 Olympic whitewater competitions, and sees increases in visitors every year. Courtesy, Chattanooga Area Convention and Visitors Bureau.*

The Tennessee Aquarium, opened in 1992, is the cornerstone of Chattanooga's downtown renewal project which has virtually revolutionized the center city. The aquarium now houses 12,000 different species and remains a major tourist destination. Courtesy, Chattanooga Area Convention and Visitors Bureau

Established in 1980 in an effort to unite Kingsport residents in a spirit of unity and cooperation, the Kingsport Fun Fest Balloon Ride now attracts over 180,000 attendees each year. Courtesy, Tennessee Department of Tourist Development.

Opened on October 1, 1928, the Tennessee Theatre in downtown Knoxville was one of the most magnificent movie palaces in the South. Recently restored, the theater now hosts films, plays, and musical events from classical to popular. Courtesy, Knoxville Tourism and Sports Corporation

The seven-time college women's basketball champions Lady Volunteers made downtown Knoxville an almost natural location for the Women's Basketball Hall of Fame, which opened in 1999. In 2008 the Hall of Fame was visited by over 45,000 basketball fans. Courtesy, Knoxville Tourism and Sports Corporation

An artist as the Main Street Festival in Franklin, which has taken place on the last full weekend in April for the past 24 years. It features arts and crafts vendors, food courts, and stages and carnivals. Courtesy, Williamson County Convention & Visitors Bureau.

McGavock Confederate Cemetery is the burial site for almost 1,500 Confederate soldiers who were killed in the Battle of Franklin. A gift of John and Carrie McGavock, it remains the largest privately owned military cemetery in the United States. Courtesy, Williamson County Convention & Visitors Bureau

In 1974 the University of Tennessee celebrated its bicentennial. The year-long event began with a kickoff breakfast at Thompson Boling Arena. Left to Right: UT President Dr. Joe Johnson, Governor Ned Ray McWherter, and Knoxville Chancellor William Snyder. Naturally, the toast was with orange juice. Courtesy, University of Tennessee Photographic Services

The medical units of the University of Tennessee in Memphis. The university's medical school originally was in Nashville but was moved to Memphis in the late 19th century. The hospital is one of the state's major medical teaching facilities. Courtesy, University of Tennessee Photographic Services.

Mule Day in Columbia has been a tradition since around 1840. Originally a livestock market, it is now an almost week-long celebration with a parade, mule and horse shows, arts and crafts, a flea market, and, of course, barbeque, homemade pies, and funnel cakes. Courtesy, Tennessee Department of Tourist Development.

*The Tennessee Walking Horse is the state's
official horse, honored each year at the
Tennessee Walking Horse National
Celebration in Shelbyville. Nearly 250,000
tickets are sold to people from over 40 states.
The walking horse was originally bred in
Tennessee. Courtesy, Tennessee Department
of Tourist Development.*

Smithville Fiddlers' Jamboree was first held in 1972 at the DeKalb County Courthouse. Dedicated to preserving traditional country music, the festival gives awards to performers of all ages as the play before an audience of over 100,000 from all 50 states and several foreign countries. Courtesy, Tennessee Department of Tourist Development.

Natchez Trace Parkway Bridge in Williamson County spans 1,648 feet and was the first segmentally constructed concrete arch bridge in the United States. The 11th International Bridge Conference named it the most outstanding achievement in the bridge industry for 1994. Courtesy, Williamson County Convention & Visitors Bureau.

All Saints Chapel at the University of the South in Sewanee. The cornerstone of this Episcopal school was laid in 1860 but, because of the Civil War, the university was not actually opened until 1868. One of the state's fine private liberal arts institutions, the university's Gothic-style buildings are constructed mainly of the state's pink sandstone. Courtesy, Tennessee Department of Tourist Development.

during most of the 1930s and indeed until 1948, when returning veterans broke his hold on the state. He brought forth Hill McAllister as a gubernatorial candidate in 1932, and through his influence the Nashvillian—although twice defeated in earlier attempts—was elected for two terms. But the state was in the grips of a financial depression during his four years, and McAllister was able to accomplish very little. Even Crump described him as "the sorriest governor" Tennessee had had in quite some time and repudiated him in 1936.

In the meantime Tennesseans, disillusioned with the president they had helped elect in 1928, voted overwhelmingly in 1932 for the winsome governor of New York, Franklin D. Roosevelt. Even many who had not voted for him approved of his appointment of U.S. Senator Cordell Hull as secretary of state. Hull already had had a long stay in Congress when, in 1930, he was elected to the Senate to replace Lawrence D. Tyson. Soon Roosevelt endeared himself to most Tennesseans by his New Deal measures, the most significant of which (for Tennesseans) was the Tennessee Valley Authority.

For years both the federal government and private developers had been aware of the potential of the river valley. Several dams and other improvements necessary to produce electric power had been built by the Tennessee Electric Power Company several years earlier, and Henry Ford had sought to lease the area to produce nitrogenous fertilizer. Twice Congress, influenced by Senator McKellar and others, enacted legislation to develop the vast area, but the measures were vetoed by presidents Coolidge and Hoover. The bill signed by President Roosevelt which ultimately established the TVA was not significantly different from the earlier ones. Inexpensive electric power soon helped raise the standard of living for people throughout the area and became a magnet for industry.

In the meantime Gordon Browning, with Crump's support, had replaced McAllister as governor. A veteran of

World War I, Browning had served with distinction in Congress for 12 years and was known across the state after an unsuccessful race for the U.S. Senate in 1934. But he and Crump, both strong-willed men, soon became enemies, and the Memphis boss began to look around for another candidate for 1938. Browning might have defeated Crump had he been more circumspect. But, knowing Crump's ability to deliver the Shelby County vote, he hastily called legislators together to consider his "Unit Bill," which would weaken Shelby's power. Browning's idea was that a plan comparable to the presidential electoral system, which gave each county "a definite influence in determining the results of the primary," was necessary to end the "invidious" power of the Memphis boss. Although the measure passed by very small majorities in both houses, it caused Browning to lose his popular support, especially after Crump took the law to the Supreme Court and had it declared unconstitutional. Then, just before the election, Browning announced that he would send the National Guard to Memphis to ensure equity at the ballot box. This threat caused him to lose what little support he still had in Memphis, including that of the *Commercial Appeal,* and brought an injunction from Federal Judge John Martin which prohibited him from sending the troops.

State Senator Prentice Cooper of Shelbyville, in the meantime, quietly had announced for governor and had readily gained Crump's support. In the primary he defeated Browning by 70,000 votes, and he won in the general election without serious opposition. Cooper, a Harvard and Princeton graduate and a scion of a respected and prominent Tennessee family, became a successful although unspectacular governor. A former attorney general, he was tough on crime and issued few pardons while in office. A fiscal conservative, he guarded the state's money as if it were his own, cutting the state's debt in half. As most people probably were paying more attention to military developments in Europe than to

state politics, Cooper did not encounter serious opposition. He became the first governor since the Jacksonian days of William Carroll to serve the full constitutional limit of three consecutive terms. He received favorite-son support for vice president at the 1944 Democratic Convention and became minister to Peru soon after his third term ended.

Tennesseans joined others in World War II when, on December 8, 1941, the United States declared war on Japan, Germany, and Italy. Indeed, more than a year before the declaration, the 30th ("Old Hickory") Division of Infantry, which had distinguished itself in World War I, had been mustered into service when Congress mobilized the National Guard and the Reserves. While about 10 percent of the state's population experienced military service, most other Tennesseans were involved in the war effort one way or another. Military bases, hospitals, and training fields were established across the state, and industrial establishments which manufactured implements of war employed thousands. When Japan officially surrendered in August 1945 (Germany had surrendered three months earlier), more than 300,000 Tennesseans had served in the armed forces—in Europe, North Africa, and the Pacific—during the four years of conflict.

Browning and most of the other political leaders not too old to fight were among those mustered into service. With Cooper constitutionally ineligible for another term as governor, the Democrats nominated and elected 65-year-old Jim Nance McCord, Lewisburg mayor, businessman, and congressman, in 1944 and again in 1946. His major accomplishment was a 2 percent sales tax levied upon a variety of sales and services. Although McCord was criticized for the tax measure, he was able to pass it because of support from Boss Crump. Revenue from the new tax was to be used primarily for education, and school officials soon were able to establish an equitable pay scale for teachers, develop a retirement system, and repair and build schools across the state.

After Browning and other veterans were demobilized, they soon returned home cherishing an active interest in politics. Most took a dim view of Boss Crump's control over governors and legislators and looked about for one of their own who could end the political dictatorship. Browning, popular among the veterans, soon announced for governor (1948). From the beginning of his campaign, he made Crump the chief issue. He was joined on the hustings by Third District Congressman Estes Kefauver, who challenged the Crump-supported

candidate for the U.S. Senate, John A. Mitchell of Cookeville.

The Nashville *Tennessean,* which had gone into receivership during the Depression, had been purchased by New Dealer Silliman Evans of Texas. It became the chief enemy of Boss Crump and the main supporter of Browning and Kefauver. Crump, accustomed to controlling state politics since the McAllister days, denounced both Browning and Evans. For years he had spoken of Browning as a "sneaky thief," who would "milk his neighbors' cows through a hole in the fence" and whose "heart had beaten over two billion times without a single sincere beat." Next Crump turned his wrath upon Evans and *Tennessean* editor Jennings Perry, who had described the Crump-supported regime as being undemocratic. Evans was a "conscientious liar" with a "foul mind and wicked heart," while Perry—that "insipid ass"—had the "brain of a quagga" and wrote "just as one would expect of a wanderoo." While voters were amused by Crump, who sent them to their dictionaries to fully understand his perverse vocabulary, they voted for Browning and Kefauver.

Browning turned back McCord's third-term bid by 60,000 votes, although the incumbent won in Shelby County by about 50,000. Kefauver won a Senate seat by defeating incumbent Tom Stewart, who had failed in 1948 to win the support from Crump that he had done six years earlier, and Crump-supported John Mitchell. Although Crump's power as a political boss was ended by the resounding victories of Browning and Kefauver, he remained powerful within Shelby County and continued to endorse candidates for statewide offices.

Browning was reelected in 1950, and by the end of that term had served six years, including the term of 1937-1939. His legislative program had included election reform, a modified "sunshine law," and the construction of farm-to-market roads. His determination to retain the sales tax had resulted in continued support for education, and his refusal to raise the truck weight limits for interstate traffic preserved the highways but incurred the wrath of trucking executives.

Toward the end of Browning's second consecutive term, his charisma began to wear thin, and some disillusioned Democrats claimed that they had traded one political boss for another. A 30-year veteran of political and military wars, by the early 1950s Browning had begun to rely increasingly upon a small "Kitchen Cabinet" in Nashville for advice. He also circulated much less among the public than in earlier years. Although he had defeated Crump-supported Clifford Allen handily in 1950, he observed with surprise a few days after the election an announcement for governor by 32-year-old Frank Goad Clement—some two years in advance of the next election.

Clement, like Browning, had returned from military service in 1946. He soon was elected state commander of the American Legion and chairman of the Young Democrats Club. In both capacities he spoke across the state to gatherings of young people, who were anxious to find a spokesman who could articulate their views and help them exert a new influence on state government. He also vigorously supported McCord's bid for reelection in 1946, and he was re-

Right: *Albert Gore, Sr., served Tennessee in the U.S. Senate from 1952 to 1970. Courtesy, Tennessee State Library and Archives*

Far right: *Buford Ellington (1907-1972) served as governor from 1959 to 1963, and from 1967 to 1971. Courtesy, Tennessee State Museum*

warded by being named chief counsel for the Public Utilities Commission—the youngest in the state's history. Clement was a popular speaker at church services across the state, and his sense of mission to render public service appealed to old and young alike. Exhibiting a boyish naivete, Clement told church and secular groups alike that not only had he dreamed since boyhood of becoming governor, but his announcement for the high office had come about because he sought "the particular place to which the Lord had called" him. The sincerity of his attempt to achieve a God-imposed calling impressed many people, and, therefore, when the 63-year-old Browning mounted the hustings in search of voter support for another term, he found that his opponent already had developed a substantial following. Browning soon also found that his own method of campaigning—one observer said it consisted mainly of telling off-color tales to "the boys"—was outdated, as the handsome and polished young lawyer appealed to a vast cross section of people seeking change. His major themes during the campaign were an "indictment" of the Browning administration for dereliction of duty and a promise that, if elected, Clement would restore "honesty, decency, and morality" to Capitol Hill.

Browning was amazed at Clement's "bold effrontery" and "disrespect" to an old political war horse; he was hurt by the charges that his administration was tainted with "corruption, graft, and favoritism" and that he might be dishonest, indecent, and immoral. As he was wont to do when flustered and angry, he responded frequently in an intemperate manner, which did nothing to help his cause. His few appearances through the new medium of television were fiascos, while those of the handsome Clement won the hearts of soap opera fans as well as serious watchers and listeners.

As the exciting campaign wound down, even the most optimistic leaders of the Browning machine held little hope. Clement's victory by 57,000 votes surprised careful observers but demonstrated the truth of the old adage that "anything can happen in Tennessee politics." In the same election Fourth District Congressman Albert Gore conducted a quiet campaign to unseat 83-year-old Senator K.D. McKellar, who sought his seventh term. Neither candidate in this race abused the other; Gore's only issue was that the aging and ill senator should be replaced by a younger person whose political and societal views were more in tune with the times. Gore won by more than 80,000 votes, and he continued in the Senate for 18 years. In addition, in 1952, Tennesseans voted for Dwight D. Eisenhower.

Clement's victory consigned the veteran Browning to political retirement and placed Clement and his campaign manager, Buford Ellington, in power for almost two decades. Clement was reelected in 1954, by which time the gubernatorial term had been changed constitutionally to four years, and again in 1962; Ellington won in 1958 and 1966.

The Clement-Ellington gubernatorial years brought substantial reform and progress to Tennessee. Clement instituted new purchasing practices during his first year to assure competitive bidding. He also created a new and separate department of mental health, reformed the tax structure to bring in more revenue, emphasized affirmative action by appointing women and blacks to responsible positions, and raised the weight limits for trucks engaged in interstate commerce.

Browning attempted a comeback in 1954, but Clement, who defeated him by more than a two-to-one majority, emerged as one of the most powerful politicians in the country. Only 34 years of age, his confident bearing and demeanor mixed with an air of wholesomeness and refinement not found generally among Southern governors, Clement soon caught the eye of national Democratic leaders. By no means the least among his developing circle of acquaintances was Billy Graham, a youthful evangelist who was well received by fundamentalist churchgoers. Association with Graham not only convinced people that Clement was assigning morality and religion an important place in his life, but also offered him an opportunity to meet prominent leaders of Graham's acquaintance.

By 1956 Clement's supporters were concentrating upon persuading national party leaders to invite Clement to deliver the Keynote Address at the party convention. With people such as Massachusetts Senator John F. Kennedy, Minnesota Senator Hubert Humphrey, Maine Governor Edmund Muskie, Oklahoma Senator Robert Kerr, and former president Truman as possible choices, Clement was signally honored when the choice was made to invite him. Friends, already optimistic about Clement's chances of being a vice presidential choice, now even began to talk about his chances of winning the presidential nomination.

The chief duty of a keynoter is to arouse interest and attention, and Clement did just that. He spoke for 40 minutes and "indicted" the Eisenhower administration just as he had Browning's a few years before. Apparently well received by the delegates, he was interrupted 44 times as he intoned repeatedly the words, "how long, oh how long, America" would the leadership of Eisenhower and Nixon— that "group of privilege and pillage"—be tolerated.

The Tennessee delegation believed the speech had won a nomination for Clement, and, early the following morning, they changed their strategy of seeking a vice presidential nomination to that of seeking the presidency. National Democratic leaders, however, while commending Clement's speech, generally ignored him during the remainder of the convention and again chose Adlai Stevenson to face Eisenhower. No ground swell of support developed for the Tennessee governor's nomination as vice president either, and Estes Kefauver, whom some Clement supporters considered a political enemy, defeated John F. Kennedy for the nomination when Stevenson permitted the choice to be made in open convention. Kefauver was, of course, much better known among political leaders than Clement, and he had actively sought the presidential nomination in 1952 and 1956. Disappointed, Clement returned to his gubernatorial duties but continued to be observant of national affairs with a view to seeking national office.

Highly significant during the Clement-Ellington years were matters of constitutional revision and legislative reapportionment. For a decade before Clement's election in 1952, reformers had talked of the need for constitutional reform. In 1953 a "limited" convention assembled. Chaired by former governor Prentice

Cooper, it increased the governor's term to four years. Delegates also gave the governor the right of the item veto, abolished the poll tax, increased the pay and allowances of legislators, and provided an option for home rule for the major metropolitan areas. The following year Clement became the first four-year governor. In other limited conventions since 1953, delegates have reduced the voting age to 18, authorized annual instead of biennial sessions of the legislature, placed legislators on a regular salary, and provided for more equitable property tax assessments.

One of the more interesting revisions of 1978 streamlined county government and abolished the old justice of the peace system which, inherited from England, had been a pillar of local government since the state had been formed. Under the traditional system each county had had a number of justices of the peace who, when acting individually, adjudicated upon minor legal infractions within their particular districts. When acting collectively, they sat as legislative bodies for their respective counties in what were called the "Quarterly Courts," each of which was presided over by a "county judge." In most counties, the justices of the peace already had ceased to hear cases, giving way to a "General Sessions Judge." The new constitutional revision called for a "county legislative body," consisting of not more than 25 "Commissioners," to replace the justices and to be presided over by a "County Executive."

The increased urban growth during and after World War II brought a demand from the cities for legislative and congressional reapportionment. Although the constitutions of 1796, 1834, and 1870 had mandated decennial apportionment, no such redistricting had taken place since 1901. Attorneys for the cities showed that approximately one-third of the voting population elected two-thirds of the legislators. In some of the small and sparsely populated counties, voters had nearly 20 times the representation that urban voters had. The result

was that the case of *Baker v. Carr,* which originated in Memphis, became the suit through which the U.S. Supreme Court ordered reapportionment in Tennessee.

The Clement-Ellington response to *Brown v. Board of Education*—the desegregation case of May 1954—was one of moderation. While most Southern governors pledged to "stand in the schoolhouse door" or otherwise defy the high court's dictum, Clement urged blacks and whites alike to eschew violence and work first "for the benefit of all our children." Although attempts to integrate brought bombings in Clinton and Nashville, and Clement was forced to send troops to maintain order in Clinton, both Clement and Ellington generally were able to accomplish integration while avoiding violence. "Tennessee Sets South an Example" was the title of a story that appeared in an Indianapolis newspaper after a feature writer's on-site visit, and across the nation Tennessee's success was commended. The tragic assassination of Martin Luther King, Jr., in Memphis in April 1968 caused disturbances which Ellington and law enforcement officers handled sympathetically but effectively.

The sales tax, mentioned earlier, had become the principal means of financing the state government by the time of Clement's first election. Funding the Clement program had become so expensive by 1955 that legislators raised the tax to 3 percent. Even those who had condemned Governor McCord a decade earlier for initiating the tax soon had accepted it as a necessary means of meeting governmental expenses.

Senator Estes Kefauver was chosen for a third term in 1960, but he died in August 1963. Clement appointed Herbert S. Walters to fill the vacant seat until the general election of 1964, when Sixth District Congressman Ross Bass defeated Clement in the primary and Republican M.M. Bullard of Newport in the general election. Then, in 1966, Clement won the party nomination when the Democrats became disillusioned with Bass, but was soundly defeated by Re-

publican Howard Baker, Jr., who won large majorities in East Tennessee and the cities. Baker's distinguished career spanned three senatorial terms, during part of which he served as senate majority leader. In 1987 he was named chief of staff by President Ronald Reagan.

As the end of Ellington's final term approached, Clement talked of seeking yet another term when the time for the 1970 election rolled around. Unfortunately, he was killed in an automobile accident in Nashville in November 1969. McCord, who had served briefly in Clement's cabinet, had died the previous year, and Ellington lived until 1972.

Despite the varied accomplishments of the Democrats during the Clement-Ellington years, Tennessee voters turned increasingly to the Republican party after mid-century. Increased wealth in the urban areas was a major factor, as indeed were the disillusionment of party stalwarts with the liberal trends of national Democratic leaders and the popularity of such Republican leaders as Eisenhower, Nixon, Baker, and, ultimately, Lamar Alexander.

After Baker's overwhelming election to the Senate in 1966, the Republicans turned their attention with renewed confidence to the presidential race of 1968 and the gubernatorial and senatorial contests of 1970. To the amazement of many political observers, they won them all. Tennesseans had not admired the liberal proclivities of Hubert H. Humphrey, and the Minnesotan finished a distant third in the balloting for president. Richard M. Nixon won the state's electoral votes, and Independent George Wallace finished a close second. In the senatorial primary, political unknown Hudley Crockett of Nashville challenged Gore and came within a relatively few votes of defeating him—a situation more attributable to Gore's increasing unpopularity in the state than to the strength or acceptance of Crockett. In the fall elections the handsome Third District Congressman Bill Brock, who won substantial majorities in six of the nine congressional districts, had little trouble in retiring Gore. After a hotly contested gubernatorial primary, Nashville lawyer and businessman John J. Hooker, Jr., was elected to face Memphis dentist Winfield Dunn, who, surprisingly, had defeated a host of better known Republicans in the primary. On the campaign trail the winsome Dunn spoke forcibly and effectively, and he defeated the Democrat by nearly 60,000 votes. In the presidential election two years later, Tennessee Democrats again could not accept most of those who sought the party's nomination, including Shirley Chisholm, Eugene McCarthy, George McGovern, and Humphrey. When party leaders finally agreed upon McGovern and Sargent Shriver, Tennessee voters chose Nixon, this time by a two-to-one majority.

By the mid-1970s the trauma of Watergate had somewhat loosened the bond of Republican control, and Dunn, although he had enjoyed a successful four years as governor, was succeeded by a Democrat. He had increased the sales tax by 0.5 percent to improve a variety of state services, including law enforcement and education. Over his veto, legislators had established a new medical school at East Tennessee State University in Johnson City. But failures in

Howard Baker, Jr., served in the U.S. Senate from 1967 to 1985. During part of his last term he served as the senate majority leader. From 1987 to 1988 he served as the White House chief of staff. Courtesy, The White House

Winfield Dunn (1927-   ) served as governor from 1971 to 1975, and ran again in 1986. Courtesy, Tennessee State Museum

Washington had stigmatized the Republican party, and the Democrats, as mentioned, regained the governor's office in 1974 and one of the two senatorial slots two years later.

Seventh District Congressman Ray Blanton defeated Lamar Alexander, a 34-year-old East Tennessee lawyer, who had served briefly with Nixon and had directed Dunn's gubernatorial election. The Republicans also lost the Eighth Congressional seat to Harold E. Ford, who became the first black to serve in Congress in the state's history.

Except for his pardoning record, Governor Blanton left the governor's office with a successful administration on record. He had even proposed that legislators consider an income tax—a proposal which tax experts had recommended for several decades. According to Blanton's plan, poor and middle income people would pay little or no taxes, and the sales tax would be decreased by one-third. But legislators, conscious of a long-time fear of a state income tax among their constituents, refused to accept it. Finally, they resorted to an increase in the sales tax. By the end of Blanton's administration, it was one of the highest in the country. Although Blanton was eligible for a second term, he announced his retirement from politics. He soon found himself in federal prison, however, after having

been convicted of accepting paybacks in allotting state liquor licenses.

Democratic victories continued. In 1976 James Sasser, a Nashville lawyer and chair of the state Democratic organization, defeated incumbent Bill Brock. At the same time Tennesseans voted for Jimmy Carter for president instead of Gerald Ford.

Republicans, however, regained the governorship in 1978, when the voters chose Alexander. Upon reelection in 1982 he became the first eight-year Tennessee governor and one of the most progressive executives in the history of the state. In the Democratic primary, prominent Knoxville banker Jake Butcher had defeated former governor Clement's son, Bob Clement. Butcher was no match, however, for Alexander, who walked across the state, stopping at schools and hamlets as he discussed issues with people in a down-to-earth manner. Although Butcher spent nearly $3 million on his campaign, Alexander won all congressional districts except the Ninth, where Congressman Harold Ford of Memphis had united the black vote behind Butcher.

A few days before Alexander was scheduled to be inaugurated, Blanton began to make extensive use of his pardoning power. On one day, for example, he attempted to grant executive clemency to more than 50 penitentiary inmates, 20 of whom were convicted murderers. Fol-

Ray Blanton (1930-   ) served as governor from 1975 to 1979. He was removed from office several days early due to the corruption of his administration, and he and several of his staff were later sent to prison. Courtesy, Tennessee State Museum

James Sasser has served Tennessee in the U.S. Senate since 1977. Courtesy, Senator James Sasser

Left: Lamar Alexander (1940-   ) served as governor from 1979 to 1987. In 1988 he became the president of the University of Tennessee. Courtesy, Tennessee State Museum

Far left: Harold E. Ford, of Memphis, in 1976 became the first black to represent Tennessee in the U.S. House of Representatives. Courtesy, Congressman Harold E. Ford

lowing the advice of the U.S. attorney of the Middle District and the attorney general of Tennessee, and with the endorsement of the Democratic speakers of the House and Senate, Alexander hurriedly was inaugurated two days before the event had been scheduled so that Governor Blanton would be denied any further exercise of the pardoning power.

Alexander assumed office as the fifth Republican governor in the state's history and the second since 1970. His conservative approach during much of his first term, occasioned in part by a decline in revenue from the sales tax below that which had been budgeted, won widespread favor. Although by 1982 the unemployment rate of 11.2 percent exceeded the national rate (Van Buren and Stewart counties each suffered a 40 percent jobless rate), Alexander still zealously courted new industry, with the result that investments by new manufacturers increased substantially over those of the previous two years.

Despite the downturn in the economy,

Alexander handily defeated Knoxville Mayor Randy Tyree and won reelection. At the same time Senator Sasser turned back a bid by veteran Sixth District Congressman Robin Beard and thus won a second term. Ronald Reagan, popular in his own right but aided by Alexander, won Tennessee's electoral votes in both the 1980 and 1984 presidential elections, as state Democrats continued to show little enthusiasm for the national candidates.

At the beginning of his second term, Governor Alexander more aggressively pushed reforms, especially in education. For some time he had talked with both educators and the public in general about a "Better Schools Program," and in 1984 legislators had enacted a measure which provided for sizable salary increases for those who qualified. More funds for teaching supplies and equipment were provided to enhance computer, mathematics, and science skills, as well as a basic skills program. Fortunately, an improved economy brought in

In 1979 the disgraced former Governor Ray Blanton was ousted as Tennessee swore in her new governor. Blanton had made sweeping and ill-considered use of executive pardoning power. The Tennessean reported that federal investigators warned state leaders that Blanton might free convicts involved in a pay-for-freedom investigation. Courtesy, The Tennessean

Alexander Sworn In; Blanton Pushed Out

By LARRY DAUGHTREY and DOUG HALL

Lamar Alexander was sworn in as governor of Tennessee three days early last night after a federal prosecutor warned state leaders Ray Blanton might free convicts involved in a pay-for-freedom investigation.

Alexander, 38, a Republican who walked the state to gain public confidence, raised his right hand in a moment unprecedented in Tennessee history and repeated after Chief Justice Joe Henry:

Alexander, 38, a Republican who walked the state to gain public confidence, raised his right hand in a moment unprecedented in Tennessee history and repeated after Chief Justice Joe Henry:

"I, LAMAR ALEXANDER, do solemnly swear that I will perform with fidelity the duties of the office of governor of the state of Tennessee to which I am elected and which I am about to assume."

Seconds before, he told a crowd of friends, supporters and legislators in the Supreme Court's courtroom:

"It is not a happy day for me."

BLANTON, AT HIS new home on Jefferson Davis Drive, heard of what amounted to his ouster from office from a television news bulletin, and two hours later emerged from his house to talk with reporters.

Ray Blanton
'No bitterness'

much-needed revenue to fund the extensive program, but legislators in 1985 increased the sales tax to 5.5 percent, with options for local governments to add 2.25 percent to assure that funds were adequate. Although improvements in education were obvious, Tennesseans also noted that they paid the highest sales tax in the nation.

Tennessee unfortunately experienced unprecedented white collar crime during the early 1980s. Soon after he vacated the governor's chair, Blanton was sentenced to federal prison for three years on charges of extortion, conspiracy, and mail fraud in the issuance of liquor licenses. Several aides were convicted and received lesser sentences. Blanton's brother, Gene Blanton, and his uncle, Jake Blanton, were sentenced and fined for rigging bids on road construction projects. Former gubernatorial candidate and wealthy Knoxvillian Jake Butcher was imprisoned in 1985, after pleading guilty to bank fraud and failure to properly report income taxes. His United American Bank of Knoxville had collapsed earlier due to "large and unusual loan losses," and soon his entire banking empire, which stretched from Bristol to Memphis and into several surrounding states, had collapsed. Also sentenced in the fiasco were his brother, C.H. Butcher, Jr., and other business associates. While these men were sentenced to minimum security prisons, other felons continued to be sentenced to the state penitentiary in such numbers that federal courts ordered a reduction of the prison population. In 1985 Governor Alexander called a special session of the legislature to address the overcrowded conditions. Plans soon were made to build two new maximum security prisons—one in Nashville and the other in Lauderdale County—and these are scheduled to be completed by 1990.

Alexander was not constitutionally eligible for another term, and the Democrats, determined to regain the governor's chair, nominated long-time House Speaker Ned Ray McWherter to face former governor Winfield Dunn. In a contest not as close as predicted, McWherter won a four-year term. The Democrats also regained both Senate seats.

Announcing that he would waste no time in "going to work" to accomplish state improvements and reforms, McWherter became the second Democrat to be elected governor since Ellington had been chosen in 1966. Although he presented no major new programs in his first year, he gave ample evidence of being fiscally sound, with no increase in taxes. By the end of his first year, the unemployment rate had decreased to less than 6 percent, and new industries were bringing growth and the manufacture of a variety of products.

McWherter began his second year (1988) on a note of optimism. Senate Democrats, who early in 1987 had argued vehemently over the election of a speaker, by January 1988 had mended their differences by agreeing that veteran John Wilder would continue as speaker. With expectations of a $21 million budget surplus, McWherter asked lawmakers to consider both an across-the-board raise and a merit pay raise for teachers. Mental health, services for the mentally retarded, and corrections also were recipients of the governor's attention.

Governor Lamar Alexander in 1984 signed into law the Better Schools Program, which provided salary increases for qualified teachers and funds for supplies and equipment to improve mathematics, computer, and science training in the state's high schools. Courtesy, State Photographic Services

An aerial view of the University of Tennessee in Knoxville. Founded as Blount College in 1794, the university now has campuses in Knoxville, Chattanooga, Tullahoma, Martin, and Memphis with several of its programs nationally ranked. Courtesy, University of Tennessee Photographic Services.

7

INTO A NEW MILLENNIUM

As Tennessee entered the twenty-first century, many people still thought of it as an overwhelmingly rural state populated by benighted backwoodsmen who were hostile to change, suspicious of strangers, and partakers of "hillbilly" music and homemade moonshine. Indeed, this stereotype was deftly "sold" to tourists, especially at the Grand Ole Opry in Nashville, the fiddlers' convention in Smithville, and throughout the entire city of Pigeon Forge.

Yet by the year 2001 this popular image was considerably at odds with the realities of a people who were experiencing rapid and profound changes in virtually every aspect of their lives and work: population, economics, education, recreation, the environment, health care, government and politics. And while some of these changes were disturbing and even painful, in the main, Tennesseans confronted and/or embraced them with a strength, maturity and courage that many did not realize they possessed.

The 2000 federal census reported that 5,689,283 people lived in Tennessee, an increase of 16.7 percent over 1990. With the average family size declining, this impressive growth was due to large numbers of individuals moving to the state, not a few of them people from the Midwest in search of a milder climate, a gentler pace of life, and a place where their dollars would go farther. In 1990 it was reported that 11 percent of all Tennesseans had moved to the state within the past five years.

At the same time that Tennessee's population was growing, it also was becoming less rural. By 1990 only 39 percent of Tennesseans could be classified as rural. Marginal family farms increasingly were abandoned, either combined into large agribusiness enterprises or sold to real estate developers who subdivided them into lots for eager homebuyers.

At first glance one might assume that Tennessee's cities were the major beneficiaries of rural out-migration as well as of people moving to Tennessee from other states. A closer look, however, would show that the state's four largest cities grew principally through annexation or, in Nashville's case, through unified government. Indeed, in the 1980s Memphis, Knoxville, and Chattanooga actually lost population (if the annexed areas are not counted) and Nashville grew by an anemic 7 percent. Older parts of these cities declined drastically and these areas were increasingly inhabited by the poor and the elderly, men and women who needed police and fire protection, public transportation, public health facilities, and other services which their tax dollars alone could not support, a principal reason why cities needed to increase the number of taxpayers through annexations.

Nationally the major population boom was taking place in the suburbs, and Tennessee was no exception. As Nashville was experiencing numerical stagnation, adjoining Williamson County increased by a staggering 69 percent in the 1970s, 39 percent in the 1980s and 56.3 percent in the 1990s. The same held true of Chattanooga, which was losing population while the surrounding counties of Bradley, Meigs, and Rhea were booming. For

Suburbanization began in Tennessee in the 1920s–1930s but moved into high gear in the 1950s–1960s. This photograph is an aerial view of a suburban development in the Karns community in northwest Knox County. Courtesy, Knoxville-Knox County Metropolitan Planning Commission

its part, Knoxville's growth was flat, even as the six counties that made up the Knoxville metropolitan area increased by 44.3 percent in the 1980s. And as the state's interstate highway system allowed people to live farther and farther from their work places, small cities within commuting distance of larger urban areas mushroomed. Towns such as Franklin, Murfreesboro, Dickson, Lebanon, Springfield, Gallatin, Cleveland, Germantown, Maryville, Sevierville, Jefferson City, etc. all far exceeded the population increases of the larger nearby cities.

The population shifts had crucially important ramifications for Tennessee's economy and politics. As people moved from the farms and center cities to the suburbs, retail establishments followed them, often setting up business in the new shopping malls which featured new stores, entertainment facilities, and acres of free parking. Malls such as Oak Court, Overton Square, Wolfchase Galleria (Memphis), Green Hills, Rivergate, Opry Mills (Nashville), West Town, Knoxville Center, Turkey Creek (Knoxville), and Hamilton Place (Chattanooga) attracted shoppers from wide radii—even from neighboring states. Since Tennessee cities and counties were allowed to add percentages to the state's sales tax, the financial gap between the wealthier and

poorer counties widened markedly. Fighting for their lives, center cities embraced several attempts to lure residents and shoppers back downtown, with mixed results.

The population shifts also led directly to one of the most important and far-reaching Supreme Court decisions in modern American history. No redistricting of the state legislature had taken place since 1901, and urbanization and later suburbanization in the twentieth century meant that rural voters had considerably more power than people who lived in cities and suburbs. Indeed, by the 1950s it was estimated that one-third of Tennessee's voters elected two-thirds of the state's legislators. A class action lawsuit filed in Memphis in 1959 challenged this unjust system, resulting in the Supreme Court decision in *Baker v. Carr* (1962) which mandated redistricting on the basis of "one man, one vote." Almost immediately, cities and suburbs gained a near domination of the legislature, thus forcing that body to take up issues more important to urban and suburban residents.

Finally, in addition to Tennessee's population growth and the urbanization and suburbanization of its people, the state's population was growing more diverse. As noted earlier, a smaller and smaller percentage of Tennesseans had been born in the state, with immigrants from other southern states as well as from the Midwest bringing new traditions and new ideas. This trend was dramatized in 1994 when both Republican and Democratic candidates for governor (Don Sundquist and Phil Bredesen) had been born elsewhere (Illinois and Massachusetts).

At the same time the state was ethnically enriched by the arrival of Asians, who began coming to Tennessee around the time of the Vietnam War. A later, and considerably more important trend, was the influx of people from Latin America. These men and women took jobs in construction, manufacturing, and tourism and gradually began working their way steadily up the economic ladder. In Sevier

County in East Tennessee, a major tourist destination, Latinos and Latinas filled an increasing demand for workers. In that county, second to the flood of job seekers from Central and South America, were young people from Russia and Eastern Europe who were escaping those areas' fragile economies. In all, these immigrants added a great deal to Tennessee's labor force as well as to an increasingly diverse culture.

As Tennessee's population was changing as the state approached the 21st century, its economy was changing as well. Once primarily a farm state, by 1990 only 2 percent of Tennessee's gross state product was agricultural. Moreover, the industries that had been established in the state in the late nineteenth and early twentieth centuries (largely textiles, apparel, leather goods, chemicals, wood products, iron, and railroad, establishments that had been attracted to Tennessee in part because of low wages) by the late 20th century were fleeing the state in pursuit of even lower wage scales in Mexico, Taiwan, Korea, and China. Between 1978 and 1987, the state lost 42,860 manufacturing jobs, with 2,844 factories closing in 1980–1985 alone. In 1987 a study was done in Knoxville of 174 manufacturing workers who had been laid off. Fifteen months later, 44 percent of those workers were still unemployed, and of those who did find work 53 percent were working only part-time. By 1990 only 29 percent of Tennessee's gross state product was industrial.

And yet as Tennesseans approached the millennium the manufacturing picture was anything but bleak. Even as low-wage, lower-skilled jobs were disappearing, higher-wage, skilled jobs were being created, the results of aggressive recruitment by the state government, as well as by local and regional industrial recruitment agencies, chambers of commerce, and local and county governments. The most dramatic gains were in the area of transportation when Nissan and Saturn opened major production facilities in 1983 and 1990 respectively.

Almost immediately smaller enterprises sprang up to provide parts for these large automobile manufacturers. By 1994 Tennessee had the same number of manufacturing jobs as it had in 1978, although these jobs paid considerably better. Partially as a result, by the end of the twentieth century the percentage of Tennesseans living below the poverty line had declined from a troubling 39 percent in 1959 to fewer than 15 percent. To be sure, for many men and women the transition had been difficult and painful, but in the end the state's industrial sector was far healthier and the workers who did make the transition were much better off.

The big gainer in Tennessee's economy in the latter decades of the twentieth century was the service sector. One of the most impressive areas of the service sector to grow was the movement of products and people. In 1973 the Federal Express Corporation was established in Memphis. As the demand for the movement of airfreight mushroomed, in 1995 FedEx opened a $36 million airport maintenance facility in Memphis. Because Memphis was a hub of two major airlines and was the home of Fed-

CoolSprings Galleria Mall, outside Franklin, contains over 1 million square feet of store space, theaters, and a 500 seat food court. 55.7 percent of its shoppers have household incomes of $75,000 or more. Courtesy, Williamson County Convention & Visitors Bureau.

World's Fair, held in Knoxville from May to November 1982. The event attracted 11 million visitors and was a great psychological boost for the city. Courtesy, University of Tennessee Video Center.

eral Express, by the turn of the century the city's airport was one of the busiest in the nation. Nashville's airport also was a hub and by 1986 was offering 144 daily flights. In 1987 a new terminal was opened.

Another major service sector was health care. Each of the state's major cities had a number of hospitals, many of them servicing vast geographical regions with increasingly complex and up-to-date technology. The state also was home to four major medical schools, the most recently founded being the Quillen College of Medicine in Johnson City that was named for Congressman James "Jimmy" Quillen (1916–2003) of the First Congressional District who played a major role in securing the school for East Tennessee. It opened in 1978 and by 1994 provided 13,000 full-time jobs in Washington County and put $771 million into the region's economy.

Perhaps the most dramatic growth in the service sector, however, was in tourism. The virtual completion of the federal interstate highway system in the 1980s put Tennessee within easy driving distance of a majority of the country's population, millions of whom visited the state each year and spent approximately $8 billion per year in hotels, restaurants, gift shops, campgrounds, amusement

parks, etc. By century's end the Great Smoky Mountains National Park in East Tennessee and Western North Carolina, the most visited national park in the United States, played host to 8.5 million visitors each year. Dollywood, in Pigeon Forge near the major eastern entrance to the park, named for and partially owned by country music star Rebecca "Dolly" Parton, attracted 1.9 million tourists per year, making it one of the most-visited attractions in Tennessee.

Efforts to pump tourist dollars into local economies prompted just about every town and city to establish departments of tourism and create attractions to lure visitors—and their dollars. Memphis could boast of Beale Street (although critics claimed that urban renewal projects had "destroyed" the original flavor of this musical locale), the late Elvis Presley's home Graceland (opened in 1982), the Civil Rights Museum (1991, expanded 2002), the Memphis Pyramid (1991), the Memphis Rock and Soul Museum (2001), and the FedEx Forum (2004). Nashville, long a tourist destination, continued to lure visitors with the New Grand Ole Opry (1974), Opryland (1987), the attraction of the Tennessee Titans professional football team (1996), and other attractions. Chattanooga's highlight was a remodeled attractive riverfront whose primary feature was the Tennessee Aquarium (1992). For its part, Knoxville hosted a World's Fair in 1982 that boasted 11 million visitors, the Women's Basketball Hall of Fame (1999), a new Convention Center (1999), and diverse University of Tennessee sporting events. Bristol's chief attraction was the Bristol Motor Speedway (originally built in 1960–1961 and expanded to seat 147,000 people in 2000). In smaller towns, Smithville had a fiddlers' festival, Oak Ridge the American Museum of Science and Energy (1975), Dayton an apple festival, Jonesborough a world-famous storytelling festival, and a number of other towns hosted events that stimulated local tourism. Also attractive, especially to sportsmen and women, were the towns and marinas on the lakes created by the Tennessee Valley Authority dams. A fine state park system also attracted campers, hikers, birdwatchers, and nature lovers.

In all, Tennessee's service sector was the most robust part of the state's economy by 1990, accounting for an impressive 69 percent of the gross state product. In fact, by 2006 there were more jobs in the service sector than there were potential workers to fill them. Major tourist destinations such as Sevier County (Pigeon Forge, Gatlinburg, the major eastern entrance to the Great Smoky Mountains National Park, and the state's largest per capita collector of the state sales tax) had to hire recruiters to find and attract workers. Some recruiters went as far as Eastern Europe and Russia to locate people to fill jobs in the booming tourist industry. In 2006 a Knox County survey revealed that between 2004 and 2006, employment in restaurants increased 7.45 percent and jobs in retail establishments grew by 6.4 percent. To be sure, many service sector jobs did not pay very well and did not offer fringe benefits such as health care. But many service jobs in transportation and health care did pay well and came with increasingly vital benefits.

Perhaps the greatest obstacle to Tennessee's reach for economic prosperity was its lack of an educated labor force. From the mid-twentieth century, several large corporations had decided not to locate or relocate in the state because of their fears that the labor force lacked sufficient education and training to hold down high tech jobs. And in spite of almost constant hand-wringing and efforts to address the problem, Tennessee consistently lagged behind almost every other state in per-pupil expenditures, in part leading to the state's troubling drop-out rate and its inability to keep educated and well-trained people from leaving Tennessee in search of better salaries and opportunities elsewhere. Indeed, even many good teachers left Tennessee entirely in pursuit of higher paying positions in neighboring Georgia and other states. In addition, some school systems remained mired in politics. In all, according to a former president of the Alcoa Corporation, by the 1980s fewer than 10 percent of the state's public school systems could be rated on a par with the United States' better public schools.

In his second term, Governor Lamar Alexander had introduced his Better Schools Program. At first many teachers balked at the introduction of "career ladder" requirements which linked additional education and training as well as job performance to salary increases, but that part of the program was so popular with the taxpayers (who were financing Alexander's program through an increase in the state sales tax) that ultimately most teachers—albeit grudgingly—accepted it. Also popular was the introduction of a basic skills program and an emphasis on computer training, mathematics, and science. Alexander's successor, Governor Ned McWherter, increased funding for the schools and worked to close the growing gap between suburban schools and inner city and rural systems. In the case of one rural system, the State Department of Education had to threaten to take over the system because the county commission had not appropriated enough money to allow the schools to open in the fall.

As the state's public education systems struggled courageously with a number of difficulties, new sets of challenges arose. Not a few parents and other citizens were loudly unhappy with the banning of prayer in public schools (many teachers and school officials simply ignored the Supreme Court decision), the teaching of evolution in biology classes, the teaching of sex education (including contraception), and other practices. Private church-related schools increased in enrollments and a surprisingly large number of parents withdrew their children from schools entirely in favor of home schooling. In addition, some other parents and other Tennesseans were critical of what they claimed was the schools' lack of quality and

Interstate I-81 near Erwin. Tennessee's interstate highway system, completed in the 1980s, was a major stimulus to manufacturing and tourism. Courtesy, Tennessee Department of Tourist Development.

be evaluated on how well their students performed on these tests.

In the 2002–2003 school year, Tennessee received $67.3 million from the federal government, approximately one-third of that from the president's No Child Left Behind legislation. The funds from President Bush's plan went to roughly one-half of Tennessee's 1,560 public schools (810 out of 1,560, or 52 percent), all of them disadvantaged schools based on the number of free and reduced-cost lunch qualifiers.

Critics attacked the program immediately. Many charged that the funds were insufficient to accomplish the ambitious goals. Others claimed that the plan was too test driven and that some teachers would simply teach the test. Still others worried that there simply were not enough computer science, mathematics, science, or reading teachers and that some teachers would abandon the profession entirely.

Promising that his second term would be devoted to education, in 2007 Governor Phil Bredesen, who while running for reelection in 2006 described the No Child Left Behind program as "almost scandalous," unveiled his own educational package, to be financed by a 42-cent increase in the sales tax on cigarettes. While in 2000 Tennessee ranked 50th in per-pupil education spending, in the first decade of the millennium gradual but steady gains were made in expenditures, test scores, and graduation rates.

The key to economic modernization rested with higher education as well, especially if the state hoped to attract new, information-based industries. And yet, while there were a number of encouraging bright spots, such as the University of Tennessee at Knoxville's College of Veterinary Medicine and College of Business Administration, Quillen Medical School's rural practice emphasis, Middle Tennessee State University's historic preservation and entertainment programs, Tennessee Technological University's College of Engineering, and others, in all, Tennessee's public higher education suffered from a top-heavy

academic rigor. Magnet schools (public schools which emphasized one specialty, such as science, the arts, etc.) satisfied some of the latter critics, but the former groups continued their assaults on what they considered to be immoral school systems and hoped that the federal government would provide vouchers that would allow parents to withdraw children from public schools and send them, partially at taxpayers' expense, to private institutions of their choosing. But the so-called "voucher system" remained bogged down in Congress and surely would face court challenges were it ever approved.

For many critics of public education, President George W. Bush's No Child Left Behind initiative provided a needed stimulus to get public schools moving in the right direction. Signed into law in January 2002, No Child Left Behind was based on a series of tests given to students from the third grade on. School systems in which students failed to perform adequately would be given assistance for a period of time, after which, if students continued to perform poorly, the state could take over those systems and run them itself. Teachers also would

bureaucracy, two competing systems of higher education—the University of Tennessee system and the Regents system— too many four-year and community colleges, and a distressing duplication of academic programs (too many engineering programs, for example). Efforts to streamline the state's public higher education system often met resistance from the two competing systems, state legislators seeking to protect their local and regional institutions, and some individuals in the Tennessee Higher Education Commission, the body charged with overseeing the state's higher education.

As with other states, the efforts in Tennessee to improve public higher education, increase faculty and staff salaries and benefits, and maintain the physical plants of the state's many campuses, led to inevitable increases in student tuition and fees, in much of the 1980s and 1990s exceeding the overall costs of living. Thus institutions once committed to open access for all gradually became schools that served middle-class and upper-class families, with many other students enrolling in the many, and less expensive, public community colleges. Scholarships helped somewhat, but college costs often outran these efforts.

In 2003 a virtual revolution in higher education took place when the state legislature approved a lottery, the proceeds from which would create scholarships for Tennessee students to attend any public or private institution in the state that would admit them. The criteria were reasonable and several thousand students benefitted from the lottery. For the colleges and universities themselves, however, the lottery proved to be a mixed blessing. Many schools were overwhelmed by the increases in applications by qualified students, and both faculty and facilities had to be quickly added to serve the surge of new students. Second, the criteria for *maintaining* those scholarships were high, and it was feared that the dropout rate would increase as well. Lastly, many legislators

and private citizens believed that at least some of the lottery proceeds should be used to improve K-12 education, a notion that was shared by Governor Bredesen, who was able to divert some money to pre-school and early education efforts. In the end, the state's public colleges and universities were not perceptibly wealthier than they had been before the lottery, although the public perception was that they were rolling in lottery money.

In addition to the public colleges and universities, Tennessee also was home to a number of private institutions of higher education. Some of them, including Vanderbilt, the University of the South, and Rhodes, had fine national reputations, while others provided good educational opportunities for students who preferred them to the public institutions. As with their public counterparts however, Tennessee's private colleges and universities suffered from spiraling costs, increasingly expensive tuitions and fees, and what they saw as the necessity of attracting students with new programs of study. Most were able to hold their own and even prosper, although for others opening the doors each fall became a struggle.

Another important challenge that confronted Tennesseans in the modern age was that of the environment. In its effort to attract industries, increase agricultural productivity, rapidly build suburban development, and play host to a virtual tsunami of automobile-borne tourists, the state had made considerable ecological sacrifices, until by the 1980s Tennessee had one of the worst pollution records of any state in the nation. In the Green Index final rankings, Tennessee ranked 45th in overall air pollution, water pollution, uses of toxic chemicals, endangerment to plants and wildlife, and environment-related health hazards to humans. In the Great Smoky Mountains National Park, average visibility during summer months, when visitors pour into the park in their automobiles and tour buses, has decreased by 80 percent since 1948, and the average

Former Vice President Al Gore (right) with former Senator Howard Baker, Jr. (center) at the 2005 Clean Air Conference held at the Baker Center, University of Tennessee. The conference highlighted the need for a major initiative to make the nation's air free of unhealthy pollutants. Courtesy, Nissa Dahlin-Brown, Howard Baker, Jr. Center for Public Policy.

sulfate concentration, in part from the Tennessee Valley Authority sulfur dioxide emissions, is 10–42 times higher than the national average.

To be sure, Tennesseans were not unaware of the problems in their environment. TVA, in part as a result of a 1978 lawsuit, made strenuous efforts to clean up emissions from its coal-fired steam plants and many private corporations did likewise. TVA also ran into difficulties with its nuclear power program. The first TVA nuclear power plant went online at Browns Ferry in 1974, but soon was shut down due to safety concerns, and did not reopen until 2007 . . . and was closed again only hours later because of similar problems. In Chattanooga, a nonprofit network of citizen groups called Chattanooga Venture set out 40 goals for the city in its bold Vision 2000 study. One of those goals was to make Chattanooga "the Environmental City." In 2005 a well-publicized Clean Air Conference focused public attention on environmental challenges. Perhaps the most well known Tennessean who has called repeatedly for Americans to recognize and address their environmental problems is former Vice President Albert Gore, Jr. His book Earth in the Balance (1992) was an early attempt to awaken Americans to their self-destructive despoiling of their envi-

ronment. Even so, Tennesseans had a long way to go before they could boast of a good environmental record.

Unquestionably, the most critical immediate challenge for modern Tennesseans was that of health care. By the 1970s it was clear that a significant revolution was about to take place in the American health care industry, although dire warnings often went ignored by the general public.

Most disturbing was the rise in costs. Health insurance premiums increased significantly as physicians, frightened by the threats of malpractice lawsuits, ordered a growing number of tests and procedures for their patients. Also as a result of malpractice suits and enormous jury awards to litigants, physicians' insurance costs skyrocketed, causing them to raise fees. At the same time, new technology allowed physicians to gain important information to diagnose illnesses that was unavailable a mere two decades earlier, but the costs to hospitals and physicians—and ultimately to patients—was huge.

To make matters even worse, the number of Americans who could not afford health insurance, visits to physicians, or medicines grew alarmingly. With no other access to health care, many of these individuals wound up in hospital emergency rooms, which increasingly were becoming the entryways into the health care system for the poor. Hospital emergency rooms, and budgets, were overwhelmed by patients who could not pay. And the Medicaid system, designed to serve this population, did not keep up with rising demands and rising costs.

As in other states, the situation in Tennessee was grave, plagued as it was by a burgeoning population of uninsured and needy people and corresponding escalating costs. In 1990, 694,000 Tennesseans were eligible for Medicaid coverage, whereas by 1994 that number had mushroomed to 1.1 million, an increase of 37 percent. In 1988–1989 the cost of Medicaid in Tennessee was $692 million, but by 1993–1994 it had more than tripled to $2.7 billion, and the state faced a projected budget deficit of over $250 million.

Faced with a myriad of unpalatable options, in 1992 Governor Ned McWherter appointed a task force to recommend how Tennessee should deal with its health care issues. The result was TennCare, implemented on January 1, 1994, a plan by which the state would receive federal Medicaid funds, supplement them with a controlled amount of state dollars, and then set up a series of managed care organizations that would negotiate hospital, physician, and pharmacy fees in an effort to keep the rising costs under control. The number of enrollees was to be capped at 1.775 million individuals, many of whom were Medicaid eligible but also others who were not eligible for Medicaid but who were either uninsured or uninsurable (the latter group would pay some of the cost of their care).

Initially the state's health care industry was leery. Angered by what they perceived as low fees set by the MCOs, many physicians at first refused to see TennCare patients, although over time 97 percent ultimately participated. As for hospitals, many of their costs exceeded what the MCOs had agreed to pay and payments often were late in arriving. As for the MCOs themselves, some complained that their own costs were more than the state allowed, and some actually were forced to close their doors.

And so Tennessee had one of the best—and, many claimed, the best— health care systems for the poor, uninsured, and uninsurable in the nation. But it was a system that tottered on the brink of complete collapse. Not a few people had moved from other states to Tennessee to take advantage of the system; some individuals who continued to live in other states maintained false addresses in Tennessee for the same purpose; and some ineligible people had been able to get on the TennCare roles through chicanery or political connections. By 1995 TennCare's budget was $3.3 billion and by 2001 the system faced a $342 million shortfall with the promise of even

more disturbing figures in the future. The state had tried to reform the program on more than one occasion, but a plethora of lawsuits had either slowed or stopped the process.

Thus in November 2004 Governor Phil Bredesen threatened to dissolve TennCare and return to the old Medicaid system, citing increased costs, reductions in federal funds, and lawsuits that blocked his efforts to reform the system. The threat, if that's what it was, awakened the state legislature and the general populace to the need for an overhauling of TennCare. Therefore, few were surprised when two months later Bredesen proposed dropping roughly 323,000 adults from the program and instituting limits on the benefits that those remaining in the program would receive. This was clearly a temporary solution, since 6.3 percent of the Tennessee population still was uninsured. But unexpectedly large tax collections allowed the reform to work and some who had been cut

Governor Phil Bredesen (2003–2011) addresses the American Legion. A former businessman, Bredesen brought a more businesslike approach to government finance in Tennessee. Courtesy, Governor's Office of Communications.

*James "Jimmy" Quillen (1916–2003), a
popular and powerful congressman from
Tennessee's First Congressional District, who
was a major force in securing a medical
school for Upper East Tennessee, now
named in his honor. Courtesy, James H.
Quillen Papers, Archives of Appalachia, East
Tennessee State University.*

from TennCare's rolls actually were able
to rejoin the program.

In 2007 Governor Bredesen proposed
a major reform of the system, which he
dubbed Cover Tennessee or Cover TN.
TennCare would still serve those eligible
for Medicaid but Cover TN introduced
affordable portable health insurance to
the approximately 600,000 individuals
who were not eligible for TennCare but
who either had no health insurance where
they worked or were unable to afford
programs offered by their employers,
since rising costs forced many employers either to raise the cost to their
employees or drop insurance plans altogether. Bredesen's plan was for private
insurers to come up with health insurance plans costing $150 per month, $50
to be paid by the employer, $50 by the
individual, and $50 by the state. Modest
co-pays for office visits and procedures
also were included. CoverKids and
Access TN would expand coverage for
children and provide insurance for those
who could afford it but who, for various reasons, had been unable to secure
insurance. At this writing many Tennesseans were cautiously optimistic about
Bredesen's reform proposals, although

some feared that, like with TennCare
earlier, costs would spiral out of control. But the state at least had recognized
the problem and taken steps to address it.

Tennessee's health care challenges,
however, were not limited to health insurance. Hospitals in Tennessee and other
states were experiencing rising costs for
rooms, tests and technology, surgeries
and other procedures that exceeded insurance companies', MCOs' and
HMOs,' as well as individuals' abilities
or willingness to pay. Some hospitals
simply went out of business while others were bought out by larger hospitals.
In 2007 there were 300 fewer hospitals
in the United States than there had been
in 2003. Many community hospitals
therefore became funnels to the larger
urban hospitals that owned them and
ceased doing certain procedures altogether. Also, in efforts to reduce
mounting costs, hospitals were forced
to reduce their work force and/or
outsource functions such as housekeep-
ing, laundry, food services, etc. which
often resulted in declines in patient
satisfaction. Many nurses retired early
or left the profession altogether, as they
believed, often correctly, that they were
being required to do more with less. By
2010, it is estimated that the nation would
need 1 million new nurses to fill vacant
positions.

Physicians also saw changes in their
own practices. In an effort to save in
overhead costs and increase their
leverage with insurance companies, many
physicians banded together in larger
groups and engaged professional business
managers to organize and administer their
practices. By the new millennium, the
single practicing physician in Tennessee
was almost a rarity.

It was hoped that the shortage of
physicians, especially in the state's rural
areas, would be alleviated by the establishment of a second state medical
school, at Johnson City. Powerful Congressman James "Jimmy" Quillen, who
represented Tennessee's First Congressional District from 1962 to 1997, used
his considerable influence to pave the way

for federal funding. But Governor Winfield Dunn opposed the founding of a second medical school (the University of Tennessee's medical units were in Memphis) on the grounds that the state couldn't afford it, but his veto was overridden and the new medical school, named the Quillen School of Medicine, greeted its first class in 1978. In less than a decade the school had earned high national marks for its program in rural practice.

Finally, Tennesseans in the new millennium needed to recognize the benefits of preventive medicine. Teenage smoking and childhood obesity were serious problems that threatened to saddle the state with enormous health care costs. Type 2 diabetes, for example, was on the rise and was predicted to increase health care costs over a person's lifetime. Unsound diets and the consumption of junk food by young people also was an increasingly serious health risk, and some Tennessee school systems carefully monitored lunch programs and tried to eliminate or limit excessive sugar and sodium intakes through soft drinks and snacks in food dispensing machines. Finally, although fitness centers had popped up all over the state in the 1980s and 1990s and a growing number of Tennesseans were working out, a disturbing number of individuals, and many young people, were getting significantly less physical exercise than they were a generation ago. Thus while they cheered professional and amateur teams and athletes, many did so from their couches or their computer workstations.

For all the challenges that Tennesseans faced concerning health care, it must also be noted that by the millennium Tennesseans generally were healthier, living longer and were less likely to suffer from chronic illness. For the state's poor, children, and uninsured blue-collar workers, however, the situation in many cases was the reverse.

Almost certainly the greatest change in American life in the twentieth century was the increasing role of government at all levels in the lives of the nation's citizens. At the beginning of the twentieth century, few Americans would have looked to government to address problems in their daily lives. The transition of the United States from an agricultural and rural nation into an industrial and urbanizing one, however, forced an increasing number of Americans to recognize that even in a land that prided itself on its rugged individualism, government at some level would have to play an increasing role in America's economic and social life. And while eventually the federal government came to be the only institution powerful enough and large enough to deal with the country's increasingly complex and difficult problems, local and state governments were still critically important to citizens in the twentieth century. Thus, in Tennessee, local and state elections continued to be followed and participated in by a majority of the state's people. Indeed, on many occasions voters turned out to cast ballots in local and state elections in greater numbers than they did for national contests.

In Tennessee the modern political landscape was reshaped by two critically important events: the 1962 Supreme Court decision *Baker v. Carr* and the emergence of a genuine two-party system in the state. As Tennessee became increasingly urban and suburban, the state legislature, dominated by representatives of primarily rural counties, was in desperate need of reapportionment, a move that was blocked by rural legislators unwilling to give up their power. The Supreme Court decision mandated reapportionment based on the principle of one man, one vote which would take representatives from rural areas and give them to urban and suburban counties. Even then the General Assembly was not able to come up with a true reapportionment plan, which finally was undertaken in 1968 by the United States District Court. As urban and suburban areas gained influence in the state legislature, issues of interest to those areas came more to the fore.

East Tennessee had voted Republican for generations, but Middle and West

Tennessee for the most part had remained faithful to the Democratic Party. The dominance of the national Democratic Party by its liberal wing gave pause to an increasing number of Middle and West Tennesseans who were coming to distrust Democrats because of their stands on gun control, civil rights, and increasingly expensive programs to help the poor. Dwight Eisenhower had attracted some Tennesseans to the Republican fold, but it was the 1964 campaign of Barry Goldwater that caused many voters, especially white voters in West Tennessee, to abandon the Democratic Party. It is true that Goldwater was crushed by President Lyndon Johnson, but in the South he had carried 233 counties that had never voted for a Republican. After 1964 white Tennesseans voted for a Democratic presidential candidate only three times, in 1976 (Carter), 1992 (Clinton), and 1996 (Clinton again). Even native son Al Gore could not carry his own state against Texan George W. Bush in 2000.

In state elections Republicans were less successful, although the new coalition of Republicans in East and West Tennessee generally did well in statewide elections. In 1966 Republican voters in the senatorial primary crossed party lines to nominate Frank Clement who, it was assumed, correctly, as it turned out, was at the end of his political career and could not beat Republican Howard Baker in the general election. Baker carried every county in East Tennessee and a majority of counties in west Tennessee to emerge with 56 percent of the vote and a victory over the wounded Clement. Then, with massive defections from the Democratic Party in 1968, in which Democratic presidential nominee Hubert Humphrey ran a distant third in Tennessee behind Richard Nixon and George Wallace, Republicans won control of the General Assembly for the first time in modern history. That majority would be extremely brief, although Republicans were a strong minority in the state Senate and briefly became a majority in 2006. And in the ten gubernatorial elections since 1970, Republicans won five

of them, 1970, 1978, 1982, 1994, 1998, and many viewed Democrat Phil Bredesen, who won gubernatorial elections in 2002 and 2006 as an ideological Republican, which in some ways he was.

The close balance between the two political parties often discouraged leaders in either party from taking bold stands on issues that were important to the progress and welfare of the state. In the 1960s and early 1970s over 49,000 Tennesseans served in Vietnam, with 1,289 losing their lives. As the war grew increasingly unpopular nationally, Tennesseans in general supported United States involvement. Anti-war demonstrations, such as the one that took place in 1970 in Knoxville during the Billy Graham crusade, were frowned on and generally dealt with harshly. Thus the war was mot a fact was not a political issue in Tennessee. However, in addition to the issues noted earlier, (economic modernization, public education, the environment, and health care), perhaps the most important issue that needed to be addressed was that of tax reform. The state government relied for most of its revenue on a comparatively high sales tax on all purchases, and in addition allowed individual counties to add their own sales taxes to that figure. By the new millennium, most Tennesseans were paying sales taxes of just under 10 percent, which encouraged those who could do so to shop in neighboring states or make purchases through the Internet. While some tourists were astounded and outraged by the high sales taxes, for the most part Tennesseans accepted them as a way to keep property taxes low and stave off calls for an income tax.

Most leaders understood that sales tax collections were highly unpredictable and could vary significantly from one year to the next. They also recognized that a sales tax was a regressive one, in that poorer Tennesseans paid a higher percentage of their incomes in taxes than did their wealthier fellow Tennesseans. Yet many people considered the embracing of an income tax by any political leader or would-be leader as political suicide,

and the vast majority of leaders from both parties avoided the issue as if it was a fatal disease. Instead, they sought other sources of revenue, such as a statewide lottery, increased levies on tobacco and alcohol, etc.

To be sure, some political figures were willing to advocate major tax reform. In his second term, Governor Ned McWherter supported an income tax, as did Governor Don Sundquist, also in his second term. Their proposals went nowhere. Indeed, the worst thing that could be said about a political opponent was that he or she was in favor of an income tax. Lamar Alexander had to consistently deny that he favored one and, ironically, in the 1994 gubernatorial race, Don Sundquist accused Phil Bredesen of supporting an income tax, a charge that Bredesen fervently denied. Just over four years later, Sundquist himself announced that he had changed his mind and now supported major tax reform. The issue continues to surface from time to time in Tennessee politics, but most political leaders continue to believe that advocating it would bring an abrupt end to their respective political careers. As of this writing, they may be correct.

Indeed, the state's voters were frustrated not only by the unwillingness of many of their political leaders to deal with the important issues and problems Tennessee faced but also by charges of political corruption which surfaced on a regular basis. As noted earlier, Gover-

nor Ray Blanton was removed from office a few days before his term expired and ultimately served a sentence in federal prison stemming from charges of corruption having to do with road contracts and pardons of state prisoners. In the mid-1980s Knoxville banker Jake Butcher, an important figure in the Democratic Party, went to federal prison for bank fraud. Reports of the excessive influence of lobbyists in Nashville arose from time to time. Finally, in 2004 a Federal Bureau of Investigation sting operation nicknamed "Tennessee Waltz" led to indictments of eleven individuals for taking bribes, five of whom were incumbent or former state lawmakers. Surely these seamy incidents captured headlines and took both time and attention away from the pressing issues that needed attention.

On the national stage, Tennessee made significant contributions to the country's political leadership. Especially prominent was Howard Baker, Jr. who won reelection to the United States Senate in 1972 and 1978. While in the Senate he, as vice-chairman of the 1973–1974 Senate Watergate Committee, won praise from all sides of the political spectrum as a fair and courageous leader. In 1977 he was elected Senate minority leader and in 1980 the majority leader. Retiring from the Senate in 1985, he was called back to public service as White House Chief of Staff to President Ronald

Groundbreaking for the Howard Baker, Jr. Center for Public Policy at the University of Tennessee, Knoxville. Left to right: Board of Trustees member James A. Haslam, II, U.S. Senator Lamar Alexander, Vice President Richard Cheney, Howard Baker, Jr., UT President John Petersen, Governor Phil Bredesen, Second District U. S. Congressman James Duncan. Courtesy, Howard Baker, Jr. Center.

Senator Fred Thompson, a protégé of Howard Baker, Jr., served as an attorney with the U. S. Senate's Watergate Committee, was a successful lawyer and lobbyist, and had a career as a motion picture and television actor before serving one term in the U. S. Senate (2003–2007). Courtesy, U. S. Senate Historical Office.

Peerless Price scores the winning touchdown as the University of Tennessee Volunteers defeated the Florida State Seminoles 23-16 to win the 1998 NCAA National Championship at the Fiesta Bowl. The team went undefeated in 1998, the first time that had been done in almost 50 years. Price went on to a career in the National Football League. Courtesy, University of Tennessee Sports

Reagan. From time to time Baker was considered as a person who should seek the presidency, although he stood little chance, largely because conservatives in his own party feared his independence, did not like his judicious stand during the Watergate scandal, and opposed his support of the Panama Canal Treaty whereby the United States ultimately gave the waterway back to the Republic of Panama. In his honor the University of Tennessee established the Howard Baker Center.

Another prominent Tennessean on the national political stage was Albert Gore, Jr. Like Baker, Gore was the son of a prominent Tennessee politician and, also like Baker, won election and reelection to the United States Senate. In addition to his advanced position on the environment, he was considered a moderate Democrat on most issues. In 1992 Bill Clinton tapped Gore to be his running mate, and the Tennessean served well as vice president from 1993 to 2001. In 2000 he was nominated by his party to run against Republican George W. Bush. The election was so close that many believed that Gore actually had won, although considerable confusion in Florida over vote counting obliged the United States Supreme Court to issue a ruling that essentially made Bush president. In general, Gore was graceful in defeat and many people believe his political career is not over.

Other Tennesseans who recently have made their marks on the national political stage include Lamar Alexander, Fred Thompson, and Harold Ford, Jr. After two successful terms as governor, Alexander became president of the University of Tennessee, leaving that post after three years to become Secretary of Education under President George H.W. Bush. He made two unsuccessful presidential runs before winning election to the United States Senate. A protégée of Howard Baker, Alexander has won respect as a Senator.

Another protégée of Baker is Fred Thompson who was a well-known attorney and lobbyist before his election to the United States Senate, defeating Representative Jim Cooper in a campaign that featured Thompson driving a red pickup truck. Also well-known as a movie and television actor, Thompson retired from the Senate after one term to devote full time to his role on the successful television series "Law and Order." In 2007 many Republicans urged Thompson to become their party's presidential nominee, an idea that he explored briefly, but from which he soon withdrew.

Harold Ford, Jr. is one of the politically prominent Ford family of Memphis. He succeeded his father in the U.S. House of Representatives in 1996 and in 2006 made a spirited race for the United States Senate against former Chattanooga mayor and successful businessman Bob Corker. Although the two candidates for the most part remained above the fray, the campaign was a particularly nasty one, even for Tennessee, with the Ford supporters charging that Corker's campaign had strong racist overtones against the African American Ford, an accusation Corker vehemently denied. Still a comparatively young man, Ford may resurface as a political candidate and national leader in the near future.

Perhaps the only thing that can divert Tennesseans' interest from politics is competitive sports. Sports at all levels, from Little League to professional teams, are followed by Tennesseans with great interest and support. As for professional sports teams, many cities throughout the nation competed with one another for new team franchises or to lure teams interested in relocating. But until the advent of modern transportation, especially charter airline travel, most professional sports franchises were located in the Northeast, with no National Football League teams south of the Washington, D.C. Redskins.

As professional leagues expanded, Tennessee cities were among those vying for professional teams that, it was hoped, would bring a great deal of revenue to those respective cities. Finally, in 1996 the Houston Oilers moved to Tennessee and were renamed the Tennessee Titans. Eventually the Titans played their home games at a newly constructed stadium in downtown Nashville, and in 2000 the entire state was thrilled when the Titans made it to the Super Bowl, although they lost to the St. Louis Rams, 23–16. Nashville also secured a National Hockey League team, the Predators, while Memphis greeted the Grizzlies, which moved from Vancouver in 2001 and played their first game in the FedEx Forum in 2004.

Exceeding professional sports interest and attendance in Tennessee was college sports. Small colleges as well as large fielded teams in a number of sports. Perhaps most popular were the University of Tennessee football team, which played in one of the largest college football stadiums in the country and in 1998 won the NCAA national championship, and the University of Tennessee Lady Volunteers basketball team, which won its seventh national championship in 2007, and was coached by Pat Summitt, a UT Martin alumna and one of the most well-known and respected college coaches in modern basketball history. But Carson Newman University in Jefferson City also won a number of smaller college football championships and the University of Memphis consistently fielded a fine men's basketball team. In all, Tennesseans loved and supported college sports throughout the state.

High school sports offered more people a chance to participate and state tournaments in football and basketball were followed throughout the state. One perennial football power was Maryville High School, but Oak Ridge, Brentwood Academy in Nashville, and other schools also earned trophies. In terms of participation, probably the fastest-growing sport was soccer, which began forming youth leagues in the 1970s and grew rapidly in the 1980s and 1990s.

Just before the dawning of the new millennium, Tennesseans celebrated their 200th birthday. In 1992 Governor McWherter had established a bicentennial commission and the General Assembly created Tennessee 200, Incorporated to plan for the celebration and develop programs that would bring the birthday party to every area of the state.

The highlight of the celebration was the creation of the 19-acre Bicentennial Capitol Mall State Park in Nashville, a magnificent undertaking that was intended to be a permanent monument to the state's history. At the same time the park was being dedicated in Nashville, simultaneous celebrations were held at Tom Lee Park in Memphis and in parks throughout the state. In Knoxville at Blount Mansion's visitors' center, U.S. Postmaster-General Marvin Runyon and Governor Don Sundquist jointly unveiled the new commemorative postage stamp honoring Tennessee's 200th birthday. For a moment, Tennesseans put aside their regional, political, social, religious, ideological, and racial differences and together remembered the state's founding, growth, trials and triumphs.

In August 2000 the University of Tennessee's Agricultural Extension Service's Cloning Project announced the successful birth of a Jersey calf named Millennium, or "Millie" for short, produced through a cell-culturing process. Although Millie lived for only nine months, succumbing to a bacterial infection common among calves, Tennesseans quickly recognized how much the state—and themselves—had changed over the past three decades. The stereotype of an alternately clever and slothful hillbilly who quaffed homemade moonshine, shot at strangers, and sang "Rocky Top" until his tonsils fell out might survive, especially in areas that catered to out-of-state tourists. But Tennessee and Tennesseans by the new millennium had become modern Americans, facing forward to a new age of great opportunities and equally great challenges.

The Tennessee Bicentennial U. S. postage stamp. The stamp was officially unveiled by U.S. Postmaster-General Marvin Runyon and Governor Don Sundquist at the Blount Mansion in Knoxville, the state's first capitol building. Courtesy, Tennessee State Library

University of Tennessee Lady Vols basketball coach Pat Summitt. Her teams have won more games than teams coached by any other person — male or female. Her teams hold seven national basketball championships. Courtesy, UT Lady Vols Media Relations.

The solution, in part, to soil erosion was
found in contour plowing. This corn crop is
being planted utilizing contour plowing in
1939. Courtesy, Tennessee State Library and
Archives

CHRONICLES OF LEADERSHIP

From the very beginning, Tennesseans have valued the land, knowing or sensing that it would sustain them if they cared for it properly. Whether the land grew crops; provided pasture; nurtured forests for houses, barns, fuel, and commerce; contained minerals that could enrich them; offered space for growth and development; provided home places to leave and to come back to, the land was important to all Tennesseans. They celebrated it in prayers and songs that recognized its bounty as well as its beauty and hold on their minds and hearts.

Even before white explorers, traders, and settlers pierced the mountain passes and found a new Eden in Tennessee, Indians who had lived there for centuries had constructed villages, grown crops and hunted its woodlands for game, and tried as best they could to live in harmony with the land and with nature itself. For their part, white settlers sought to *tame the wilderness* rather than live in harmony with it, and blazed trails that others would follow, to settle in Tennessee or use it as a stopping-off place in their journeys further westward. Those who stayed built towns, some of which would become prosperous cities.

Farmers not only lived off the land but also produced products for regional and even national markets. Cotton, wheat, and livestock, along with pigs, turkeys and chickens were raised and shipped either down the rivers or to the growing towns of Knoxville, Chattanooga, Nashville, and Memphis. The coming of railroads to Tennessee in the 1850s ultimately extended the markets

for agricultural goods grown or raised on the land.

After the Civil War the railroads also served to ship minerals and lumber either to out-of-state markets or to the growing mills and factories of Tennessee. Iron, coal, copper, and marble all were extracted and millions of board feet of lumber were felled, sawed, and sold. Cities virtually blossomed with new wealth and a new commercial-industrial elite was born in the state's cities. In the country, however, overpopulation, economic hard times, and a desertion of farms by young people created a tale of two Tennessees: one urban, growing, prosperous, and the other distressed, eroding, and increasingly poor.

Yet, as in the past, the land did not desert its people. New crops were found, such as tobacco, which gave many farmers a new lease on life. In the 1930s the New Deal helped to restructure the state's agriculture and industry. At the same time, the Tennessee Valley Authority brought electricity to rural areas, established thousands of test demonstration farms to show farmers better ways to use their land, and provided much-needed off-the-farm jobs building a series of dams along the Tennessee River. Finally, World War II brought full employment to the state and created Oak Ridge, an entirely new city in Anderson County where parts of the atomic bomb were secretly developed. At its peak, Oak Ridge, the "city behind the fence," had a population of 75,000. During the war, many women were able to take good paying jobs once reserved for men, jobs which some were unwilling to leave when the troops returned after the war.

In The Interstate Highway Act of 1956 prompted the construction of a national network of modern roads in America, which benefited Tennessee immeasurably. Products manufactured in the state could be carried via a new trucking industry to all corners of the nation. Also, many industries located in other states relocated to Tennessee, in part because of the new way to transport their products. And these new roads were beneficial to farmers as well: many could remain on their land and commute long distances to jobs in cities and newly-established industrial parks (a new census designation, "part-time farmer," claimed an increasing number of Tennessee agriculturalists). Finally, tourists "discovered" Tennessee in ever-growing numbers, especially after the dedication of the Great Smoky Mountains National Park in 1940, the fine network of state parks, and the ability to use those new highways to reach the state's beautiful and bounteous streams and lakes as well as tourist destinations in all three of the "grand divisions" of the state.

In the 1970s and 1980s Tennessee lost a number of its traditional manufacturing enterprises and jobs (in textiles, apparel, iron, and railroads), many of which sought lower costs and wages overseas. And yet, they were more than replaced by high-tech manufacturing jobs (the most dramatic of which was automobile production) as well as by a burgeoning service sector, especially in the health care industry and tourism. Suburbs mushroomed, many of them filled by people who were moving to Tennessee from other states because of climate, cost of living, and comparatively low taxes. By 1990 the erosion of population had been halted and reversed, in large part because of the new opportunities the state provided.

As Tennesseans became more affluent, better educated, generally healthier, and more urban or suburban, they never lost touch with their land or their traditions. Country music was more popular than ever (the country music cable network [CMT] enjoyed growing popularity); the art of quilting enjoyed an enormous revival with Nashville hosting the American Quilters Society show at the Opryland Hotel and suburbs were filled with pickup trucks with umbrellas in their gun racks. As retirees moved to Tennessee and melded into the population, more diverse in-migrants from Asia, Latin America, and Eastern Europe attempted to do the same.

As they loved and respected their land, Tennesseans made great efforts to preserve their rich history. Historical societies, museums, and various historical sites are thriving. Reenactments of battles dot the summer landscape. The state's history is taught to every schoolchild. And books such as this one preserve in print and illustrations Tennessee's rich and diverse past. The organizations whose own stories are told on the following pages believe it important to save our collective past and pass that legacy on to those who will come after us. As the state continues to face daunting challenges, in health care, the environment, public education, better jobs, etc., the grounding in and respect for the land and an understanding and appreciation of the state's history help Tennesseans face their collective future with confidence and courage.

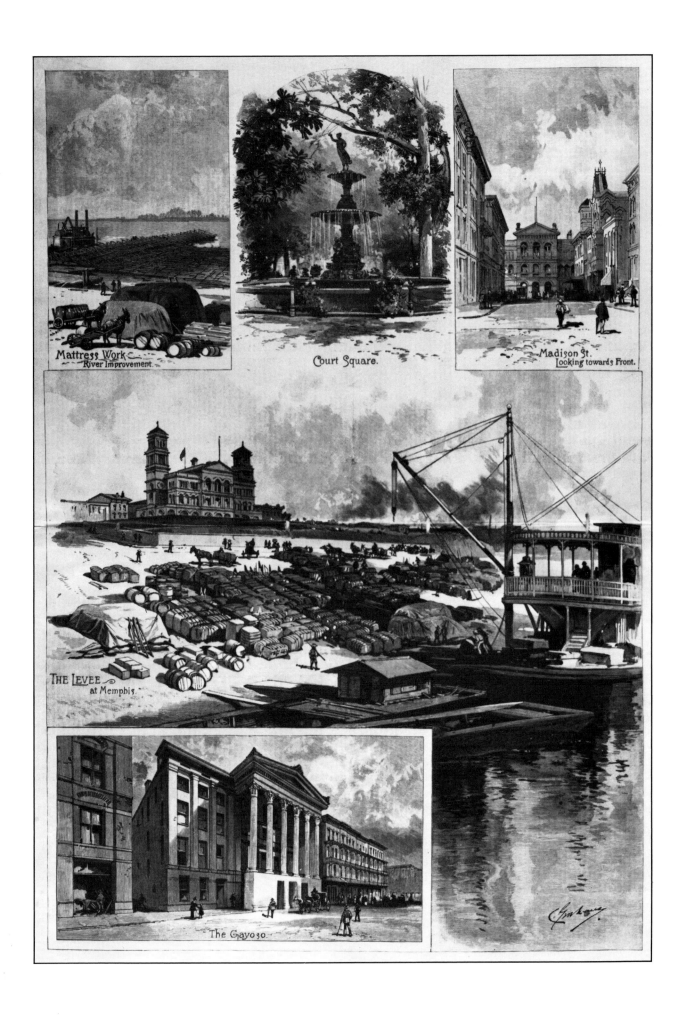

Mattress Work.
River Improvement.

Court Square.

Madison St.
Looking towards Front.

The Levee
at Memphis.

The Gayoso.

BARRETT FIREARMS MANUFACTURING

From the time that Ronnie Barrett was a young boy, he has enjoyed an appreciation and a fascination with guns. He grew up in a home where guns were a way of life, both for protection and recreation. Like many youngsters in his neighborhood he was a hunter and became a pretty good marksman. As an adult he competed in several shooting competitions and was a reserve deputy for the Rutherford County Sheriff's Department for a period of time.

Barrett became more than just a gun enthusiast in 1982 when he launched a fledgling firearms company with lots of dreams but little capital. Today, Barrett Firearms Manufacturing is known around the world as a leader in the production of long-range rifles with applications for military, law enforcement, and civilian sport shooting.

Back in the 1970s and 80s, Barrett had a successful photography studio in Murfreesboro and a modest garage workshop at his home where he would tinker when not earning a livelihood. It was there that the famous Barrett Rifle was born. He received a telephone call one day that would forever change the course of his young entrepreneurial career. He was asked to photograph a gunboat on the Stones River near Nashville. Barrett turned that opportunity into an award-winning photograph receiving top recognition from the Tennessee Professional Photographers Association.

Something else happened when his camera zeroed in on a Browning .50-caliber machine-gun, mounted prominently on that boat. The image was burned into his mind; a great, big gun, one with a reputation for having a strong thrust and recoil while hitting targets.

Even though Barrett had never fired a .50-caliber, he became almost obsessed with it. He wanted to own one, but didn't think that he could afford the price tag. While mesmerized, he was wide-eyed with confidence that if he couldn't afford it, he would just make one himself.

He became a man on a mission poring through books looking for pictures, talking to people who had shot a .50-caliber and trying to understand the mechanics of how he could make a more practical gun for firing the cartridge. His thoughts were to make a rifle for a shooter that would be lighter and easier

Ronnie Barrett holds the world-famous Barrett .50-caliber M82A1 rifle. The rifle was adopted by the United States Army and named the M107 for military purposes.

to handle, even shoulder-fired without landing a person in the hospital with a broken jaw or dislocated shoulder. And he also wondered if people would be willing to purchase it for sport shooting or as a collectible. Barrett resolved to find out.

Within two months, he hand-drew a design for what was to become the Barrett .50-Caliber. When he approached some machine shops to help with the creation, instead of getting praise and encouragement, he was greeted with laughter and sneers. The response was that it could not be done. And if it would have worked, someone before him would have made it.

Barrett's determination never wavered for one moment. A few days later, he was introduced to Bob Mitchell by a mutual acquaintance. A tool and die maker and machinist at Greer Manufacturing Company in Smyrna, Tennessee, Mitchell agreed to help the young gun dreamer and artist, using Barrett's three-dimensional drawings as a guide to better understand how the rifle should be crafted.

Barrett knew very little about tooling, but knew how to draw the gun that he wanted and the parts to make it work. While many a naysayer had said that it would never work, Barrett remembered the story about the bumblebee which is not supposed to fly, but the bumblebee doesn't know that, and it flies anyway. Mitchell and Barrett would get together daily after their respective regular jobs and sometimes work all night fine-tuning Barrett's latest ideas. Like the bumblebee, Ronnie Barrett did it anyway.

As he continued developing the .50-caliber rifle, Barrett went to the shooting range countless times, often tromping through the mud and wet weeds. After shooting it, he'd get a new idea, head back to the shop to make the changes and then back to the shooting range to try it out. Finally, he was pleased.

Then he had another major challenge. How was he going to mass produce it? Had he been financially able, people could have been hired to do that. His only option back then was to do the research and development, quality control and all the work himself.

Remember, Barrett had a "day job" which was his photography studio. He also had a passion to create a unique .50-caliber rifle which included finding and

purchasing the raw materials, while being the chief manufacturer, assembler, advertising department, salesman, order taker, and the shipping department. He never entertained the idea of failing; he just showed up for work every day and did what had to be done."

Ronnie Barrett is shown with the George M. Chinn Memorial Award given in 2004. Named in memory of Lieutenant Colonel George M. Chinn, a noted author, weapons designer, and career United States military officer, the award recognizes an individual who has contributed significantly to Small Arms Weaponry Systems based on excellence in research, development, engineering, manufacturing, and management.

Through it all, Barrett became a self-taught engineer whose .50-caliber rifle has become a hallmark in gun manufacturing. The Barrett Rifle has helped defend America's freedom and wage the war on terrorism in places like Afghanistan and Iraq. Law enforcement agencies and civilian sport shooters throughout the United States also sing the praises of the Barrett Rifle.

The Barrett .50-caliber served the United States well

The modern state-of-the-art Barrett Firearms Manufacturing building in Murfreesboro; a far cry from the original manufacturing facility that was located in Ronnie Barrett's garage in 1982.

during Desert Storm. When the conflict began, only a handful of the rifles were with the U.S. military, mainly for demonstration purposes. There were a lack of manuals, formal training procedures and certainly spare parts.

Barrett took the initiative when he learned that our military men and women were being deployed to the Middle East. The situation was urgent if our brave soldiers were to have the battlefield advantages the Barrett Rifle could provide. They needed support from its creator.

He quickly assembled manuals and related materials and set out on a personal whirlwind tour traveling at his own expense to several U.S. military locations to demonstrate the incredible weapon, even providing his own ammunition. With Barrett shooting the rifle, touting its merits, and training the trainers, U.S. military officials liked what they saw and heard.

The United States Army recognized Ronnie Barrett's .50-caliber rifle in 2004 as one of the Top Ten Greatest Inventions. In the last 100 years, only four individuals including Ronnie Barrett have invented guns adopted by the United States military. Designs by the others were turned over to another industry or to the government for further perfection and then production. Barrett is the only one to create, manufacture, market, and mass-produce his firearm for the U.S. government.

Barrett rifles have appeared in motion pictures, thousands of shooting sport magazines, military magazines, reference books, and even a novel. The rifle has been the topic of many radio shows, numerous television shooting sport shows, including "The American Shooter," The History Channel's "Tales of the Gun" and The Discovery Channel's "Future Weapons" program.

Ronnie Barrett stands five-feet, seven and three-quarters inches but walks tall where he travels; from an award-winning photographer, entrepreneur, successful firearms inventor and manufacturer, and accomplished businessman.

Born on March 5, 1954 in Murfreesboro, Tennessee, his parents Joe and Hazel Barrett taught the importance of being thrifty, having a good work ethic, possessing strong character, and using common sense.

As a child tugging at his mother's apron strings, he had an inquisitive mind that expressed itself many times in drawing images of people, animals, houses, and most often a gun. His creativity was reinforced and encouraged by his mother who is also talented in art although without formal training.

Some things appear to have come easy for Barrett. His self-confidence and can-do-anything attitude radiated, winning him friends and influencing people throughout his early life, from his days at Murfreesboro Central High School up to the present.

There were other things about school that were difficult. Math and literature were not his forte.

What got him excited was art, which is probably the reason that he found an affinity with Jean (Craig) Butler, the art teacher at Murfreesboro Central High School. He understood what she was try-

ing to teach the students because he is a visual person. But most times, it was more enjoyable to draw things that stirred his interest, especially images of a gun.

It was his art teacher's encouragement and recommendation that placed Barrett on the path to a career in photography. Ed Delbridge, a successful Murfreesboro businessman, photographer, and studio owner would sometimes employ talented high school art students to work part-time doing touch ups to portraits and general chores at his business.

Delbridge gave him a job working after school until 6 p.m. Barrett's fascination with photography was like a sponge soaking up whatever anyone would share. He even volunteered without pay to assist on projects that included after hours and weekends.

Ronnie Barrett holds the award that recognizes the United States Army naming the Barrett M107 rifle one of the Top Ten Greatest Inventions in 2004.

Inspired by Delbridge's success, Barrett dreamed of having his own photography business, and in 1973, while talking to Eloise Elrod, he learned that she had a building for lease on South Church Street in Murfreesboro. He didn't have $250 for the first month's rent, but convinced Ms. Elrod that he was good for the debt and could pay her at the end of the month because a wedding was scheduled to be photographed and more would soon be added to the books.

With his shingle secured, he began planning to open Barrett's Photography.

Having no serious cash and with only some pocket change, he drew on his creative talents; using his own hands to make easels, cabinets, backgrounds and other necessary items to furnish the business.

Five years later, he purchased the building for $25,000, a large amount of money for Barrett at the time. By 1975 he was winning a significant number of awards given by the Tennessee Professional Photographers Association, and became the youngest to receive its Certified Photographer's Degree that normally takes years to achieve.

One interesting aspect of his photography studio was that when the door was opened from the reception room leading down the hall to the back wall, it presented a fine 200- foot straight line that was perfect for a bullet trap where he and some of his neighbors from the Murfreesboro Police Department would shoot handguns at night. He regularly competed in regional pistol and rifle contests and won most.

Ronnie Barrett's journey from being a gun enthusiast and professional photographer to a world-class manufacturer, entrepreneur and businessman has taken many twists and turns. He would be the

Ronnie Barrett has a good grip on business and on life as a former professional photographer turned entrepreneur, gun inventor, and firearms manufacturer. The name Barrett is known around the world, making him an icon with military, law enforcement and civilian sport shooters.

first to admit that it has not been easy, but the reward has been worth the effort.

As a visionary, he created a market for a .50-caliber rifle that could be shoulder-fired before there was a market for it. The name Barrett became a proven brand that is recognized around the world.

Barrett's two children joined the Barrett Firearms team after they graduated from high school. Son, Chris Barrett, is following in his father's footsteps and is expected to exceed past successes while designing guns, by being involved in research, development, and engineering. Daughter, Angela Barrett, also has her father's creative eye and mind and has developed her own expertise in graphics and marketing.

Ronnie Barrett has worked hard to earn his legacy. It required many long hours in the early days tweaking the

Ronnie Barrett stands with the next generation of Barrett Firearms Manufacturing. Son Chris is following in his father's footsteps as a gun designer in research, development and engineering. Daughter Angela uses her creative talents in marketing, graphics and trade show productions.

prototype rifle, convincing bankers to loan him money, honoring his word and commitments while making sales, and positioning the company for the future with solid business and financial principles.

Ronnie Barrett and Barrett Firearms Manufacturing are a great success story, proving that the American dream is still possible for anyone with the courage to set goals, work hard and overlook the naysayer when he or she fails to see the dream.

BETHEL COLLEGE

Bethel College was founded more than 150 years ago in northwest Tennessee with the aim of providing students with a Christian environment that fostered both scholastic and spiritual growth. Today, Bethel is a thriving, rapidly growing academic institution that confers on its students much more than a degree. It also develops within students the knowledge and confidence to excel in the world and make it a better place.

Bethel was originally established in 1842 in the frontier town of Mc-Lemoresville as an extension of McLemoresville Academy, also known as the "Brick Academy." It was initially founded as Bethel Seminary, operating under the guidance of the West Tennessee Synod of the Cumberland Presbyterian Church, and it was granted a charter by the state in 1847. Early years at Bethel focused heavily on classical learning, with freshmen completing courses in Herodotus, Virgil, and Cicero, as well as upper level mathematics, Greek, and Latin courses. In later years, courses included botany, surveying and navigation, philosophy, and the United

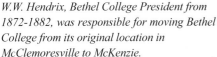

W.W. Hendrix, Bethel College President from 1872-1882, was responsible for moving Bethel College from its original location in McClemoresville to McKenzie.

The first building at Bethel College's new site after it was moved from McClemoresville to McKenzie.

States Constitution. Students could attend Bethel College for $20 a semester, while board (which included washing and firewood) was an additional $30.

Enrollment through the 1850s fluctuated between 130 and 175 students, but the onset of the Civil War brought an end to Bethel's auspicious beginning and the most difficult time in the school's history dawned. Much of the school's population was lost, with students fighting on one side of the fray or the other in an area with deeply divided loyalties. The school itself was also a casualty of the war, frequently occupied by troops, with school buildings commandeered as barracks. Much of Bethel's equipment was lost as well. A notable loss was that of an impressive refracting telescope, which had been purchased for $3,000 in 1852 by C.J. Bradley. Suspecting that the brass barrel was really a Confederate cannon, Union troops captured the telescope, which had resided in a laboratory building that had been renovated to serve as an observatory. Happily, though, through the efforts of Will Calhoun, the telescope was eventually returned to the college, where it now resides in the college vault.

Eventually, Bethel, like the nation, was able to survive and rebuild after the war. It reopened in 1865 under the leadership of the Reverend Benjamin Wilburn McDonnold who opened the school's doors for the first time to women students.

Shortly thereafter, during the administration of President Reverend W.W.

Hendrix, Bethel moved from McLemoresville to McKenzie. This move put the college in closer proximity to the recently built railroad, which had bypassed McLemoresville. J.M. McKenzie deeded the land upon which the school still sits to the Board of Directors on February 2, 1872, and a brick building large enough to accommodate 300 students was erected. This single building comprised all of Bethel College for 50 years, complete with classrooms, dormitory rooms, kitchens, and an auditorium.

Hardship was still to come for the school. As a result of a Church Union in 1906, ten Cumberland Presbyterian colleges transferred sponsorship. Only Bethel College remained as the sole Cumberland Presbyterian college.

The 1920s, under the leadership of school president Professor N.J. Finney, signaled a time for growth and construction at Bethel College. The main building remained for some time, evolving as other buildings were added to the campus, such as a boys' dorm as well as married couple housing. However, after new dorms were built for both male and female students, the old building was torn down.

This period of growth was followed by more challenges not only for the college, but the nation as well. Both the Great Depression and World War II took their toll on the college community which suffered at the height of the war with a rock bottom enrollment of only 75 students. Amazingly, the school was able to survive again, coming back after the war with record numbers—508 matriculated in the fall of 1951. The 1960s saw a continued rise in enrollment and continued assurance that the school was strong and thriving.

In recent years, Bethel College has again set new enrollment records, with enrollment topping the 1,000 mark shortly after the turn of the century and with enrollment numbers quadrupling during the 10-year-period from 1998 to 2008. By providing equally significant athletic, performing arts, and general scholarships and also by offering a non-traditional degree program tailored to working adults, Bethel College has made a private, Christian liberal arts education more accessible to a broader base of education seekers. Its 2007 fall enrollment number of 2,155 students is evidence of that success. This incredible growth distinguishes Bethel College as the fastest growing private school in Tennessee— an identity it intends to maintain through a master plan commissioned by the school's board of trustees to expand the campus' physical facilities and accommodate a residential student body of twice its current size, an adult degree program of similar size and master's degree programs to accommodate 500 students.

Bethel College, which remains in beautiful McKenzie, Tennessee, typifies the small-town values of the local citizenry. Tucked away enough to give students a contemplative and peaceful learning environment, it is only 45 minutes from the amenities of Jackson, and only two hours from major cities Memphis and Nashville. McKenzie offers full access to outdoor recreation, with Carroll Lake, one of the Tennessee Wildlife Resource's family lakes, just across town, and Kentucky Lake, Tennessee's largest lake, a short drive away.

Laughlin Hall was a boys' dormitory that once stood at the present site of Prosser Hall, a residence hall built in 2004 that faces the Bethel courtyard and is adjacent to the Burroughs Learning Center and the Marrs-Stockton Student Center.

Today, Odom Hall Science Building is one of Bethel's oldest existing buildings. Built in 1951 as a seminary, it has served as a library and now as a space for math and science classes and laboratory work.

Bethel takes a hands-on approach to student success, making sure each person enrolled at Bethel has every educational advantage. This includes keeping class size limited to ensure a personal learning environment, as well as giving adult students the opportunity to earn their degrees while working. Bethel College pioneered the use of laptop computers, when it became the first school in Tennessee to give each entering full-time student his or her own laptop.

Bethel College is accredited by the Commission of Colleges of the Southern Association of Colleges and Schools and awards both undergraduate and master's degrees. A wide range of majors is offered, including three different business administration programs (with emphasis on accounting, management or computer information), education, humanities, science and mathematics, as well as social sciences. Students are also offered the unique opportunity to tailor their major to suit their career goals with a student-initiated major, which can be pursued for either a bachelor of arts or bachelor of science degree.

Bethel recently added an honors program to its curriculum that is aimed at stoking intellectual growth through small-group discussions, accelerated course work, and cultural events in nearby Nashville and Memphis. For many undertaking the honors program, an undergraduate degree may just be the first stepping stone in their academic career. The school recognizes this and therefore puts strong emphasis on preparing these students for ongoing analysis, research, and composition in their chosen fields of study. Additionally, the college awards each student accepted into the program a significant scholarship, to help defray costs and to help give each student extra time to devote to his or her studies.

Master's degree programs are also available at Bethel College, with popular courses of study including education and teaching tracks. Bethel is one of only three schools in Tennessee to offer a master of science degree in physician assistant studies. Accredited by the ARC-PA, this select program consists of 12 months of classroom studies reinforced with fifteen months of clinical medical experience.

The college offers a master's in business administration that focuses on creating opportunities for adult learners to hone their business skills. Two tracks are available for students with different degrees of real-world experience: the executive track offers those who are already experienced managers in the workplace, training to help improve their

This log cabin was the home of Reverend Samuel McAdow in Dickson County, Tennessee in which the Cumberland Presbyterian Church was organized in 1810. A replica of this building stands on the Bethel College campus.

particular workplace, while the academic/practitioner track teaches skills across a wide spectrum of business administration areas, such as management, marketing, economics, ethics, and strategy. The two emphases give both students continuing on from undergraduate degrees and working adults the opportunity to open doors through higher education.

Students at Bethel enjoy a wide variety of extracurricular activities in addition to their academic pursuits. Sports play an important role in the Bethel College tradition with the school fielding competitive men's and women's teams in every major sport disciplines, including football, basketball, baseball, softball, soccer, cross country, track and field, and golf, among others. Bethel is a member of the National Association of Intercollegiate Athletics (NAIA). The football program is a member of the Mid-South Athletic Conference. Intramural sports and activities are also available for the enjoyment of all and range from flag football to dodgeball.

During recent years, Bethel has incorporated

a renewed focus on the performing arts through its Renaissance Performing Arts program, which provides choral, instrumental and theatre opportunities to close to 250 students. And most recently, Bethel has expanded music major opportunities and theatre coursework opportunities by adding majors related to the commercial music industry and by expanding the school's theatre minor.

An active student government association is a vital part of the Bethel College community, allowing students to actively participate in the planning and organization of student activities. Greek life is popular at Bethel, with numerous sororities and fraternities, some in existence for more than 80 years. Students can also apply for membership in the service and scholarship society, *Gamma Beta Phi* or in service organizations like *Arete*, a social sciences club.

Another hallmark of student life at Bethel College is the strong Christian community, seen in every aspect of the academic environment, including student activities. Through daily events, such as chapel services, ongoing club participation and annual events like Bethel College Youth Festival, students can feed

Bethel's log cabin was constructed in 1928 by the freshman class as a replica of the log cabin in Dickson County, Tennessee where the Cumberland Presbyterian Church was organized.

This two-story building was used as a student center and music building at Bethel College until 1970 when it was demolished and the Dickey Fine Arts Building was erected.

Student Life and the Career Development Center.

Throughout its many years in Tennessee, Bethel has thrived and struggled along with the surrounding community. Yet it has always remained a safe haven for young people seeking a strong Christian community supportive of learning and growth. By continuing this tradition, Bethel not only ensures that young men and women will become scholars, but that they will live up to their potential to serve themselves and others through a thoughtful, ethical, Christian approach to life.

their Christian spirit through worship, fellowship, and service. Off-campus activities, including mission trips to developing nations, give students the opportunity to go beyond their borders and live out their personal faith.

A full range of support services are offered to help students achieve balance in their academic, spiritual, physical, and emotional lives. Tutoring and academic counseling are available for all students to help them improve study skills, manage their time more effectively, and navigate test-taking. These services are offered free of charge for those having specific difficulties in particular classes or those who may be a bit overwhelmed by their overall schedule. Confidential counseling is also available to help students transitioning from structured home life to the freedoms and responsibilities of college, and is just one more way that Bethel addresses the wider needs of its students.

As part of Bethel College's four-year plan for incoming students, comprehensive career planning and guidance is available beginning with freshman

orientation. The administration at Bethel College believes that planning for graduate education or for a first job after college should not be delayed until the junior or senior year. Instead administrators encourage students to pro-actively consider their options and career path early in their college experience to take advantage of all possible opportunities.

More than 500 students live on campus in one of five residence halls: McDonald Hall, Morris Hall, Prosser Hall, West Hall, and Wildcat Cove. The residence halls are all located in close proximity to the Marrs-Stockton Student Center, which houses the school bookstore, post office, a pizza parlor and coffee house, as well as the Offices of

In 1966, workers completed construction on Morris Hall, a structure that still serves as a men's residence hall on the present-day campus of Bethel College.

BRADFORD FURNITURE

Celebrating its 120th year in business, Bradford Furniture is a Nashville institution and one of the country's finest full-service home furnishing resources, offering furniture, both new and antique, oriental rugs, accessories, lamps, mirrors, and art. The company is also acclaimed worldwide for its custom interior design services provided by talented and knowledgeable designers, and its fabric and wall-covering library is one of the most extensive in the south. Focused on quality products and fine service, the reasons for Bradford's longevity are clear.

In 1889 J. H. Bradford founded Bradford Wholesale Furniture Manufacturing Company in Nashville, Tennessee. At the time, Benjamin Harrison was

Bradford's on Broadway, downtown Nashville in 1912.

president of the United States, and the South was still recovering from the Civil War. Railroad transportation was rapidly transforming the West from the age of "cowboys and Indians" to a growing economical environment. Montana, North Dakota and South Dakota had just become states, and the local Daily American National Bank boasted an astronomical capital sum of $1 million. It was a time of great promise and countrywide optimism.

J. H. Bradford started the company on Broad Street (now Broadway) in a building that, while a bit modified, is still there. He was a furniture manufacturer as well as a wholesaler to retail stores, and also sold at the retail level to walk-in customers. This was a time when a business owner did it all. As the company grew, it began manufacturing in its own

factory at a building on North First, which also still stands.

Sometime between 1912 and 1916, the company's legendary founder was ready to retire. Word has it that the entrepreneurial Mr. Bradford opened one of the first movie theater chains in Florida that actually had some form of air conditioning. He sold Bradford Furniture to his clerk, Joseph William Rowland. As business grew, Rowland moved Bradford's to a larger space on Third Avenue North. The manufacturing and wholesale end of the business became less important, particularly as the Depression hit the country, and in the mid-1940s the company changed its major focus to the retail market, where it remains today.

In the 1940s Rowland's son, Bill Rowland, Jr., who had been working for his father since he was a teen, took over

the business after graduating *magna cum laude* from Vanderbilt University in 1933 with a degree in economics and many years already under his belt working for his father full-time. In 1945 a devastating fire put the company out of business for four months and later, in a freak accident, a ceiling above Bradford's warehouse caved in due to the weight of tons of stored walnuts, turning all the company's inventory into kindling.

Amid this adversity, the business has also enjoyed many amusing incidents over their long history. One of the most famous is the time a large white-faced steer wandered through the company's door on Third Avenue, proceeded halfway to the office, abruptly turned around and then bolted at full-speed out the door. Fortunately, there was no damage to either furniture or person.

After these incidents, and believing that downtown Nashville in the late 1940s was not a location where the company's customers—particularly females—wanted to shop, Rowland moved the company to Green Hills, when the area was still primarily nothing but just that—green hills.

"Both my grandfather and my father," says Bill Rowland III, who has served as president and CEO since 1996, "were visionaries. My father moved us to Green Hills 20 years before it began to develop into the growing community it has become."

While Bradford's had always enjoyed an outstanding reputation for the manufacture and sale of quality furniture, in the early 1950s, interior design was

J. W. Rowland, Sr.

coming into vogue. When the company made the move to Green Hills, Rowland Jr. took in three partners. The most actively involved was Joe Murphy, who worked for the company for more than 45 years. Says Bill Rowland III, "He had an eye for interior design and was a powerful force in fine-tuning that aspect of our business. We already had fabulous furniture, a fine reputation and offered quality service, but he took the

interior-design ball and ran with it. My father recognized this potential in him and encouraged him to do so."

Since then, Bradford's has continued to employ talented and knowledgeable designers and buyers. One, who has been with the company for 38 years and is current senior vice president, Buell Sullivan, is known internationally. He has a staff of people who read, travel, and research the latest trends. "People come to them," says Rowland, "because we have a reputation for being the best."

The Murphy family and the other two family partners, both Davis and Daugherty, have been involved with Bradford's since 1951. Murphy retired in 1998 as chairman of the company. For 58 years, the same four business associates and/or families are still owners of Bradford's—"something," says Bill Rowland, "we are very proud of."

"My father," says Rowland, "was only a teenager when the Depression began. He saw his father struggle to keep the doors open. They had trouble acquiring wood and other materials they needed to make furniture. The company resorted to three-day workweeks." During wartime, Bradford's employees supported their much-needed livelihood by making gunstocks for the military.

After World War II, Bradford's became trendsetters, beginning to incor-

Rendering of front of Green Hills store.

porate antiques, rugs and other high-end home furnishings into the business. Whatever brand of furniture the company sold, it was the Bradford name that sold it. Bradford's reputation for quality and top-notch service was what both the company and its customers valued most.

In the early 20th century, furniture, reports Rowland, was more utilitarian and included the arts and crafts style, along with reproductions of English pieces. Bradford's made its own bedding and mattresses and served people within a radius of 50 to 100 miles, delivering many times by horse and wagon. Everything was made of the finest quality materials and fit the styles of the time.

In 1950 the company incorporated. One year later, long before there was a Green Hills Mall and H. G. Hills Center, Bradford's decided to move outside the city to Hillsboro Pike. The company set up shop at the south end of its present center. To the north was a vacant lot used only during December to sell Christmas trees, and across the street was a small market. The site of the current mall consisted of such poor, rocky soil that even the hardy cedar trees that dotted the landscape could not grow. The area had a spring running through it. Bradford's portion of this land was a low spot that would flood during heavy downpours. After wading through the spring's water and salvaging furniture several times, the company expanded onto the vacant Christmas-tree lot and built its current three-story building. "At first," says Rowland, "we still had to deal with flooding, until we reconfigured and built a state-of-the-art building in 1963."

In 1989, the company, whose name had morphed from Bradford Wholesale Furniture Manufacturing Company to Bradford Interiors, celebrated its 100th birthday. Rowland states that 100 years in this industry is remarkable because the furniture business has changed greatly over time; it has become far more competitive. "Like any other business, we've gone through cycles. The people still in it are the successful ones. Our niche has been as a leader in fine furnishings in a city that appreciates what we have for sale.

"Nashville," Rowland conveys, "is known as the Athens of the South" because a world renowned Parthenon replica was

created for Nashville's centennial." The city has always been proud of its intelligent, philanthropic residents. "There is a level of taste here," says Rowland, "that's been here for years, that continues to support not only fine furniture but the arts. The community has been a great place for us to thrive. There is a sophistication here that has been on the upper end of the southern city experience. We consider ourselves fortunate to be here.

"Our reputation," he says, "is also based on the way we treat our customers. They come back time and again because we do business in a positive way. Our business is based on the golden rule:

A picture of popular polish from Bradford's 1910 catalog.

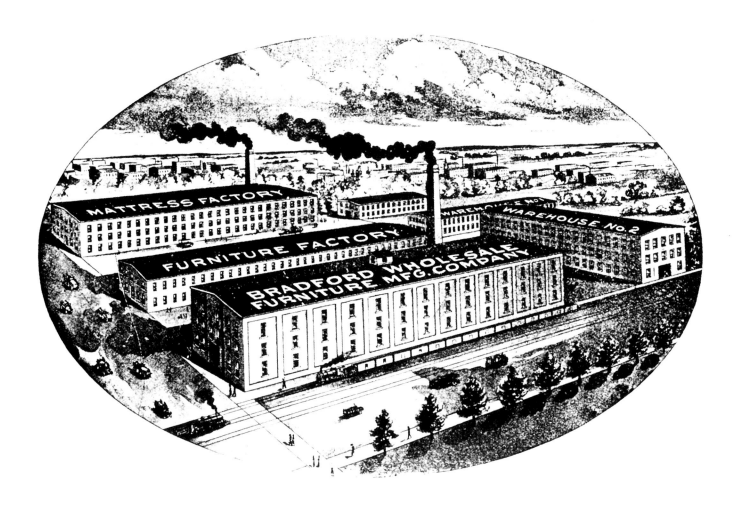

Do unto others as you would have them do unto you." This newest CEO claims that they would forego profits for customer satisfaction. "In the long run, it pays off," he asserts. "If your goal is to stay in business and employ people to be the best at what the company does, you must focus on customer satisfaction."

In the last 15 to 20 years, with this third-generation Rowland at the wheel, Bradford's has been recognized as a true leader in the antique import and rug business. While the furniture business has been a slow-moving one, within the last 10 years it has begun to change more rapidly, with manufacturing leaving the United States. "We have become," Rowland says, "a one-world economy when it comes to furniture."

Still, the company continues to thrive. "I have been surrounded," he continues, "by people who have been successful long before I became a part of this company. They have all given me the opportunity not only to learn from them, but also to continue to use their talents and introduce new people to the business. Bradford's was doing well before I entered the picture. I am simply a steward of what was put in front of me. All I've attempted to do is to continue to perfect and fine-tune what they created."

In 1996, Bradford's was recognized as Retailer of the Year by the Oriental Rug Retailers of America, the equivalent, Rowland reports, of an Academy Award for rug dealers. As a one-store operation, the company believes this is quite an honor. With 14 designers on staff, Bradford's continually strives for excellence and works to maintain ongoing relationships with their customers in the world of interior design.

Of the 57 employees currently on board at Bradford's, 18 have been with the company for more than 15 years. Four employees have been there for more than 20 years; three more have been there for 25; four others, for more than 30; and another three for close to 40 years.

Bradford's was founded on quality furnishings, and plans to continue forever to deliver only that. The company has seen many trends come and go but

Rendering of East Nashville factory from 1920s catalog.

remains dedicated to value, quality and service. Its owners pride themselves on one of the most experienced design staffs in town plus on-hand inventory and a seven-day trial period to ensure that any item customers fall in love with on the showroom floor is everything they thought it would be in their home.

The accelerated growth of the city and Bradford's dedication to service and quality home furnishings has ensured the prosperity of the company from its very beginning through the development into what it is today. Says Rowland, "We're good at providing our patrons with something they want. We offer competitive prices and stand behind everything we sell. The best thing about our past is the thing that's brightest about our future— our customers."

CHARLES HAMPTON'S A-1 SIGNS INC.

A bastion of American entrepreneurship, Charles Hampton's A-1 Signs has impacted both central Tennessee and American history since its founding in 1966. The signs A-1 expertly manufactures and installs provide the faces by which hundreds of businesses across the United States are known. Through innovation, dedication to quality, and an abiding concern for the community, A-1 Signs has created the face of commercial America.

A-1 Signs is located in Dickson, Tennessee, now the largest city in Dickson County at just under 20,000 residents. Since its founding at a railroad stop in the late 1800s, Dickson has always been known in Tennessee as a place of industry. Today, Dickson is home to a number of large industries, including TENNSCO Corporation, Quebecor Printing, Teksid Aluminum Foundry, and many others.

It was not the town's industrial history, however, but a family connection that led Charles ("Charlie") Hampton to found A-1 Signs here in 1966. Hampton grew up in North Little Rock, Arkansas, where an aptitude test he took sometime around the sixth grade showed that he had exceptional artistic ability. Upon graduating from high school in 1957, Hampton went to work for Arkansas Sign & Neon Co. to make use of that ability. There he learned everything he could about crafting neon signs, and about three years later he moved on to Shreveport, Louisiana to finish his sign-making apprenticeship. His plan at the time was to

Employees in 2007

Aerial view in the 1980s

become a sign painter, thereby making commercial use of the artistic ability he had discovered as a child.

In 1965, however, Hampton's father passed away and left him unexpectedly with some land in his hometown of Dickson, Tennessee. Hampton decided to use the land his father had left him to start his own business, and by January 1, 1966, Charles Hampton's A-1 Signs was open for business. Most of Hampton's initial business was for hand-painted signs in a variety of styles and for a variety of companies—"gold leaf, truck lettering, real estate signs," he summarizes. Thanks to his dedication to providing products of the highest possible quality, the business grew, and by 1971 Hampton was able to buy the five acres on Highway 96 where A-1 Signs now stands.

By the time Hampton and his staff moved into the new building, most of the company's business came from doing installations for oil companies. Before long, however, Hampton noticed that there was a need for quality sign manufacturing in the area, and he transformed A-1 Signs into a custom sign manufacturer. Soon, A-1's creations would be seen across the United States at hundreds of well-known locales, including Cracker Barrel, Applebee's,

Drury Inn & Suites, and Nascar Café.

Today A-1 Signs provides a unique combination of services that are not available from any other sign manufacturer/installer in the country. Through the company's one-of-a-kind Sight Flight Survey Service, A-1 specialists fly on company aircraft to the airport nearest a potential client's location to provide the fastest available site survey. Proposals are completed within six days of the survey, more quickly than any other U.S. sign manufacturer. Within six weeks of an agreement, A-1 installs the signs with its local installers, located in most major towns throughout the country.

Company aircraft also comes in handy in backing up A-1's one-year guarantee. "We build an excellent product, and we stand behind it," Hampton says, and he provides his employees with the tools they need to do it. The company aircrafts are available to carry A-1 specialists to variance meetings, maintenance checks, and emergency repairs—the kind of on-the-spot assistance necessary to keep things running smoothly in today's fast-paced world. In addition, A-1 works with local installers to insure that there is always someone available to maintain the signs in top condition.

The idea of providing his own company aircraft is the kind of innovation that has allowed Hampton to stay ahead of the competition for over 40 years. He puts it down to necessity: "When you live in a small town, you have to think differently," he says. But Hampton's success is based on much more than a response to necessity. It comes from that unique entrepreneurial talent that defines the American business leader: the ability to identify what needs to be done and to find newer, smarter, and better ways to do it.

As Hampton is clearly aware, however, innovation takes more than a dream; it takes good people to bring that dream to life. He cares for his employees in a

Charles Hampton's A-1 Signs headquarters in 1970

that he and his staff sometimes have trouble keeping up with them.

Nevertheless, the basic principles on which Hampton founded A-1 Signs remain as solid today as they were over 40 years ago: providing the highest quality product and customer service available. By continuing to focus on these principles, A-1 Signs will continue to lead its competitors and represent the best of American small businesses for many years to come.

Charles Hampton's A-1 Signs many designs

way that shows he recognizes them as A-1's greatest resource. "I furnish 60 percent of the insurance for all my employees—healthcare, disability, life insurance—because I think it's important. I want them to have that." Hampton's dedication to his employees is returned in kind by their long-term dedication to the company: many employees have been with the company more than 20 years. Forty-eight-year-old Vice President Mark Burns, who also serves as the company pilot, started with the business working part-time when he was 14 years old. Business Coordinator Bobbie Lamply has also been with the company for more than 20 years.

Hampton's dedication to others extends beyond the walls of his own business, however, and into the Dickson community, where he has provided every area school with a lighted sign and marquis. "We did that so they could advertise their events," he says, "which I think is important." The company has also recently provided a new college in the area with a lighted sign, free of charge.

Business has changed over the years, and, according to Hampton, not always for the better. One of the greatest challenges small businesses face today, he says, is the trend towards increasing government involvement. "The hardest thing in this business is getting the permits," he says, adding that the Tennessee legislature passes so many new laws each year

Workers used a crane to install part of South Central Bell's sign.

CHATTANOOGA STATE TECHNICAL COMMUNITY COLLEGE

Since opening its doors in September 1965 as Tennessee's first technical college and Southeast Tennessee's first public institution of higher education, Chattanooga State Technical Community College has remained a key contributor to the community and the state's growing economy. Originally known as Chattanooga State Technical Institute, it was a two-year, coeducational, college-level institution with 150 students enrolled the first semester. In less than 45 years, the College has expanded to become a full comprehensive community college that offers a curriculum with more than 50 majors, concentrations and certificates ranging from nuclear medicine technology to masonry to theatre arts to early childhood education to civil engineering technology. There currently are 10,000 students enrolled at the College.

In the early 1960s there was tremendous growth in higher education as post-World War II children entered Tennessee's colleges and universities. The Tennessee State Board of Education then began efforts to establish community

colleges across the state that would provide technical education to bridge the gap between engineers and craftsmen. J. Howard Warf, the state's former commissioner of education, led the charge for community colleges. Chattanooga, with its long history of manufacturing and engineering-based companies, was the location on which Mr. Warf focused his attention. He worked closely with engineers of the Chattanooga community to develop the College's early curriculum in engineering and computer science. The technical programs offered were Associate in Science and Associate in Engineering degree and certificate programs, while remaining flexible to offer customized training to meet industry needs.

Due to the support of the state and the surrounding Chattanooga community, just two years after opening, the College was able to move to an 80-acre campus within a few short miles of the downtown area. A 75,000-square-foot facility was built, which now is called the Albright Omniplex in honor of Ray C. Albright,

Front entrance marked by 65-foot John Henry Sculpture "Transformations."

state senate education chair and a proponent of the College. There were 92 students in the first graduating class; more than 1,200 now graduate each year. Since the first class, more than 90 percent of the College's graduates have remained in the region to spur the area's economic development.

With the introduction of Senate Bill 1010 in 1973, Chattanooga State Technical Institute became Chattanooga State Technical Community College. Specifics of the bill included that the College: 1) provide comprehensive one and two-year occupational, college parallel, continuing education, and community service programs; 2) offer quality technical and scientific occupational programs; and 3) serve as a regional technical school to train engineering technicians or technical workers in the fields of production, distribution, and service.

Center for Business, Industry and Health Professions

Up until 1974 the State Board of Education oversaw the College. However in 1974 that changed when the College became part of the State Community College and University System under the Tennessee Board of Regents. Later that year the College announced specific service areas including Hamilton, Rhea, Bledsoe, Sequatchie, Marion, and Grundy counties in Tennessee and border counties in Georgia. The student enrollment in fall 1974 increased to 2,245.

With the merger of the State Area Vocational-Technical School with Chattanooga State Technical Community College in July 1981, the College revised its mission to include vocational education. The Tennessee legislature officially recognized the merger in July 1983. With this merger, unique in Tennessee, the College offered one-year certificates in fields such as plumbing, industrial electronics, automotive technology, and welding.

In 1990 Dr. James L. Catanzaro became the president at Chattanooga State Technical Community College, which profoundly increased the momentum of the College's advancements. Dr. Catanzaro has served for more than 30 years as president of different community colleges throughout the United States. Now having served 18 years at Chattanooga State, Dr. Catanzaro is the longest-serving president at the College. When he arrived in Chattanooga, Dr. Catanzaro had three priorities. He wanted to develop the College's response to community needs, including corporate training. He also planned to strengthen the quality dimensions of the College's instructional programs. Finally, he sought to expand the main campus, establish satellite campuses and further advance the curriculum.

Among his many contributions to Chattanooga State, a key advancement occurred in the late 1990s when Dr. Catanzaro led the development of a unique and effective early college high school for underperforming students in their junior and senior years. By 2000 the College partnered with the Hamilton County School System to establish the Middle College High School (MCHS) program. The program is offered to students who meet the following main criteria: 1) have an ACT composite score of 19 or better; 2) have a parent or guardian who will attend at least four meetings with school officials each school year; 3) have a record of under-achievement, drop out or independence from the school system.

The program is structured so that all MCHS students attend a high school English class taught by a Hamilton County School teacher on the College campus. MCHS students then take their remaining course work required to earn their high school diploma by choosing from more than 1,000 regular college courses at Chattanooga State, which are taught by college professors with college students in attendance. MCHS students accumulate at least 48 college credits, which they then apply to an associate's degree. The biggest advantages of the program are that underperforming students have the chance to learn in an adult environment and compete with students ranging in age from 18 to 65; and they have access to the College's library services, state-of-the-art technology and different cultural and social activities.

The results of the MCHS program speak for themselves. Nearly 26 percent of current seniors are expected to be awarded simultaneously their associate's degree from the College and high school diploma from Hamilton County Schools. Approximately 85 percent of MCHS students earn the highest writing scores, according to the TCAP Writing Assessment. Students enrolled in the program exceeded the district and national average for ACT scores with an average of 22.4. Lastly, all graduates have continued their education past high school graduation, and many have been accepted at major colleges and universities throughout the nation and even the world.

Dr. Catanzaro also conceptualized and hosted *Fast Forward*, a 30-minute weekly PBS television program to advance the image of the College. The program features interviews with authors, researchers, and other prominent figures from throughout the community and nation. The interviews focus on local and societal issues important to viewers. From the television program, Dr. Catanzaro, who earned his Ph.D. in the philosophy of religion at Claremont Graduate University, developed an online course called Religions of the World as Practiced in America. The course, which was created from more than 50 interviews with clerics, authors and scholars, was highly acclaimed and accepted as a "best practice of education," according to Monterey Institute for Technology and Education on the Stanford University campus.

By 2000 the College expanded its curriculum by offering associate of arts, associate of science and associate of applied science degrees as well as technical and institutional certificates. The physical accessibility of the College expanded as well by providing classes at seven different satellite campuses and through video and Internet-based courses. The main campus on Amnicola Highway included 10 major buildings with more than 675,000 square feet. During the 1990s athletic fields as well as the campus amphitheater were constructed. In 2006 the College acquired the world headquarters of Olan Mills, Inc., adding 59,000 square feet of space and 40 acres. The 1987 vintage former Olan Mills facility is now the Center for Business, Industry and Health Professions. An 11th building is under construction

C.C. Bond Humanities Building at night.

based on a grant from the state in the amount of $28.5 million dollars. The new Health Science Center will house the College's 20 programs in the health sciences.

With specialized study areas, like a professional acting program and motorsports engineering technology, the college currently attracts students both locally and from throughout the region. A specific feature of the College that sets it apart from other community colleges is its partnership with the Gallup Organization and its StrengthsFinder program. Every degree-seeking student at the College is required to take the Renaissance 100 course, which is centered on Gallup's StrengthsFinder program. The course guides students to develop strategies of learning and helps them make sound career selections that complement their strengths. In fact, Chattanooga State was the first such college to establish a strengths-based program for its students and faculty. As Dr. Catanzaro said, "College and university education should begin with learning about yourself so you can more effectively learn about what is around you." The Renaissance course helps students better navigate college and discover career choices that play to their scientifically identified personal strengths.

According to Dr. Catanzaro, one of the most distinct elements of the College is the powerful role it has played in preparing a workforce for Chattanooga business and industry. As a key partner with city, county and state governments, the

College has worked to attract major companies to the Chattanooga region. Companies like T-Mobile, Blue Cross Blue Shield of Tennessee, Cigna, McKee Foods Corporation and others have located or expanded operations in the region with the assistance of the College in workforce selection and training and technology transfer.

The College developed the Business and Community Development Center (BCDC) to become the primary provider of customized training needs for business, industry and government in the Chattanooga area. Each BCDC program, seminar and workshop meets the specific needs of businesses. The College works with local companies not only to develop their future employees, but also to train their current workforce. Instructors from the College and trainers retained from business travel to the offices, plants and laboratories of different partner companies in the area and teach the staff recent technological advances that they can apply to their jobs. The BCDC has become equally as popular as the College's on-campus training. The BCDC soon will operate out of a new Advanced Manufacturing Training Center at Enterprise South, the region's developing industrial mega-site.

One of the greatest developments at Chattanooga State was the evolution of its Nursing and Allied Health program.

Healthcare is the largest industry in the Chattanooga community with many major hospitals, insurance companies and retirement homes in the region, increasing the need for nurses and other trained medical professionals. Since 1975 the College has offered healthcare-related programs that range from nuclear medicine to ultrasound technology to radiological technology. The College's specialized programs provide training for the core of the healthcare workforce, not only in Southeast Tennessee but in Western Virginia, Kentucky, Georgia and the Carolinas.

Another important development at Chattanooga State came in 2008, with the creation of the Build Your Own Business (BYOB) online program. The program addresses a dilemma that small business owners in America often face. They have a viable product and start a small business, but their company soon folds—not because their product is poor, but because they do not possess the entrepreneurial skills needed to remain afloat or the time and money to acquire them. Many do not know how to market their product, navigate the accounting process or manage human resource issues. Under

the direction of Dr. Catanzaro, Chattanooga State developed an online tool that helps small business owners sharpen their competitive edge with resources and tutorials to increase efficiency and help them make more money. The program is being piloted with the Chattanooga Area Chamber of Commerce and local banks, with encouraging results.

Chattanooga State also boasts its appreciation of culture through its Outdoor Museum of Art (OMA), which is the only gallery of its kind in American higher education. Established in 2003 under the direction of world famous sculptor John Henry, the museum contains seven galleries. Art pieces have been acquired from student and faculty artists in addition to local, regional and international sculptors. The museum is supported by Chattanooga State and private donors and administered by its own board of directors. The museum's permanent collection is comprised of 40 works. Every six to nine months temporary exhibits are installed as well. The outdoor sculpture program complements the gallery by combining the College's sheet metal, painting, welding, machine tool technology, engineering, computer-aided design,

The Outdoor Museum of Art contains international, regional, faculty and student sculpture.

metallurgy and art programs. The uses of the OMA range from classroom instruction and school field trips for children to simple individual appreciation and meetings of the International Sculpture Center.

With a basic philosophy centered on creating a culture that embraces contagious warmth and energy which includes respected faculty who prepare students to respond to community needs, it is apparent that Chattanooga State will continue to lead the way for other community colleges in the nation. "Our faculty and students always are seeking to discover what is coming over the horizon," said Dr. Catanzaro. "At Chattanooga State Technical Community College, we are gearing up to respond to community needs and meet those challenges and opportunities as they come into view. Because of this, the College will remain the flagship college of the region and a leader in higher education and corporate training nationwide."

CRESCENT, INC.

Change does not come quickly to the small town of Niota, Tennessee, tucked away in peaceful northern McMinn County, but progress does by way of Crescent, Inc., a leading hosiery manufacturer. It is the oldest U.S. hosiery mill still in operation and a historic landmark that has provided an economic and influential anchor to the town of Niota since 1902. Crescent has survived and grown due to a strong vision, hard work and a commitment to the community.

It began as the dream of James L. Burn, a Southern Railway agent, who, together with the support of the Niota community, started Crescent Hosiery Mills as a way to bring jobs to the community and improve the quality of life for its citizens. However, it was not easy. Several times in its history, Crescent faced severe threat and great adversity. Yet, because of Crescent's unfailing support of its community and constant care for its workers and their families the firm was able to remain a stalwart during the worst of times.

A crisis during World War II threatened to shut the mill down due to the shrinking availability of cotton yarns. Severe rationing closed many of Crescent's competitors and second-generation owner, James L. Burn, Jr. vaulted into action. He approached the War Production Board and argued that

Cathy Burn Allen and Sandra Burn Boyd.

without Crescent, Niota would not survive economically. The Board agreed and rationed enough yarn to Crescent to keep it running through the war years.

Learning how to survive under the toughest circumstances is something Crescent has always done well. William H. "Bill" Burn, son of James Burn Jr., mastered all the operations at the mill from the day he began in 1946. His formula for success was based on integrity, dependability and doing whatever it took to satisfy a customer's needs. As the decades passed and many competitors found cheaper ways of manufacturing by cutting quality, Mr. Burn invested in new and more efficient machinery to offset the cost of labor advantages his competitors were enjoying.

In 1966 a devastating fire consumed a major portion of Crescent. Cathy Allen, Burn's daughter and vice president of marketing & business services/distribution recounts, "Two days after the blaze, with assistance from mill employees, community volunteers, and a neighboring mill, full production was restored. The business never failed to ship an order. A new site was quickly secured and a new mill was built and running within months." My father later said, "We were out of business but I was too stubborn to know it."

Crescent believes in rewarding those who have worked hard to help them succeed and offers some extraordinary benefits. One such benefit is the installation of a Wellness Center with state-of-the-art exercise equipment for employee use. "We've had some great success stories emerge from the Wellness Center," Sandra Boyd, another of Burn's daughters and vice president of human resources shares. "My favorite is the employee who literally cured herself from diabetes by sticking to an exercise routine at the center and keeping a healthy diet."

Keeping it personal is truly a way of life at Crescent. "We're all on a first name basis here," continues Boyd. "And I think based on the long-term tenure of many of our employees, they like the personal

The original 1902 building burned in February 1966 with snow on the ground.

touch." Amanda Presley has been with Crescent for 11 years and recently reached out to her employer to say, "Thanks for working so hard to keep jobs here for local people." Cherrie Birge, a 12-year veteran agreed, "It is such a blessing to work for Crescent." Its suppliers also boast about Crescent's personal way of doing business. "They set the standard for suppliers to work with. You always feel like part of the family when you are there," says Ginnie McCallie of R.L. Stowe, a long time supplier to Crescent. Unifi's Rolf Landry states, "I've been selling yarn to Crescent since 1968. Bill Burn personally trained me in the value of personal relationships for which I am grateful."

In 2000 Burn was looking to bring the company into the new millennium. Robert H. "Bob" Yoe, a close friend and associate was chosen as president due to his tactical strengths and strong business acumen. The appointment was also a great fit for Yoe, who wanted to work alongside Burn, a man he considers a legend in the hosiery industry. Yoe believes that Bill made products far better than anyone he has ever known and was anxious to learn from the master.

Under Yoe's guidance the company has transformed from a manufacturing plant to a marketing company. Prior to

The plant today showing the depth and many additions behind the original 1967 building. (2007)

this new business plan, Crescent was primarily a converter for brands like Liz Claiborne®, Banana Republic® and Land's End®. Now their core business is licensed product. While keeping distribution and specialty manufacturing in Niota, Crescent has remained price competitive by partnering with international sourcers to supplement their production. Almost two-thirds of the company's revenues are derived from brands like Head® and Columbia Sportswear Com-

Bill Burn and his daughters, left to right: Cathy Burn Allen, Pat Burn Cotton and Sandra Burn Boyd at the formal anniversary celebration. (2002)

pany™, and most recently, the popular brand Life is good®. Crescent also produces its own brand, The World's Softest Socks®. Encouraged by its wild success, the brand now offers plush robes and wraps in its World's Softest™ Spa Collection.

In September 2002 Crescent celebrated its 100th anniversary with two spectacular events. A formal dinner was held at the local country club where distinguished guests included friends from the hosiery industry, long-time suppliers, retired management and close friends of the Burn family. Also present were Congressman John Duncan and Dr. W. Carl Jacobs of Atlanta, Georgia. Mr. Burn claims Dr. Jacobs kept him alive to see Crescent achieve this milestone by successfully performing a quintuple bypass surgery. A second event was held in Crescent's backyard where current and retired employees were invited for an outdoor celebration that included inflatable games for kids, dunking booths loaded with supervisors and plenty of food. As a fitting end to a great day, 100 balloons were released as the "family" watched them float up into the sky.

Crescent has been involved with The Hosiery Association (THA) for many years. THA supports leg wear manufacturers and suppliers while serving as the information gateway to consumers, retailers, legislators, and the media. Crescent is the first to have three of its own elected THA chairman of the board. In 1985–1986 Bill Burn served, followed by Bob Yoe in 2000–2002. Cathy Allen assumed the role in April 2008. Crescent's involvement with the association has been an inspiration to the hosiery industry.

"We are certainly following in our father's footsteps by meeting challenges head-on along with taking the time to honor traditions," relates Boyd. On the 20th anniversary of the fire, Bill Burn decided to invite everyone who had been with the company on that fateful day in 1966 to join him for lunch to celebrate. It was such a hit that it has continued every year, inviting anyone who achieves his or her 20-year anniversary as well as retirees.

As fourth generation owners, the sisters have made a commitment to family ownership, maintaining a close-knit cooperative spirit with the employees and the community. Boyd is a 30-year veteran of the company and Allen returned home in 1995 to join her father and sister after a 20-year accounting career in the banking industry in Alabama. Their younger sister, Pat Cotton, is a pediatric practitioner in Birmingham, Alabama but keeps up with Crescent's operation and success through her sisters.

It is no secret that Crescent's longevity can be attributed to its cherished relationships. Treating everyone with respect and kindness, sharing life's triumphs and tragedies and never compromising excellence has made Crescent a model for businesses everywhere. It is a philosophy that has defined life in Niota and its families for generations. Indisputably, Crescent has a huge heart and it has proven that good business means being the best in every way. At Crescent, people are valued, hard work is rewarded, and life is celebrated.

Portions of this information first appeared in Hosiery News *written by Karen Koza.*

Employees and retirees with 20 years or more of service having lunch together, celebrating the continued success since the fire in 1966. (2007)

On the 50th anniversary of Bill's employment, he was presented with a "golden broom" since he always told people that his dad started him with a broom in his hand and he climbed his way to the top. (1990)

Crescent management team preparing to release 100 balloons in celebration of their 100th anniversary. (2002)

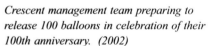

CUMBERLAND UNIVERSITY

Cumberland University has a very distinguished past, one that traces its history to the early 1800s. In the late 18th and early 19th centuries, the leaders of the Cumberland Presbyterian Church began creating colleges and universities throughout the South. One such institution, Cumberland College, got its start in the 1820s in Princeton, Kentucky. Unfortunately, financial troubles plagued the college and the founders decided to move it by seeking bids from neighboring communities.

A $10,000 bid from Lebanon, Tennessee, along with a commitment to erect a new building to house the institution, secured the rights to the college. Most of Cumberland's faculty made the move from Kentucky to Lebanon where the college was reestablished in 1842. Forty-five male students enrolled at Cumberland during its inaugural year.

The city of Lebanon, which was incorporated only a few decades earlier in 1819, may have seemed like an unusual choice for an institution of higher learning. However, the small town's unique locale made it an attractive choice. Situated just 10 miles from Andrew Jackson's Hermitage and 30 miles east of Nashville, Lebanon lay at the intersection of a major east/west highway and a highly traveled north/south road. In addition, it offered nearby access to one of the state's most important waterways, the Cumberland River.

Although Cumberland began as a liberal arts college, it soon branched out

into other areas. These additions came out of a practical need rather than the pure pursuit of knowledge. Cumberland's founders were keenly aware of a growing number of Americans venturing out to the new frontier in the West and Southwest. They looked at the emerging workforce demands that were being created because of this movement and designed educational programs to fill those needs. In particular, they anticipated an increased need for lawyers, preachers, and engineers. In an historic move in 1847, the college added a School of Law, the first in the state of Tennessee and the first west of the Appalachian Mountains. Soon after that it added a theology school and an engineering program.

One of the first ten law schools in the country, Cumberland took an innovative approach to teaching the subject. At the

Constructed from 1892 through 1896, Cumberland University's Memorial Hall is listed on the National Register of Historic Places. The distinctive clock tower remains the tallest landmark in the City of Lebanon.

time, most law schools relied solely on a teacher to impart knowledge to students. At Cumberland, however, teachers encouraged students to read law books themselves. This practice eventually became the standard in law schools. Cumberland's law school also held a moot court every week whereas other law schools typically did so only once a year.

The unique approach worked, and by 1857 the law school was as large as

Members of the Theta Chapter of the Kappa Sigma Fraternity at Cumberland University in 1903.

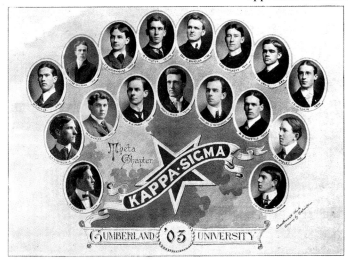

Members of the 1924 Cumberland University women's basketball squad pose for a team photograph.

Harvard Law School, the best known law school in the country. The college's forward-thinking approach to teaching law is just one example of the educational innovation that quickly became a trademark of Cumberland.

The college's growth throughout the 1850s came to an abrupt halt during the Civil War, which began in 1861. Most of the college's faculty and students fought in the war—some for the South, some for the North. During the Civil War, the Yankees occupied Cumberland's University Hall, the college's first campus building designed by famed architect William Strickland. This regal structure was sadly burned to the ground during the war, and there are two conflicting stories about how it happened. One tale indicates that the Yankees burned it down; the other claims that students burned it down since the Yankees had desecrated it.

A Cumberland student is said to have written across one of the building's ruined columns the Latin term *resurgam*, which means "I will arise." This inspired the college to adopt the mythical phoenix as its symbol.

This statue stands outside Cumberland University's Labry School of Business and Economics as a tribute to the workers of the Works Progress Administration, who built the first gymnasium in Wilson County, Tennessee on the site in 1936.

Dr. Edward L. Thackston (left), chairman of the Cumberland University Board of Trust and Cumberland University president, Dr. Harvill C. Eaton stand alongside the Cumberland University Law Degree of Samuel Sydney Gause, who was Thackston's great-grandfather.

Cumberland did rise again. In fact, classes resumed immediately following the end of the Civil War in 1865. By the following year all departments were in operation in various locations throughout the town of Lebanon. In 1892 construction of Memorial Hall began and the college moved to its current location on 46 acres. The Memorial Hall building, which became the focal point of the campus, was completed in 1896 and is currently listed on the National Register of Historic Places.

In the late 1800s Cumberland created a business school. At the time, several colleges offered courses in business, but Cumberland was one of the first to offer a full-fledged program in the subject. This endeavor once again fulfilled a practical need as the nearby city of Nashville began expanding as an economic hub.

Cumberland continued to grow throughout the early 20th century and maintained its reputation for academic excellence. The college underwent several changes, however, following World War II. In 1946 the Presbyterian Church handed over the reins of the institution to the Tennessee Baptist Convention. The Tennessee Baptists didn't hesitate to

initiate sweeping changes at Cumberland, deciding to close down the College of Arts and Sciences and to operate only the School of Law.

A decade later the Board of Trust amended the college's charter and Cumberland became a private, independent corporation. The Board of Trust reversed the decisions made by the Tennessee Baptists and reopened the College of Arts and Sciences as a two-year junior college called Cumberland College of Tennessee. To complete the new focus on a liberal arts education, the School of Law was shuttered in 1962 and its assets were transferred to Samford University in Birmingham, Alabama.

In 1982 the junior college expanded its academic programs and became a four-year, degree-granting institution. That year, the college changed its name to Cumberland University. Since then, Cumberland has continued to expand its academic offerings, adding graduate programs to its undergraduate courses.

Today, under the leadership of president, Dr. Harvill Eaton, Cumberland University boasts nearly 1,400 under-

Constructed in 1989, the Doris and Harry Vise Library serves the needs of Cumberland University's students, faculty and staff, plus provides limited access to its collection to the community.

graduate and graduate students enrolled in more than 40 majors. Although the number of students is growing, Dr. Eaton plans to cap future enrollment at about 2,000 students in an effort to maintain small class sizes and an individualized education.

Since taking over as president in 2004, Dr. Eaton has firmly led the institution into the 21st century. The new president's first major undertaking focused on technology, which he recognized as an indispensable tool for communication, education, and business. To modernize Cumberland, the campus was reconfigured to be 100 percent wireless.

At the same time, Dr. Eaton has maintained some of Cumberland's long-standing educational values such as a commitment to creating educational opportunities that are responsive to the changing needs of society and the workplace. For example, the economy in nearby Nashville has blossomed, in part, due to expansion in the healthcare and music industries. In response, Cumberland has bolstered its school for nursing and health professions. And considering that Nashville is home to a quickly growing number of songwriters and musicians, Cumberland has taken the innovative approach of gearing its music program to performers. Many other colleges cater to the business side of the music industry rather than to performers.

Memorial Hall, the focal point of the Cumberland University campus, houses administrative, faculty and staff offices, classrooms and Baird Chapel.

Cumberland University professor of marketing Dr. Jack E. Forrest leads a classroom discussion on marketing as business students follow the lesson plan on University-issued laptop computers.

Dr. Eaton, who earned his own degree in engineering, is also spearheading the creation of a new engineering program that will be designed around biotechnology and computing. Scheduled to start in fall 2008, the engineering program will be part of the business school. Although this program promises to be on the cutting edge, it also harkens back to the college's earliest days when engineering was part of the curriculum.

Creating innovative educational programs such as these that meet the practical needs of society and the workplace continues to be one of the hallmarks of Cumberland University. Providing individualized attention in small classroom settings is another long-standing tradition that has defined learning at Cumberland. Indeed, the faculty/student ratio is one faculty member for every 16 students.

In addition to being distinguished for academic excellence, Cumberland also offers a variety of athletic and social experiences to enhance the education of its undergraduate and graduate students. The men's and women's sports teams regularly compete for conference and national championships. And a vast array of service organizations, honor societies, fraternities and sororities, provide social opportunities for students.

With all of the educational, athletic, and social opportunities available, it's clear that Cumberland's leaders and faculty are committed to helping students succeed in college and after graduation. In fact, Cumberland has earned a well-deserved reputation for producing leaders throughout its history.

Among the more prominent Cumberland alumni are former United States secretary of state and Nobel Prize winner Cordell Hull and Myles Horton, a pioneer in the cause for social justice and founder of the Highlander Folk School which was attended by Martin Luther King Jr. and Rosa Parks. Cumberland alumni also include U.S. Senators, more than 80 Congressmen, two justices of the U.S. Supreme Court, 13 governors and scores of other leaders. In fact, by the 1950s there were more people serving in the U.S. Congress from Cumberland University than from any other college.

Although Cumberland University boasts such a distinguished list of alumni, it refuses to rest on its laurels. The university and its leaders remain focused on the future and on educating the next generation of leaders.

DREXEL CHEMICAL COMPANY

With one of the most comprehensive lines of agricultural chemicals available today, nationally and internationally, Drexel Chemical Company continues to innovate, expand and, at the same time, meet challenging standards in the agricultural industry.

Robert D. Shockey, the company's founder, grew up on a tobacco farm near Campton, Kentucky. His father owned a small sawmill and store and also had a small farming operation. His mother ran the local post office. Their entrepreneurial leadership and farm lifestyle helped train their son Robert for the agrichemical field.

Shockey began his agrichemical career as a sales representative for the Niagra Chemical Division of the FMC Corporation in 1960, followed by several years as a sales representative for tobacco states. He then worked nine years for the Ansul Company, which relocated him to Memphis, Tennessee. At Ansul, he worked his way up to national sales manager and later became their national marketing manager.

In 1972, with twelve years experience in agricultural chemical sales, Shockey founded Drexel Chemical Company using his middle name for the company and locating his first office in a spare room

Robert Drexel Shockey, founder and CEO

of the family home. In its first year the company operated mainly as a manufacturer's representative. By 1975 however, Shockey began contracting for the manufacture of agrichemicals for resale and, in 1977, purchased many of the labels and product technology from his former employer, the Ansul Company. That same year, he purchased a manufacturing facility near downtown Memphis.

The company grew from a sales volume of less than $1 million in its first year to $10 million by its fifth year. Shockey attributes this jump to the move into manufacturing and to offering commodity products in a new way. "Most other companies that had commodity products handled them like a stepchild," he says. "We believed that by offering good service, consistent and high quality products in an attractive, sturdy package, and being a reliable source of supply, we would be favored with a lot of business." The product line began to expand as Drexel placed more emphasis on acquiring additional agricultural chemical labels to complement its line.

Today, Drexel's product line includes growth regulators, herbicides, insecticides, fungicides, adjuvants/surfactants and micronutrients. In fact, Drexel Chemical now owns 550 product labels; 250 EPA-registered and 300 other specialty agricultural products. Further, Drexel is a member of numerous task forces that generate data and support the continued use of various agricultural chemical products. In addition, its regulatory staff monitors and maintains Drexel's product line by working closely with the U.S. Environmental Protection Agency as well as laboratories, consultants and other government agencies, both domestically and internationally. This ensures that Drexel products are in compliance and incorporate the latest application methods and sites. Bob Shockey says, "We must all do whatever it takes to provide a product that the grower can afford to use and that will help him produce a more profitable crop."

Drexel Chemical Company executives: Ben Johnson, Jim Pelt, Bob Shockey and Leigh Shockey

Drexel Chemical's manufacturing facilities began to grow as well. Today Drexel has seven warehousing and/or manufacturing facilities in Memphis, Tennessee; two in Cordele, Georgia; and others in Leavenworth, Kansas; Tunica, Mississippi; and Guatemala City, Guatemala. Each manufacturing facility has its own Quality Control Lab and the Memphis headquarters houses both a research and development laboratory as well as a formulation lab. Shockey says that the Memphis plant facility's location gave him an edge in transporting products across the nation and around the world because he could transport more cost effectively from Memphis than anywhere else.

Drexel's plants and laboratories are constantly upgraded with necessary equipment and people to consistently produce quality products and reduce costs.

The Memphis lab complies with Good Laboratory Standards (GLS) as well as with Collaborative International Pesticides Analytical Council (CIPAC), the Environmental Protection Agency (EPA) and the World Health Organization (WHO).

From its inception, Drexel Chemical has been active in the international marketplace. Shockey was committed to exporting and began targeting those countries closest to home and with similar crops. He looked for ways to incorporate the needs of the international customer with his domestic business by locating and/or developing packaging and formulations that could easily be adjusted to fit the needs of both markets. He developed an in-house typesetting department to allow for more label flexibility, including labels required in other languages.

As Drexel's international presence grew, the company began to acquire more registrations and set up new

distributors. Today the Drexel brand is sold in more than 40 countries and its distributor network includes many of the same distributors that joined them 20 years ago. Bogdan Diaconescu, Drexel's international sales manager, works with Drexel's export shipping personnel as well as Drexel's distributor network to keep a steady pace of sales growth and market expansion. Each year he hosts numerous grower groups that come to learn not only about Drexel's product line but also about new and innovative application methods practiced by U.S. farmers.

From the beginning, the Shockey Family has played a supporting role at Drexel. Robert Shockey's wife and two daughters have worked within the organization in various capacities. The family atmosphere is also present among Drexel's longtime management team. Ben Johnson, the company's president; Jim Pelt, vice president of sales and other Drexel personnel have been with the company about 20 years or more. Other key Drexel management dedicated to the organization and its mission include Stanley Bernard, vice president of growth and development; Jim Reagor, director of purchasing; Mark Stewart, national sales manager; Roy Olson, business development manager; Mike Shankle, product development; Bruce Tonkle, quality control manager; Hattin Grillette, surfactant/adjuvant manager; Luz Chan, production registration specialist; Rodney Howard; environmental safety manager; Dan Kim, accounting operations manager; Karen May, director of office operations; and Gray Senter, corporate regulatory manager. Drexel's marketing specialist, Don Spikes, though with the company only a few years, has worked closely for a number of years with Drexel's sales team via a Drexel distributor and thus feels right at home in his present employment.

In 1984, after a life-threatening illness, Shockey sold 80 percent of his company to the Sweden-based Nobel Industries; two years later, he sold the balance of the company. He went into semi-retirement but remained active by running another chemical business for Nobel—Chapman Chemical Company. With Shockey's help, Nobel sold Chapman Chemical. In 1990 Shockey bought

Robert Drexel Shockey, founder and CEO

Drexel Shockey, Drexel Allen Shockey Membreno and Tennessee senator Bob Corker., acknowledging their win at the 2008 Veterans Corporation Entrepreneur Event.

Drexel Chemical back. "I didn't have anything to do," Shockey says.

Through the years, Robert Shockey has received numerous awards and recognition for his industry successes. A few of those include the Mid South Exporter's Exporter of the Year, U.S. Small Business Administration Small Business Exporter of the Year, and the *Memphis Business Journal* Small Business Executive of the Year. Shockey most recently received the American Veteran Entrepreneur of the Year Award, presented to him by the Veterans Corporation. This award came about through his grandson Drexel Allen Shockey Membreno's nomination-submission of an essay that acknowledges Shockey's service during the Korean War (his grandson's award-winning essay follows.) Shockey has contributed time and money to many nonprofits in his community. In 2003 Lausanne Collegiate School dedicated a new state-of-the-art "Shockey Science Center" made possible by his generous donation.

Since Shockey's return to the company, he has led the organization to new sales levels every year. "I am blessed with a dedicated and skilled team of people," Shockey says. When asked about retirement, his response is: "Been there, done that."

My Grandfather/My Hero
By Drexel Allen Shockey Membreno,
Rossville, Tennessee

Nominee for Veteran Entrepreneur of the Year: Robert Drexel Shockey My grandfather should be this year's "Veteran Entrepreneur of the Year" because he exhibits all the qualities that make me proud to be an American and his grandson. My grandfather joined the army when he was 17 years old. I am not sure he really knew what he was getting himself into because before that time, he had never been anywhere outside Wolfe County, Kentucky. I do believe, however, that he was looking for an adventure and he certainly found one. He spent time in Germany and at 19 he volunteered to go to Korea.

I think the training my grandfather got in the Army has been paramount to his success in business today. His superiors obviously had the management skills necessary to instill the much needed discipline I am certain my grandfather needed without breaking his spirit. He learned from them to be fair but firm and to lead by example while never misusing that position of power. Thus, they gained his respect and motivated him to surpass his own expectations.

From his comrades, he learned to appreciate the strength of diversity. Living and working in close quarters with a variety of men allowed him to understand, firsthand, the heart and mind of individuals he might have, in another place and time, found no connection with. By understanding their background, their culture and their life experiences, his perspective and assumptions changed, as did his value for each individual's uniqueness.

At the same time, he discovered many areas of common ground among his fellow soldiers including a love of country and freedom. One of the most valuable lessons I learned on putting diversity in perspective came from my grandfather's story of being injured while out on patrol one evening in Korea. He stepped on a land mine, which blew his foot off and riddled his body with shrapnel. He lay there for hours while going in and out of consciousness and questioning as to whether he was dead or alive.

Eventually, my grandfather was

rescued by another soldier, who picked him up and carried him out of enemy territory back to his unit. What he did not mention, in previous accounts, was that his rescuer was African American. When I asked my grandfather why he had never mentioned that before, he looked puzzled and replied, "Why would it matter?" I thought about it for a moment and realized it did not. His rescuer was simply, at that moment, another American comrade fighting for a common cause and belief. Nothing else mattered.

Today my grandfather runs a business that is known and respected throughout the world. He is determined, tenacious and a true motivator of people. He never falters in the face of adversity; always believing that justice will prevail. He sees a blessing in some of the most unlikely

Shockey Family: Alex Carlew, Leslie Shockey, Leigh Shockey and Drexel Membreno; Bob Shockey and Wanda Shockey (seated).

predicaments and always gives of his time and money to those less fortunate and/or struggling. Those are qualities I believe he developed while an American soldier.

He wears his purple heart with pride and that ever-so-slight limp in his walk never slows him down or prevents him from pressing on. There is no one I admire more and there is no one that makes me more proud to be an American. I wear his name with pride and I only hope I live to be half the man and entrepreneur he is. I believe if you meet him, you too will be proud.

EARL SWENSSON ASSOCIATES, INC.

To merely call Earl Swensson Associates (ESa) a world-class design firm hardly does the organization justice. Led by Chairman Earl S. Swensson, FAIA, ESa goes beyond this distinction. In addition to offering a design vision that melds form and function with aesthetics and the fabric of a project's locale, the firm is known for its personalized service.

Since its 1961 founding, ESa has put its imprint on projects across the globe. ESa provides a full range of services, from architecture, interior architecture, master planning to space planning for healthcare facilities, hospitality venues, education and library facilities, corporate offices and senior living communities. ESa has 190 employees, which include 48 architects and 22 interior designers. Its architects are licensed to practice in every state as well as Washington, D.C. The firm is actively managed by its four owners and principals: Mr. Swensson, company president Richard L. Miller, FAIA, and vice presidents Joe D. Crumpacker and Raymond Pratt.

Nashville residents are well aware of ESa's local work, as one of the city's icons soars across the downtown skyline in the form of the A T & T tower's twin spires (formerly the BellSouth Tennessee Headquarters), which inspired the affectionate name "the Batman building." The exterior's design is not only visually

The AT&T tower rises over Nashville as one of the city's icons. Photo by Jon Miller © Hedrich Blessing

arresting, but the interior offers an 8,000-square-foot winter garden. This building is just one example of ESa marrying design and technology to create wellness environments.

While Mr. Swensson has often been called visionary for his and his firm's designs and design approaches, this insight extends beyond design prowess. His philosophy is based upon creation of human-centered environments that fulfill the needs of clients. He also believes that a facility's spaces should be both aesthetic and designed around its users.

Belmont University's Beaman Student Life Center and Curb Event Center are joined together by the Maddox Grand Atrium. Photo © Kieran Reynolds Photography

Nowhere is this more apparent than in the design of healthcare facilities, which account for over 80 percent of the firm's work. ESa has been a trailblazer in innovative healthcare design, commissioning a university-based research project in the early 1980s to independently assess the future needs of healthcare facilities. This forward thinking move and subsequent work in this area has paid off, giving ESa unique insight to the technical needs of this area of specialization. ESa is also a member of the Health Care Industry Committee of The Advisory Board, a firm that provides strategic insight and best practices research for over 2,600 hospitals, health systems, and healthcare companies. Notably, ESa is also consistently ranked one of the Top 10 healthcare design firms in the United States by *Modern Healthcare* magazine.

One of ESa's significant Nashville medical projects is Centennial Medical Center, which includes a 476,400-square-foot, 239-bed patient tower addition that was completed in 1994. An atrium lobby provides easy access to outpatient areas and also serves as a wayfinding tool.

While ESa's design incorporates flexibility for technology advances, it is also functionally efficient, yet comfortable for patients. Nashville's nationally acclaimed Monroe Carell Jr. Children's Hospital at Vanderbilt embodies these concepts. In order to make young patients and their families more at ease, the interiors feature soothing, colorful animal and nature themes and curved elements, such as the sweeping grand staircase accented with swirling, starry "ribbons," which soften the hospital environment, while helping families feel more at home under taxing circumstances. In ESa's healthcare projects, great care is always taken in the design of patient rooms to ensure that they are comforting spaces allowing patients to focus on healing and wellness.

ESa also applies these principles to the design of senior living residences, one of which opened recently in Nashville. The English Manor design style of The Cumberland

Centennial Medical Center's atrium lobby enhances wayfinding to all outpatient and public areas. Photo © Norman McGrath

at Green Hills, an assisted living/memory enhanced complex, seamlessly blends with the neighboring architecture. The elevated suburban site looks down upon the city's skyline, which was maximized with generous windowed views. Wood paneled wainscoting, moldings, columns and trim are incorporated to enhance the residential ambience. Seventeen of the 110 residences are secured, memory-enhanced units.

ESa's design expertise extends beyond healthcare projects. Another Nashville icon in ESa's portfolio represents the hospitality sector—Gaylord Opryland Resort & Convention Center. ESa designed the original hotel and convention center and the three subsequent expansions of the 2,881-guestroom venue. Notably, this facility has nine acres of indoor gardens enclosed in climate-controlled atriums. The fourth phase, The Delta, an antebellum city enclosed in domed glass, boasts boat rides along the quarter-mile indoor river. This setting also includes a 400-seat restaurant, a multi-outlet food court and a wedding pavilion. Walkways connect the Delta to the convention center and other areas of the hotel.

As for education design, ESa's local presence is seen in a number of facilities for lower, middle, and upper schools and

Curving architectural elements of Monroe Carell Jr. Children's Hospital at Vanderbilt soften the approach to the facility. Photo by Scott McDonald © Hedrich Blessing

Gaylord Opryland Resort & Convention Center has nine acres of indoor gardens enclosed in atriums. Photo © Jonathan Hillyer

colleges and universities in the Nashville area. At Belmont University, for example, ESa designed Beaman Student Life and Curb Event Center, which are joined together by the Maddox Grand Atrium to form a single campus building. The Curb Event Center, a 5,000-seat entertainment and athletic venue, has hosted a number of nationally broadcasted events. A later addition to the campus, the Gordon E. Inman Center-College of Health Sciences and Nursing building, brings all of Belmont's health sciences and nursing programs to picture-postcard positioning at the front of the campus.

These are but a few of the local examples that are among ESa projects worldwide that reflect the firm's innovative artistry and commitment to people-focused design.

With a driving creed "The Job Is The Boss," ESa has created a vital niche in the design industry. Its focus on excellence and customer satisfaction has propelled the company to a pinnacle of respect within the Tennessee design community and bolstered its reputation nationally as an inventive, forward-thinking design firm.

The Vanderbilt Children's Hospital features a sweeping grand staircase accented with swirling "ribbons." Photo by Craig Dugan © Hedrich Blessing

GASTROINTESTINAL ASSOCIATES

Knoxville, Tennessee leads the region in culture, history and economy. As the historic capital of the Southwest Territory in the late 1700s, and home to one of the nation's first colleges, Blount College, now The University of Tennessee-Knoxville, it is a proud city of firsts. Currently it is home to a group that leads the nation in technology for the treatment and diagnosis of gastrointestinal diseases.

Gastrointestinal Associates (GIA) was the first private practice in the country to develop a state licensed, Medicare certified, endoscopic ambulatory surgery center (ASC) to care for patients suffering from digestive disease system disorders and diseases involving the esophagus, stomach, small intestine, colon, liver, pancreas, and gallbladder. The center has served as a model for other practices around the country. However, only a few have achieved the same level of technical excellence developed by GIA, which has included the introduction of colonoscopy, endoscopic ultrasonography, and radiofrequency ablation of esophageal diseases in their ASCs, serving as a model for other groups.

Founded by Dr. Bergein Overholt with his partner Dr. R. Leslie Hargrove in 1971,

the growth of GIA has been a story of success driven by a constant focus on providing the best and most advanced care in the specialty of gastroenterology. Every group has its own culture, its own direction. GIA is no exception. With a service culture that is patient centered first and foremost, doctors and nurses and, in fact, all their staff place the "highest priority on taking care of patients the right way the first time."

By the mid-seventies the practice had built and relocated into its own office building to improve patient convenience and satisfaction. The group has expanded and now has 13 gastroenterologists, a nurse practitioner, almost 100 staff, three offices and three ASCs to geographically better serve their patients and their community. In addition to being one of the largest outpatient practices in gastroenterology in the country, GIA has established one of the first GI Hospitalist programs, serving Saint Mary's Medical Center to dramatically improve GI services to hospitalized patients.

GI Associates is proud of introducing new technology in the early diagnosis and treatment of certain GI diseases. Dr Overholt pioneered flexible fiberoptic sig-

The physicians of Gastrointestinal Associates, PC: back row (left to right): F. Raymond Porter, R. Kent Farris, J. David Lee, Bergein F. Overholt, John M. Haydek, Sarkis J. Chobanian, Stanley L. Miller, Charles M. O'Conner, Jr, Meade C. Edmunds and front row (left to right): Barry V. Maves, Raj I. Narayani, Maria B. Newman, Steven J. Bindrim

moidoscopy, developing an instrument which led to modern colonoscopy. GIA has formed "partnerships" with the Thompson Cancer Survival Center, The University of Tennessee College of Veterinary Medicine, and the Oak Ridge National Lab focusing on developing new technologies and treatments. Collectively, the group pioneered the development of photodynamic therapy (PDT) for Barrett's esophagus. GIA is now the leading practice in the country for the use of PDT and more recently, radiofrequency ablation of Barrett's esophagus, essentially eliminating the need for surgical removal of the esophagus for this disease. GIA is one of few practices in the country that provide endoscopic ultrasound studies in an ASC to better image the gastrointestinal tract. The practice is also taking a leading role in the endoscopic treatment of obesity. GIA continually strives to advance endoscopic treatments for GI diseases in ASCs to provide better care more conveniently and at a lower cost

Great doctors, great technology, great facilities. Yet perhaps the single most important thing that GIA provides is having great staff. By offering individualized care and attention in the treatment and diagnosis of GI diseases, GIA's staff helps each patient receive a comprehensive evaluation and an understanding of their condition and what can be done to treat, cure and prevent future problems.

Patients are offered the opportunity to educate themselves through GIA's website (www.gihealthcare.com), looking over specific diseases, frequently asked questions, and scrolling through an easy to read glossary of terms and symptoms. Online registration, scheduling of appointments, medications refills, and selective e-mailing will be available in 2008.

The Knoxville community has been good to GIA and in turn, GIA strives to be a good community citizen. Physicians have served on the Knoxville school board and the boards of the opera, the local zoo, the Chamber of Commerce board and in church leadership positions. Several physicians have been elected to Leadership Knoxville.

The nursing unit surrounded by recovery and prep gurneys. The Endoscopy Center, 2005.

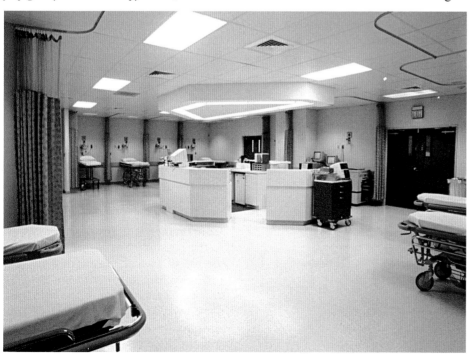

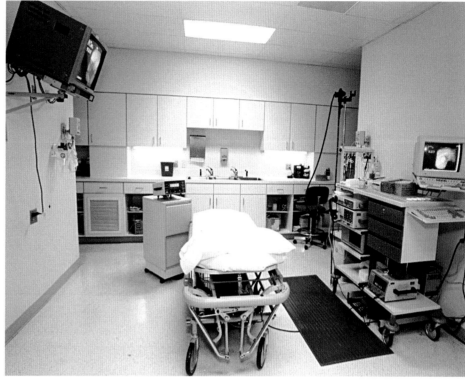

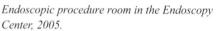
Endoscopic procedure room in the Endoscopy Center, 2005.

To become a physician member of GIA requires reaching a level of professional excellence. All its physicians are board certified in both internal medicine and in gastroenterology. Two of the physicians have served as presidents of national professional organizations, an unusual accomplishment for a single group. Four have been chief-of-staff at their community hospital. The group continues to encourage and to lead in certain areas of clinical research in gas-

troenterology and in teaching of advanced procedures to visiting physicians. One of its physicians has over 100 publications in scientific journals.

Leaders in gastroenterology—absolutely! Yet from the time physicians join this group, they know that family is most important. Medicine is a privileged opportunity but GIA, its physicians and its staff, place strong emphasis on being an active part of their families.

GIA physicians have achieved a great deal personally and professionally. They have contributed to their community. They have elevated the level of care for patients in gastroenterology in Knoxville and East Tennessee. They have developed new technologies and treatments for GI diseases that have been adopted across the country. They have trained other physicians in the treatment of certain GI diseases. They have trained physicians from around the world in ways to improve their own GI practices. And through it all, they have maintained a balance between family and profession. These are reasons GIA serves as a model for other GI groups in the USA.

INTERMODAL CARTAGE COMPANY INCORPORATED

Intermodal Cartage Company (IMC) is a Memphis-based provider of intermodal transportation services specializing in import-export cargo shipments. Founded in 1982, Intermodal Cartage continues to be a trailblazer in the industry, always just ahead of the growth curve of intermodal transportation. The company sets the standard for excellence in innovative technology, customer satisfaction, and impeccable reputation. Its founder and CEO, Mark H. George, has a corporate philosophy which spearheads the vision for the company: "Your success is our final destination." Whether referring to his employees, his customers or the community in which he resides, George's deliberate focus on others' success has insured his own.

The term intermodal means two or more modes of transportation combined in a single shipment: ship to truck, truck to rail, air to truck, etc. In the early 1980s, these modes of transportation were in direct competition in terms of transporting freight. "When I started this business 26 years ago, railroad companies and trucking companies were bitter enemies, they didn't cooperate with each other," states George. At that time most trucking companies avoided working with railroads and ocean carriers. They did not want to encounter the process of U.S. customs and heavy railroad regulation. George, instead, saw potential. If there could be collaboration between modes of transportation, then all would benefit.

Mark H. George, founder and CEO

He also saw great potential in transporting ocean containers when most trucking companies avoided it altogether. "I took advantage of an opportunity," George says. "Nobody wanted to carry ocean containers at that time. I steered my company to capitalize on it. Containerization changed our industry. Transporting international shipments around the world via containers grew rapidly. IMC's primary focus and long-term strategy became servicing international shipping clients. I happened to be at the right place at the right time." Now, 26 years later, IMC is a forerunner in transporting overseas shipments offering marine container storage, and repair of equipment for world-wide ocean carrier customers.

Custom designing a plan to meet customers' transportation needs has been a trademark of IMC, one that has helped build a stellar reputation in the industry. Since the beginning, Mark George has set forth a precedence of professionalism in all aspects of operations. Drivers wear a uniform identifying them to the company. Upper management dresses in appropriate business attire, men wear ties to work in the corporate offices. IMC utilizes only late model tractors to ensure reliable, on-time customer deliveries. Company trucks are on a three year trade-in cycle. Every truck is equipped with the latest technology which helps drivers keep perfect accuracy with shipment specifications and delivery instructions. IMC facilities are state of the art. Buildings and grounds are well maintained. Paved areas for container parking add to the overall organization and efficiencies. Expansion is ongoing at several locations.

Technology has played a significant role in the growth of the company. The company has been progressive in automation and information management systems, even to the point of developing its own software. Transitioning modes of transportation with any shipment is open to the possibility of human error. With the use of specialized tracking technology, the chances for error are virtually eliminated. "It's very easy for us to track shipments, whether we're working with something currently being delivered or whether it's a shipment we handled two

Grand opening of shop facility

years ago—that information is readily available to us. Employees process over 1,000 shipments per day. We depend on a competent, proficient operating system in order to meet customer expectations." states George.

Mark George seems to have an innate ability to see where improvements can be made in the intermodal transportation industry and where challenges are really opportunities. This is partly due to his keen sense of business and understanding of profit margins, but it is also because the transportation service industry is in his blood. His grandfather began a warehousing business in Nashville and his father owned and operated a refrigerated trucking business, Tennessee Cartage Company and Quickway Carriers. He never worked for either company, but being around it, he learned of the daily challenges and the annual revenue possibilities.

In 1982 George and his wife, Melinda moved to Memphis to attend the University of Memphis. George was 20 years old, a newlywed, attending college and in need of a job. His parents gave him an opportunity to start his own trucking company. He relied on his father's business expertise and became a third generation trucker.

By 1987 IMC had two locations and annual sales of $3 million. By 1997 the company had seven locations and brought in annual revenue of $27 million. In 2007 the company had annual revenue of $78 million, a 20 percent increase from the previous year.

Fifty-acre Memphis expansion completed in 2008

Intermodal Cartage's two most tenured drivers, Tony Coleman with the company since 1989 and Percy Jackson since 1985.

IMC had one driver when the company started, now it has approximately 500 drivers. In the beginning, Mark George, himself, handled sales and operations, now he has over 300 employees who work in customer service, sales, operations, accounting, and administration. In addition to the Memphis location, the company has hubs in Dallas, Houston, New Orleans, Nashville, Savannah, Atlanta, and Charleston.

George has been recognized for his accomplishments within the industry. He was a finalist in the 1992 *Memphis Business Journal* Small Business Award and a finalist in the 1997 *Memphis Journal* Entrepreneur of the Year Award for business–to–business services. He is the recipient of the

Mobile communications devices for tracking real time shipments

Tennessee Business Quality Award in 1994. He also is a member of the American Trucking Associations, Tennessee Trucking Association (director in West Tennessee), Intermodal Association of North America, Memphis Uniport Association, Memphis Chamber of Commerce and Memphis World Trade Club.

In addition to his success in the industry, George is dedicated to the success of his community. He is a strong supporter of AGAPE, a Christian organization that provides children with foster care and adoption opportunities. The organization promotes the idea that every child deserves a loving family and a healthy home environment. George and his wife, Melinda, have given generously of their time and resources to help the organization serve the children in theirs and surrounding communities.

Intermodal Cartage employees also serve the community by taking part in the American Heart Association's annual heart walk. Drivers are in an occupation that fall into the high risk category for heart disease. IMC is focused on increasing the awareness and knowledge of the contributing factors of heart disease. Company employees have participated in the annual event for the past five years and Intermodal Cartage has been the presenting sponsor. IMC employees have raised donations in excess of $100,000.00 each year. IMC's employees have given personal testimonies about their experience with heart disease. These testimonies have made lasting impressions and have contributed greatly to this worthy cause and its fundraising efforts.

IMC executive team, Mark George (seated), (left to right) Randall Wright, Karen Stevens, Lynn Parrish, Bob Slaughter, Melinda George, Michael Baker and Joel Henry.

Mark George has traveled far since beginning his cargo transportation company in the early '80s. "When I started this business, trucking companies didn't want to deal with railroads, ocean carriers or U.S. customs, they wanted to deal with domestic shipping only," says George. As with any successful business, George has built a management team of knowledgeable, dedicated and committed individuals. George states, "Each employee at IMC promotes the company through excellent customer service no matter what job title they hold. Without the best day-to-day support, I could not have grown my business." Now through his persistence and expertise, intermodal transportation has revolutionized the industry in the state of Tennessee.

Intermodal Cartage is the leader of import/export cargo movements in Tennessee and Memphis has expanded from being the location of a rail hub to being a major international trade center with thousands of import-export shipments passing through the city on a daily basis. Mark George and his employees at Intermodal Cartage Company are, in many ways, responsible for that impact.

However, when you ask George what he is most proud of, he will answer, "My family. Melinda has supported me from the beginning and has been a valuable resource in helping me make key decisions." When he is photographed for business magazines or company brochures, George stands in front of a large canvas portrait of his four children. Will any of them follow in his footsteps and join ranks in the company? George answers, "It's still too early to tell, but it's a possibility. My two older children have worked part-time at the company and gained knowledge in the industry. If they decide to join the company or start a business of their own, Melinda and I will be there to offer advice and guidance just as my parents did for me."

Intermodal Cartage has matured into a leader in the transportation industry and looks forward to future business growth.

The George children, Mason, Anna, Alli and Katie.

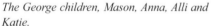

JOHNSON BIBLE COLLEGE

Ashley S. Johnson founded Johnson Bible College in 1893 as a place where poor young men could obtain an education and study to become ministers. For Johnson, born in 1857, this mission evolved from his own personal experience of growing up poor in a log cabin in Tennessee. As a young boy, Johnson saw education as the means to achieve success, but it was a struggle for underprivileged students like him to gain access to good schools. Through hard work and determination, he managed to get that all-important education and, at the age of 16, passed an exam and obtained a certificate to teach in the public schools of Knox County. At 17 he became a student at the University of Tennessee, but left a year later to enter a law office in Knoxville.

One of the biggest events in Johnson's life came in 1877 when he was 20 years old; he began studying the New Testament and was converted to Christianity. From this point on Johnson concentrated on evangelistic work. When he married Emma Strawn in 1884, he had a partner who shared his beliefs. Johnson was determined to teach the Gospel to as many people as possible. Frustrated with the realization that he couldn't reach

The original main building (far right) which contained classrooms, chapel, library, dorm rooms, kitchen and dining room burned to the ground in 1904. A solid hand-made brick building replaced it by 1906 and is still in use today.

Richardson Hall contains the teacher education and missions departments, archaeology lab, computer lab, and classrooms. It was named in honor of Mr. Lee Richardson who has significantly impacted the College as faculty and administrative staff for over 50 years.

enough people with his preaching alone, he had a brainstorm—he would teach the Gospel via the mail.

This innovative technique proved very successful, and Johnson enrolled thousands of people in his Correspondence Bible School. Johnson crafted his own books and materials for his courses, printing more than 200,000 copies of books in a 10-year period. During this time, Johnson began to contemplate creating a brick-and-mortar school where he could teach the Gospel. That dream soon became a reality.

Johnson purchased his great grandfather's farm outside Knoxville and built a large house overlooking the French Broad River. In 1890, when the house was finally completed, Johnson invited two young men—Albert Fitts and John Dickson—to move in and receive personal instruction in the Gospel. Thus, the School of the Evangelists, which would later become Johnson Bible College, was born.

The following year the Johnsons anxiously awaited yet another birth—this time their first child. Unfortunately, Emma nearly died in childbirth, and the child did not survive. Devastated by the loss, the couple turned their focus to their newfound school and its students. The pair was eventually able to find peace and perspective in the loss, saying that the Lord had blessed them with thousands of sons through the school.

In an effort to expand the College, Johnson solicited friends for help but got little response. Disappointed, the college founder decided to take an innovative approach to building his college. In 1892 Johnson took out an advertisement offering young men the opportunity to gain an education in return for their help in building the new college. The ad worked, and a number of men responded.

Within a year, building was underway. Johnson's goal was to create a completely self-sustaining institution that could teach the "whole man," meeting the physical, spiritual, social, and intellectual needs of his students. Over the next few years several structures were erected, including

the Main Building, which housed 100 men and included a chapel, a library, classrooms, dining facilities, and recreation facilities. Industrial Hall, which provided housing for 60 men, went up next, along with a spring house, a barn, a henhouse, a blacksmith shop, a laundry, a dairy barn, a bakery, and other facilities.

By 1904 the last lecture hall was finally completed and everyone was elated. But tragedy struck that same year when the Main Building caught fire and burned to the ground. Watching more than a decade of labor go up in smoke, Johnson could have given up on the College, but he continued to have faith and promised to rebuild the school. And rebuild it he did. The Main Building rose again, and the College continued to grow until Johnson died in 1925.

After Johnson's death, his wife Emma took over as president of the College. Johnson Bible College became one of the first American colleges to have a female president, but Emma's leadership didn't last long as she lost her battle with cancer in 1927.

Emma Johnson's successor was a young man named Alva Ross Brown who had graduated from JBC only the year before Emma's death. At 21 Brown became the youngest college president in the nation. The choice may have seemed unusual, but the Johnsons had come to think of Brown as a son during his time

A campus of approximately 175 acres has been developed within the 350 acres owned by the College.

as a student at the College. An outstanding student, Brown had impressed the College leaders and had begun assisting them with administrative duties. He began taking on more and more responsibilities until he eventually became viewed as Johnson's "right-hand man." Because of this, Brown didn't seem like such an unlikely candidate to lead the College.

The timing for Brown couldn't have been worse. Just two years after taking over the leadership of JBC, the stock market crashed and the Great Depression hit. Times were tough, and, not surprisingly, the College began to sink into debt. Brown did everything within his power to maintain the number of students on campus. Unfortunately, the stress of the

Depression weighed heavily on the young man who had been diagnosed with heart trouble at a young age. In 1941 Brown suffered a heart attack and died.

Ashley Johnson's will stipulated that all future presidents of the College must be graduates of Johnson Bible College. With this in mind, the College's Board of Trustees chose Robert Monroe Bell, a 1918 graduate, to take the reins. Like Johnson himself, Bell had grown up in a poor home and more than likely would not have had access to an education if it hadn't been for Johnson Bible College. After attending a revival hosted by a JBC student, the 21-year-old Georgia farmer ventured to the College with nothing more than an eighth-grade education. He worked hard and earned his degree—yet another example of the "poor man" whom Johnson had originally set out to help with his College.

When Robert Bell took over in 1941 the College was $40,000 in debt as a result of the Depression. But being an economics teacher, as well as a wise investor and money manager, the new president paid off those debts within three years. In the process, he made a lasting impression on the College's creditors, something that paved the way for future expansion. During Bell's tenure, several buildings were added to the campus, including a gym with a swimming pool, a girls' dormitory, a dormitory for married couples, the Alumni Memorial Chapel, and a new library. Expansion continued until Bell's death in 1968.

The Eubanks Activities Center, named for Dr. David and Margaret Eubanks, contains a student activity area, science lab, administrative offices, and the television and radio media center. Dr. Eubanks taught for 10 years before serving as president for 39 years.

In 1969 the role of president passed to David L. Eubanks who had earned an undergraduate degree in 1957 and a master's degree in theology in 1958 from JBC. He also earned a doctoral degree in 1965 from The University of Tennessee. Eubanks set out on a mission of expansion and modernization. The new president also turned out to be a formidable fundraiser, bringing in multimillion dollar gifts and launching the Centennial Campaign, which aimed to raise $7 million by the year 2000.

The successful campaign helped fund numerous projects, such as renovating and modernizing existing structures to make them as technologically advanced as possible. Other projects included new dormitories, additional faculty housing, a new activities center, an addition to the library, a new music center in the basement of the chapel, and an educational and technology center. Thanks to Eubanks' tireless efforts, Johnson Bible College emerged as a thoroughly modern 21st century institution.

Eubanks' successor, Dr. Gary Weedman, graduated in three years from JBC in 1964, earned a M.A. degree from Western Illinois University in 1967, and earned a Ph.D. from Indiana University in 1971. Since then he has held administrative roles at Lincoln Christian College, Milligan College, Palm Beach Atlantic University, and TCM International Institute. Weedman and Eubanks share a long history at JBC; in fact, Weedman was the first professor that Eubanks hired in his new position as president in 1969. Weedman taught homiletics, Greek, history, and Bible courses at the College until 1976.

As the sixth president of the school, Weedman faces the unique challenge of dealing with change for the future while holding on to the best of the institution's past. With tremendous respect for college heritage, Weedman insists that some things should not change even as he prepares to meet the ever-changing needs of society and the church. The College he leads today boasts over 900 students, several baccalaureate programs, and four graduate degrees. At first glance, it may not seem to have much in common with the Correspondence Bible College or the School of the Evangelists that Johnson created. But the new president, along

Dr. Gary Weedman was inaugurated in 2007 as the sixth president of Johnson Bible College in the College's 114th year.

with the board and administration, remains committed to the institutional mission and core values, including access to education irrespective of financial resources, a focus on the text of the Scriptures, and a broad-based education in the arts and sciences.

In keeping with long-standing tradition, the 360-acre campus still houses the majority of students and faculty—just the way Ashley S. Johnson envisioned it. This unique living arrangement has created a strong sense of community on campus. In addition, the most popular major at Johnson Bible College continues to be ministry. As such, the College maintains its long history of producing graduates who serve faithfully as preachers, youth ministers, missionaries, Christian college faculty and administrators, ministers of music, and church secretaries/administrative assistants. Many other graduates work in parachurch organizations and other areas of Christian service.

When contemplating the future, Weedman acknowledges that the College will face changes. New programs to meet the needs of the 21st century are under review at the graduate and undergraduate level.

Two new residence halls were built in 2000 with spacious rooms, each having a private bathroom and wired for modern technology.

LIFE CARE CENTERS OF AMERICA

A caring nurse offers a perfect single rose to a delighted elderly resident who sits in a wheelchair. The visual described is a life-size statue which stands just outside of Life Care Centers of America's home office in Cleveland, Tennessee. The bronzed figure which forever captures the personal relationship between resident and caregiver has been duplicated in smaller statuettes and printed in Life Care Centers of America's information materials. It has become the symbol for the organization which has more than 200 nursing homes across the nation. The image not only has emotional impact; it authentically depicts the focused concern of the people who make up Life Care's organization. Their highest commitment is to the well-being and happiness of the individuals in their care. This dedication began more than 30 years ago and continues to be modeled by the founding father of the organization, Forrest Preston.

In the mid 1960s, Forrest Preston had an innovative idea motivated by a compassionate spirit and an entrepreneurial mind. Growing up, he witnessed unfavorable conditions in which the elderly were often resigned to live and die; he was determined to make a change for the better. He also knew that the growing elderly population meant an expanding clientele for a new business model. His

Activity director Angela Bialkowski and resident Anna Fridell at Life Care Center of Tucson, Arizona..

A life-size statue of Life Care's logo—a nurse presenting a rose to a resident.

plan was to build a nursing home facility which was modern, attractive and inviting. The staff would be well-trained and highly motivated to make residents feel at home. Engaging activities would be a regular part of a daily schedule. All residents would be treated with dignity and respect in an environment created to foster friendships and feel like family.

Preston honed the vision for the nursing home idea with college chum and Oregon based contractor, Farrell Jones. The two men planned to build the extended care facility in Preston's home town, Cleveland, Tennessee. Based on its success, their hope was to duplicate the model and build nursing care facilities throughout the country. There was just one hindrance: no financial resources to support the venture. Fortunately, Jones knew

of someone who not only had the monetary resources, but also had a vested interest in the nursing home business. The man was Carl Campbell.

Carl Campbell was an established entrepreneur who owned 25 nursing homes throughout the Northwest. Campbell helped build the first free-standing nursing home in Washington in the early 1950s. Seeing the growing demand for extended care facilities, Campbell and his wife, Betty, opened their own nursing care facility in 1954. The industrious couple managed the facility themselves and worked all aspects of the business. Betty Campbell was a registered nurse and resident cook. Campbell wore many hats: bookkeeper, orderly, dishwasher, and janitor. By 1967 the couple owned and managed 25 nursing homes with their sights on opening more.

Jones had previously been contracted to do some construction work for Campbell on several of his nursing homes. Jones found Campbell to be a considerate man and easily approachable. When Jones and Preston brainstormed about financial resources, it was a natural that Campbell would come to mind as a possible partner for the venture.

In the summer of 1967 Preston made the long cross country trip from Cleveland, Tennessee to Oregon to visit his friend and business partner, Jones. Even though the journey was at heart a Preston family vacation, the men decided to take a side excursion to Wenatchee, Washington to see if they could get a face-to-face with Carl Campbell and share their idea. The two drove all night and at 8 a.m. arrived on the doorstep of Campbell's main office. There was no appointment set or prior call made. "We had blind faith we'd find him in," recalls Preston.

As they knocked on Campbell's office door that early morning, no one answered. The men turned to leave just as

The Corporate Plaza, headquarters for operations and administration at Life Care Centers of America in Cleveland, Tennessee.

Carl Campbell rounded the corner heading to work that day. Campbell, who recognized Jones immediately, greeted him warmly, but apologized in response to the men's request to discuss a business proposal. He explained he had a full day scheduled to inspect several of his nursing homes in the states of Washington and Idaho. He piloted his own plane for this task to make the inspection tour more expedient. Campbell thought for a moment, and then offered, "If you aren't afraid to fly with me, we can talk about your project on the way."

Preston and Jones were more than willing to join Campbell on his inspection tour. In the small cockpit of the plane, the two men enthusiastically shared their plan with Campbell who was intrigued with the idea. He not only thought the initiative of raising the standard for extended care facilities a sound one, he was impressed with the two men's enthusiasm and confidence for the project. He had experienced Jones' fine work on his own nursing care facilities, but he didn't

know Preston at all. He did, however, know of his father, Reverend Benjamin Preston, a Seventh-day Adventist minister from Oregon. Campbell had heard the senior Preston preach on several fondly memorable occasions. There was also an innate quality about young Forrest Preston that was attractive to Campbell. "He had a lot of fire and he was quite a talker," remembers Campbell, "I liked him immediately."

The three men took the quick flights to each of Campbell's nursing home sites as they continued discussing the specifics of the business venture. They stopped at a sandwich shop for lunch and while munching sandwiches at an outdoor table, Campbell made his decision. "I think you guys would be honest and fair with me, and I think you can make this happen,' stated Campbell. With that said, the wheels were in motion and the partnership between the three men began.

Because of Campbell's commitment to the project, the partners were able to borrow $305,000 from the Cleveland

National Bank to make their dream a reality. The three partners formed the company, Development Enterprises, and began their first project. Less than three years later, The Garden Terrace Convalescent Center opened its doors for residents. The 99-bed nursing home was beautifully situated on a wooded, seven-acre piece of land which overlooked Keith Street just outside of Cleveland. The facility offered professional medical care, rehabilitation equipment, recreation programs, meals planned by a dietitian, beauty and barber services, and a television in every resident's room. The facility, as Preston and Jones first had envisioned, was expertly designed with attractive furnishings, fine carpeting and tasteful chandeliers.

The Cleveland (Tennessee) *Daily Banner* ran a story announcing the

Garden Terrace Center's grand opening. Excitement about the new facility traveled throughout Cleveland and surrounding areas and the 99-bed facility filled quickly. Beecher Hunter was the editor of the *Banner* at that time. Even though Hunter had seen blueprints of the project and walked through the building site of the nursing home facility, he was still impressed with the completed project at the grand opening. "When I saw the final product, even after all the preparation I had witnessed, I was amazed," states Hunter. "This was the Hyatt Regency of Cleveland business developments." Hunter took a vocational interest in the growing company; he is now president of Life Care Centers of America's organization.

Sailing on the success of the Garden Terrace project and in keeping with their original plan, the partners began construction on their next project. The site for the company's second nursing home was in Tullahoma, Tennessee, 90 miles from Cleveland. The home was named Meadows Convalescent Center and opened in September of 1970.

Dorothy Giehm, 107, a resident of Life Care Center of Tucson, Arizona, who took up a hobby in painting at 102.

By 1976 Preston, Campbell, and Jones had opened six convalescent homes with a total of 881 beds in two states, Tennessee and Florida. The need arose for a long-term care management company to oversee and operate these and other facilities to be built in the near future. Life Care Centers of America, Incorporated was founded by the partners on January 6th, 1976. The name of each of the homes already in service changed to include the prefix Life Care Center of, followed by the name of the community in which it served. Most additional centers would follow this same pattern. Campbell and Jones eventually sold their stock in the company to Preston in order to pursue their own interests in long-term care.

Each year the company constructed or acquired additional facilities which were created or transformed to embrace Life Care's structure and philosophy. By 1980 the organization managed 24 facilities across America with 3,184 beds and had net revenues of $30 million. The growing number of facilities acquired by the company dictated a need for a sister

The Campbell Center, one of two corporate campuses of Life Care Centers of America in Cleveland, Tennessee.

company to manage the process of acquisitions. In 1982 Life Care Affiliates was created to make acquisitions and transformations run more smoothly. By 1986, the year of the organization's 10th anniversary, Life Care owned or managed 90 nursing centers and eight retirement centers in 21 states. The number of beds grew to nearly 10,000.

Since its inception, Life Care Centers of America's prioritized excellence in caring for residents first, and company expansion, second. The leadership believed that if the well-being and happiness of residents was their greatest concern, growth and success of the company would take care of itself. The mission for Life Care is consistent with that philosophy: *Providing the highest quality of service to those who entrust their lives or the lives of their loved ones in our care.* "We have never set goals based on the quantity of beds or volume of dollars," states Preston, "The goals were always predicated upon excellence of the healthcare we provide."

Excellence in healthcare at each facility not only meant surrounding residents with attractive furnishings and providing the latest in medical equipment, it also meant hiring the best staff for quality long-term patient care. Each staff member is carefully considered when hired. All employees are respectfully referred to as associates, exemplifying

Frances Wright, 92, a resident of Life Care Center of San Gabriel, California, the country's first female ranger in the National Park Service.

Alice Gumm, 100, a resident of Life Care Center of Wells Crossing, Florida, crowned Miss Orange Park Nursing Home Queen.

equality throughout the company. Although individual tasks vary, associates work together towards the common goal of improving the life of each and every resident in their care. Even though the company is not directly affiliated with a religious organization, its culture is grounded in Judeo-Christian based ethics. The company's management training adheres to The Golden Rule "Treat the resident as you would want yourself or a loved one to be treated." Employees and volunteers approach their work as a ministry and serve the needs of others as a higher calling.

The individuals who make up top management of the organization operate as servant leaders, undergirding staff with support and encouragement rather than wielding authority and intimidation. They lead by example. Members of the management team visit Life Care Centers around the country on a regular basis. They warmly greet and visit with residents first before attending to the operational business of the facility. This practice began with Preston, himself. "There's something about the founder of the company taking time to visit a facility and talk to residents and staff that is very special," states Angie Clayton, Preston's longtime administrative assistant.

Preston and his management team recognized the value of encouraging hard-working and seemingly tireless associates. The corporate managers created various awards and programs to honor exceptional work done by extra conscientious care workers. In 1992 the "Whatever It Takes' customer service campaign was introduced to recognize those associates who gave beyond themselves to help residents and their families. Also that year, the company began a tradition of bestowing performance awards presented at the annual management meeting. The fall meeting has become the organization's most anticipated event, held at Life Care's beautiful Corporate Plaza in Cleveland, Tennessee. Associates and their spouses are flown in at the company's expense for a five-day program which includes team building activities, inspirational addresses by well-known speakers, reports on goals and results and a celebration gala with spirited entertainment. The Chairman's Award, President's Award and Facility of the Year Award are among the most coveted awards to be received. Award winners are not only given a symbol of recognition for their accomplishment, they are treated to a six-day retreat and personal growth event at Useppa Island Resort in Florida.

The past decade has seen specialized growth for Life Care Centers of America. A concentrated effort in the care of Alzheimer's patients has been a direct focus. The organization now has eight facilities devoted to Alzheimer's patients and the special concerns of their loved ones. Of the more than 200 Life Care Centers nationwide, 80 have Alzheimer's wings. The organization is considered a pioneer in Alzheimer's care and dedicates many of its resources to further research the treatment for the disease.

The desire to treat the elderly with grace and respect was at the core of Forrest Preston's dream. Through Life Care of America's pristine centers and life affirming associates, Preston has added years and smiles to the residents who have made Life Care their home. "Always keep the boss happy," Preston would often quip. He was not referring to himself. He would quickly add, "The boss is each and every resident in our nursing centers."

MEMPHIS UNIVERSITY SCHOOL

Memphis University School is a college-preparatory school for boys in grades 7 through 12 and is dedicated to the development of well-rounded young men of strong moral character, consistent with the school's Christian tradition. MUS was founded in 1893 by two energetic young educators who, at the suggestion of the University of Tennessee's president, came to Memphis and opened a small college-preparatory school. Since then, MUS has been committed to the highest standards of academic performance, extracurricular activities, and personal honor for each of its students. In addition to its engaging curriculum, the school provides an exceptionally able and dedicated faculty, which nurtures critical thinking, challenging discussion, and lively exchanges of ideas. Approximately 75 percent of the MUS faculty hold advanced degrees, including eight Ph.D.s and one J.D. MUS teachers have an average of 20 years experience in challenging young minds.

The original MUS opened with only seven students, but it grew rapidly. It thrived into the 1920s, grooming numerous young men for leadership roles of various sorts in the Mid-South and beyond. In 1936, however, the Great Depression and shrinking enrollments forced the school's closure.

Memphis University School was founded in 1893 by James W.S. Rhea and Edwin S. Werts.

The new MUS, patterned closely on the methods and values of its namesake, opened in the fall of 1955 with 90 boys on a 94-acre wooded campus at 6191 Park Avenue. In the ensuing 50 years, its enrollment has grown to 650 students. Its college-preparatory program thoroughly grounds each student in traditional disciplines of the humanities, fine arts, and physical sciences. The campus includes state-of-the-art laboratories and classrooms and a library that rivals those of many colleges.

MUS focuses considerably on preparing boys to enter the nation's most competitive colleges. Its students have a 100 percent college acceptance record, and each graduating class earns several million dollars in merit-based scholarships. Mastering critical-thinking skills and self-discipline, MUS students consistently score well above national averages on standardized tests, Advanced Placement examinations, and National Merit Scholar recognition.

From its inception, the school also has emphasized physical fitness and athletic competition. Both boys and teachers played on the earliest MUS athletic teams, sometimes defeating even college squads. Today, approximately 70 percent of the student body participates in a total of 12 sanctioned sports. In recent decades, MUS teams have won numerous city, county,

district, regional, and state championships, earning the enthusiastic support of fellow students, faculty, and alumni. More important than simply winning, however, are the life lessons that the boys internalize in the areas of self-discipline, teamwork, leadership, and personal responsibility.

The school's extracurricular activities are not limited to athletics. MUS also provides an exceptional climate for student achievement and extension of their individual talents in the areas of studio and choral music, dramatics, fine arts, and student publications. Moreover, MUS government club teams consistently dominate such activities as Model UN, Youth Legislature, and mock trial competitions. Civic service to the Mid-South community is yet another area of profound student involvement.

Most important of all, however, is the school's student-operated and student-enforced Honor System. An integral part of school life from the beginning, the Honor Code epitomizes the firm bonds of faith and trust among students and faculty. Lying, stealing, and cheating simply are not tolerated.

For additional information about Memphis University School, visit the school's website at *www.musowls.org.*

Go, Owls! School spirit, school pride, and long-standing traditions bind together generations of MUS alumni.

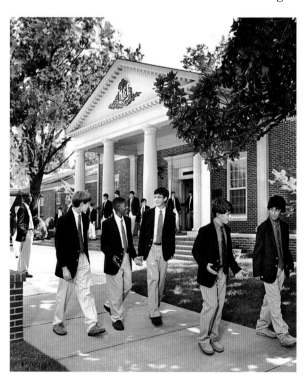

WEST TENNESSEE HISTORICAL SOCIETY

The West Tennessee Historical Society (WTHS) is one of the Mid-South's least conspicuous, yet most beneficial educational and recreational amenities. It is the umbrella heritage organization for the Western "Grand Division" of Tennessee and is a true cultural gem. Through its antecedent organizations, WTHS dates back to 1857 when "The Old Folks of Shelby County" began regularly meeting for fellowship and programs. At these gatherings, residents who had arrived in Shelby County during the 1820s and '30s told the stories of their pioneer days.

In the Civil War's aftermath, three successive local history groups had a Confederate historical emphasis. In the 1910s, the last of these groups morphed into the Memphis Historical Society. In 1935 the MHS broadened its geographical scope to include all 21 counties of West Tennessee. Reflecting West Tennessee's population distribution, however, somewhat more than half of the society's historical emphasis has stayed focused on Memphis and Shelby County. Consequently, there is no

The West Tennessee Historical Society sponsored the publication of Metropolis of the American Nile *in both its 1982 and 1991 editions. Courtesy, West Tennessee Historical Society.*

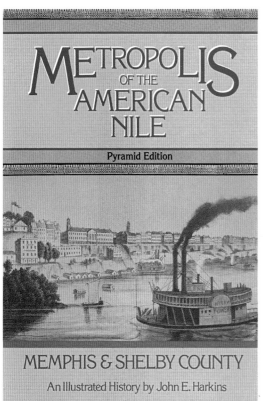

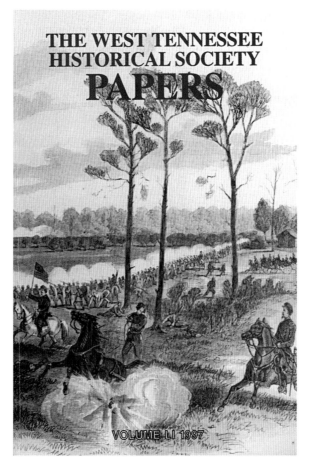

The cover of the 1997 issue of the WTHS Papers *depicts the Civil War Battle of Shiloh, also known as Pittsburg Landing. This was the most significant battle fought in West Tennessee and was symbolic of the course of the war itself. The Confederate troops prevailed during the first day's fighting, but were overwhelmed on the second day. This tinted illustration is from a May 17, 1862 supplement to* Frank Leslie's Illustrated Newspaper. *Courtesy, Memphis Public Library.*

separate historical society for either Memphis or Shelby County. Most of the other West Tennessee counties, however, do have their own county and/or town historical or genealogical societies.

From its inception, WTHS has sponsored and scheduled periodic history programs. Such programming includes both formal papers and audio visual presentations devoted to almost any aspect of West Tennessee's history. Since 1996 Memphis University School has hosted the Society's regular monthly

meetings. The November and March meetings are held in the Martin and Jackson, Tennessee areas, respectively. Some meetings are held at historic sites.

At least as important as the Society's programs has been the publication of its annual journal. Since 1947 WTHS has published an anthology of formal papers, notes, documents, and book reviews relating to West Tennessee. Nearly the entire run of the Society's 60 volumes of the *WTHS Papers* is available on the Shelby County Register's website.

Almost as important as publishing the *Papers*, is the Society's work in sponsoring and publishing books and reprints related to the area's history. Such books include: *The Old Folks Record*, J. Harvey Mathes' *The Old Guard in Grey*, Judge J. P. Young's *Standard History of Memphis, Tennessee*, James D. Davis' *The History of the City of Memphis* (facsimile reprint edited by James E. Roper), and John E. Harkins' *Metropolis of the American Nile* and *Historic Shelby County*. WTHS has also bought up inventories of excellent publisher overstock books, keeping them available for purchase at bargain prices. Examples include Robert A. Sigafoos' *Cotton Row to Beale Street* and Paul R. Coppock's six-volume set of Memphis-area historical vignettes.

The Society's other major functions include sanctioning and erecting historical markers, helping preserve historic structures and sites, and collecting and preserving publications and documents bearing on West Tennessee History. The WTHS manuscripts' collections and rare books are permanently housed in the Special Collections Department at the University of Memphis.

Finally, WTHS serves as a referral network and a clearing-house for sharing information about events bearing on West Tennessee's past. To learn more about the West Tennessee Historical Society, please visit the society's website at www.wths.tn.org.

NASHVILLE SASH & DOOR CO., INC.

Since 1926 family-owned and operated Nashville Sash & Door Co., Inc. has been guided by a commitment to excellence—providing products of exceptional value, sold in a friendly atmosphere by motivated professionals who maintain a sense of business ethics and unsurpassed customer service. In business for more than 80 years, providing windows, doors, columns, builder's hardware, moldings, shutters, special millwork, stairs and glass, the company has continually strived to balance time-honored values with modern distribution efficiencies.

The McAlister family traces its family ancestry to the late 18th century when they arrived in the historic town of Franklin, Tennessee, approximately 20 miles south of Nashville. In Franklin there is an old city cemetery where pioneer settlers are buried. The land for that cemetery was deeded in 1811 to several town commissioners, —among them, Dr. Charles McAlister.

The McAlister Family's roots in the window and door industry date back

Nashville Sash on Second Avenue

to Riddle and Company, circa 1860, which was owned by John F. Wheless and Robert Riddle. Wheless and Riddle were married to the daughters of William K. McAlister.

William K. McAlister, nephew of Dr. Charles McAlister, was the father of Harry Hill McAlister. In 1892 Harry Hill McAlister was listed in the city directory as secretary-treasurer of Riddle

Left to right: Wallace M. Green, Harry Hill McAlister III (father of Sidney) and W.L. Robertson

Left to right: Hill McAlister, Sidney McAlister and Robert Smith.

and Company. He passed away in 1893. His son, H.H. McAlister, Jr., became a clerk with that company. When Riddle Company shut down in 1915 and H.H. McAlister, Jr. left Nashville to manage Cole Manufacturing Company in New Orleans, his son, H.H. McAlister III, a former salesman for Riddle Company, stepped in and continued the sash and door business. With partner Ben Patterson, he formed Southern Door and Glass Company, located at 200 Second Avenue North in Nashville. In 1926 H.H. McAlister III and his new partners Wallace Green and W. L. Robertson sold their interests in the company to Patterson and founded Nashville Sash and Door Company, a few doors away at 152 Second Avenue North.

Thomas J. McMeen joined the company in 1936 as secretary to Harry Hill McAlister, spending more than 48 years there and becoming a full partner. The other two partners—both sons of Harry Hill McAlister III—are the current chairmen of the board, Sidney S. McAlister, who joined the family business in 1946, and Jack McAlister, who joined in 1951.

Harry Hill McAlister III ran the company with his two partners from the late 1920s. He had a "gentleman's agreement" to buy out his partners' shares after their deaths. The families of both partners honored this agreement, and the McAlisters eventually purchased the remaining shares. Would a deal

based on a handshake work in today's business environment? It was an era when a person's word was good enough.

"My older brother, Harry Hill McAlister, IV, lost his life as an aviator in World War II, so as the second son, having attended St. John's Military Academy, in the army at the age of 18 and out in my early 20s, after a year at Vanderbilt University I arrived at Nashville Sash & Door working in the warehouse, eventually getting into sales." In the 1950s the company was led by Sidney and his younger brother, Jack McAlister with Sidney becoming president in 1955.

There is a mutual respect among family members that Sidney claims is the stronghold of the business's success. Family members speak with great pride about the company and the work ethic the business has maintained over its entire history.

Jack's son, Joel McAlister, was a company sales representative and a stockholder. Sidney's two sons, Harry Hill and Sidney McAlister, now in their 40s, have both been salesmen and stockholders as well. They began their employment in the company when they were teenagers and have learned every facet of the business while also taking time to earn college degrees. Harry Hill McAlister V now owns the company. "He is a good leader and is committed to the continued success of the company. He also puts me to work daily. I get the mail, sign checks, watch the stock market—I am here four hours every day" said Sidney McAlister.

During World War II, when building materials were in short supply, most sash and door distributors sold their limited allotment directly to the highest bidder. Nashville Sash & Door decided instead to unload their windows and doors, carry them to the building on Second Avenue, and then repack them, rationing their supplies to dealers: "My father," says Sidney, "kept many of these dealers in business by doing this, and they have been very

Nashville Sash & Door today

loyal ever since. I'm sure these dealers told their sons what we did during the war to keep them in business."

The company also has loyal employees, some who've been with Nashville Sash & Door for more than 50 years. "We have a steady sense of tradition," he said. "All of our employees, many who've been with us for decades, are strong, dedicated people."

Berry Lee Pyburn began working for the company at age 15 and retired at age 74. He had retired once before, at age 64, but returned to work after the first week. What holds an employee this long? A sense of community is one factor, and security is another.

"Right after World War II, things took off for us," says McAlister. "We had more square footage than we have now and we have more than 206,000 square feet today." The building the company originally occupied, on Nashville's famous Second Avenue, was owned by family members. The company had many floors in the building, but doing business was difficult, because the doors and windows had to be moved via elevator throughout the building. As a result, flow was difficult and products could be damaged.

Nashville Sash & Door continues to serve Nashville-area architects, builders and homeowners from their modern facilities on Sidco Drive. Their newly redecorated showroom features a full millwork inventory that includes windows, interior and exterior doors, moldings, hardware, shutters, columns, skylights, stair parts and special millwork.

"We know windows, doors, and millwork," said the senior Sidney. "You can drive around the countryside and see our products—some of them my great grandfather made by hand. We've furnished homes of famous people— one recent job is listed at $40 million." Living and working in Nashville, the McAlisters have had the opportunity to serve some famous country music celebrities. "They're everywhere," says McAlister, "but we leave them alone, let them be private." One particular home they're proud of belongs to former vice president and current Nobel Peace Prize winner Al Gore. "They are new windows made by Anderson and Eagle." says McAlister,

Nashville Sash & Door showroom.

"In the winter, the window is heat absorbent, and in the summer it reflects heat. Today as we deal with global warming, features like these appeal to anyone interested in saving energy. And today, everything is maintenance-free," says McAlister, "using plastic, aluminum, vinyl you don't have to paint for 40 years—or ever.

In today's world, with businesses failing throughout the country, Nashville Sash's staying power is notable. Its current generation runs the company, but the fourth generation is actively involved and learning more about the business.

To what do they attribute their longevity and success? Sidney McAlister, Sr., now in his 80s, ascribes credit to the family's sense of loyalty to one another and those around them, along with a tried and true business philosophy of absolute honesty in all aspects of work.

Nashville Sash delivery truck

Warehouse

Customer pick up area.

OOLTEWAH MANUFACTURING INC.

Almost 40 years ago, Ooltewah Manufacturing sold different products than it does today, and it had a unique name. It was called Mr. America Manufacturing and produced exercise and body building products. Tennessee-born owner and CEO Jerry Daniels—who was raised in Georgia but has lived in Tennessee since he was 19—gave the company its original name after winning the Mr. America title in 1965 at the age of 21, and used his success in that world to begin an enterprising journey.

Today, while Daniels' business no longer makes body building equipment, and its name, Ooltewah Manufacturing Inc., more accurately reflects its hometown and its character, the company manufactures a diverse and substantial line of products. These include motorcycle products such as seating, electronics and communications, trademarked under the name Air RiderTM; rehabilitation and therapy products; and OEM and private label products. Some of the markets are seat parts that go into such large trucks as Mack, Kenworth, Peterbuilt and Freightliner. Ooltewah also manufactures air conditioning parts for Carrier Air Conditioners, bath mats for a company that sells to chain stores, upholstery parts used to restore old Jaguars to their original

Approximate time Jerry started making potholders at age 11.

Jerry Daniels in front of his business in 2008.

condition, gymnastic products, and such rehabilitation products as ankle and wrist weights, cold packs, wheelchair cushions, a variety of neck and back pillows—and these are only a few.

As a man blessed with an inventor's curiosity, whatever path Daniels tends to walk and whatever direction his interests take him, a new product emerges. Fifteen years ago, as an avid motorcycle rider, he invented a patented air system for installation in motorcycle seats to provide more comfort and adjustability. The company has since gone into electronics and communication products. Each of Ooltewah's product lines could be a subdivision, acting as its own company, but Daniels has elected instead to keep all of Ooltewah Manufacturing products under one roof.

And that roof is a big one. Having started as a one-man garage-based company, Daniels' business has grown into a 30,000-square-foot plant in Tennessee's Ooltewah Industrial Park. The plant accommodates such diverse equipment as ultrasonic welding machines, electronic sewing machines, heat-sealing equipment, and machines to make gel products for cushions.

Daniels' entrepreneurial spirit began long before he won his body building

title. When he was 11 years old, living in Georgia, some neighbors were involved in the home manufacture of socks. "They would cut off the top loops they didn't use and throw them away. There were square metal looms that one could purchase, and stretch loops onto, interweaving the loops to make potholders," the CEO recalls. "I had my mother purchase one and started making potholders. There was no cost in materials, nothing but my labor. That was my first actual product," he says. "I got lots of colorful loops, made potholders by the hundreds, and sold them all over the area. I'd sell one for a dime and two for a quarter. Most people bought two! I was good in math even at 11 years old."

Daniels' first official invention was an exercise video he produced in 1969, before VHS and Beta video machines existed. It consisted of a reel of 8mm film threaded onto a film viewer and hand-cranked. Excited about his new creations, he took his video and a waist trimmer he invented to J. C. Penney. They bought both products for a limited number of stores. The waist trimmer sold well in the stores they put them in, but the exercise video was so ahead of it's time it didn't do well enough for them to continue to keep them in the stores.

"I guess I was about 15 to 20 years ahead of my time," he says. "Today there are hundreds of exercise videos worth millions of dollars in sales every year." By the 1980s video players had become prominent. "I suppose it's a point of pride," says Daniels. "I created a product that eventually became very successful several years later for other people, but not for me. Had I been 20 years younger, I could have been a very wealthy man."

The motorcycle division of Ooltewah began 15 years ago, starting with a manually controlled air bladder that is installed into a stock seat on a motorcycle. Then Ooltewah purchased a small company that made gel cushions for the top of motorcycle seats and made that a major part of the company line. Daniels bought a small electronics company a couple of years after that and expanded that company to broaden their line even more. "We are now working on wireless communication for motorcycles that will help carry us for several years to come. We have always been very diversified, and

Jerry Daniels, "Mr. America 1965."

that's kept us strong and viable all these years."

"The key to any business is its people," says the former Mr. America. "My key personnel are very important to me." His son, Chuck Daniels, the president and manager of Ooltewah has been working for the company since he was a young teenager. Jerry's wife Martha is secretary/treasurer, and has been very involved since the company's inception 40 years ago when their office was the garage. Jerry's daughter Deanna Daniels Rogers, and daughter-in-law Mikki Daniels both work for the company part-time while being stay at home moms for Jerry and Martha's grandchildren: TJ, Trace, and Zoe Rogers, and Riley, Madison and Lily Daniels. Some of the grandchildren are already working part-time in the company. Mandy Daniels, Jerry and Martha's youngest, who is now an MRI technologist traveled with her dad several years while in school doing motorcycle rallies around the country. Tracy Rogers, Deanna's husband, handles inside sales for Air Rider along with the help of Jennifer Aubrey.

Keith Grove, the company's chief financial specialist, started as a teenager and has been with the company for almost a quarter of a century. Glenn Kilgore, plant manager, has been with the company 10 years and wears many hats.

Front view of plant as of 2008, located in the Ooltewah Industrial Park in Ooltewah, Tennessee.

Gary and Linda Theodoro and Ron and Jeanine Sherbarth have been traveling for the Air Rider division for 10 years, living out of company motor homes and taking the products direct to the consumer at motorcycle rallies. Other people who have carried big loads in production and been with Ooltewah for 10 to 20 years are Tami Bettis, supervisor of Ooltewah's new military project; Mitchell Brogdon, shipping supervisor; and James Cargile, cutting supervisor. Charles Deville is in charge of the embroidery department; Brenda McDaniel, embroidery department assistant manager; Ava Farrow, also in the embroidery department; Juanita Lake Robinson, sewing department supervisor; Retha Wafford, supervisor of the heat seal department; and Chris Wilson, supervisor of the gymnastic division. Teresa Seymore is the office manager and Valerie Fortner is in charge of the electronics division.

Only a handful of body builders have developed careers from their body-building success, but Jerry Daniels most likely holds the title for manufacturing the most wide-ranging collection of products. "And I'm proud," he says "to be able to pass all this on to my family."

PIONEER CREDIT COMPANY

In a turbulent economy, one financial services company takes pride in truly putting their customers first. At Pioneer Credit Company, "There are no bad customers, just bad financial situations." When John W. Holden Jr., President and CEO, founded the Cleveland, Tennessee-based company on April 16, 1974 his vision was to build a financial corporation that focused on the customer seeking a loan and their circumstances—not just numbers on paper. More than three decades later, this approach has proven successful and helped countless customers, who might not have qualified for loans elsewhere.

Prior to establishing Pioneer Credit, Mr. Holden began his consumer finance career in 1960 at American Credit Corporation in Charlotte, North Carolina. After witnessing the success of the company, he decided that he could offer the same service, while placing more emphasis on the individual needs of customers.

Mr. Holden gathered the support of a small group of friends to become investors in the new Tennessee business. Today, several of the Pioneer Credit's original investors have remained on the board of directors. In the 1980s the Tennessee legislature capped interest rates at 10 percent, motivating Mr. Holden to expand his operations to other states without the same restrictions. Pioneer Credit now employs more than 400 loan specialists who operate 98 offices in eight different southeastern states that include Tennessee, Georgia, Mississippi, Kentucky, Alabama, Louisiana, South Carolina and Texas.

John W. Holden Jr., President and CEO, founded the Cleveland, Tennessee-based company on April 16, 1974

Pioneer Credit, an independently owned and operated private corporation, has catered to the needs of customers, and as a result, has varied its products and services during more than three decades of operation. The company offers traditional loan services, such as personal loans, real estate loans, home improvement loans, medical, appliance, and furniture financing and auto loans. Additionally, they have diversified to include services, such as tax preparation, vehicle sales and jewelry sales—all with 24-hour same day service. Pioneer Credit previously offered mortgage loans. However, in October 2007, the company temporarily discontinued this service due to the market conditions. The company has focused on making loans available to customers when other lending institutions would not. The Pioneer Credit difference definitely has caught on. With more than $250 million in assets, the company serves nearly 100,000 customers.

The average loan at Pioneer Credit is $2,400 and is provided to customers who use funds for expenses that include vacation and holiday expenses as well as home repairs and back-to-school costs. Customers can apply for loans online at *www.pioneercredit.net* or in person at one of the many conveniently located branches. Most loans are paid within 19 months. Pioneer customers might not have a perfect credit history, but because the company has a liberal loan criterion, customers are able to establish good credit again. "We make every effort to

Corporate office in Cleveland, Tennessee.

"We try to understand"

get to know our customers and their financial needs," says Mr. Holden. "We roll out the red carpet for every person who walks through our doors. Our customers are treated with dignity and respect. That makes a difference."

Playing by the rules is very important to Mr. Holden and the employees at Pioneer Credit. He says that the company operates in a highly regulated industry and they comply with the legislature in each of the eight states in which they do business to the letter of the law.

According to Mr. Holden, what sets Pioneer Credit apart from other financial services companies is its employees. When Mr. Holden began the company 34 years ago, he hired three employees. Now 500 individuals are proud to work for Pioneer Credit and the three employees who helped launch the company continue to work there today. In fact, many employees have been with the company for more than 30 years, another indicator that Pioneer Credit not only treats its customers well, but its employees too. Pioneer Credit employees know each and every one of their customers by name. That is part of their job and has proven to be what keeps third and fourth generations coming back to Pioneer Credit for financial help. "Our employees spend a great deal of time getting to know customers and their situations, not just what they look like on paper," says Mr. Holden.

One reason that Pioneer Credit has prided itself on being a hometown finance company is that its employees are active in community service. The company's management team is encouraged to belong to civic organizations and give back to the communities they serve. As a result, Pioneer Credit employees belong to the local Kiwanis, Rotary, Boys &

Girls Club of America, etc. Among his other community activities, Mr. Holden has been an active member of the American Financial Services Association for 34 years.

Perhaps Pioneer Credit's success best can be described through a memo that Mr. Holden wrote to his employees. In it he cited a *Wall Street Journal* article that noted a dramatic increase in layoffs in the financial services industry. In the next sentence he boasted that the Pioneer Credit difference remains because the company has continued to do just the opposite and hire employees. He attributed this difference to what he called, "Sticking to our knitting and remembering what brought us to the dance for the past 34 years." More technically speaking, Pioneer Credit has conducted business in a way that has focused on well-made consumer loans. Mr. Holden continues to ask his employees to consider two questions when making a loan: Can the applicant pay? Will the customer pay? If the answer to both is, "yes," then they will continue to avoid potential losses. This approach is a stark contrast to following the strategy of the direct consumer loan business that has provided loans, regardless of the answers to the aforementioned questions.

Mr. Holden believes that the future of Pioneer Credit Company has great promise. "We receive most of our business from word of mouth referrals," he says. "If our employees continue to provide the unparalleled understanding and service to customers, I am confident that Pioneer Credit will continue to grow in years to come." Focusing on the customer and not only the numbers and the paperwork—that's the Pioneer Credit difference.

R.E. WEST INC.

Ever since he was a young boy, Robert E. "Bob" West, Jr. idolized his father. After serving in the U.S. Marine Corps during World War II, Robert Earnest West returned to his family in rural Livingston, Tennessee to make an honest living. He started by buying an old truck to transport livestock. Bob admired how his father earned his livelihood in the trucking industry. When Bob was 16, Earnest sold him the truck that then also helped Bob make a living, and along with it, fulfill dreams of building a nationally recognized interstate and intrastate truckload carrier business based on hard work, integrity and family values.

In 1969 Bob West founded R.E. West Inc. with the late 1930s KB8 International that his father had driven to transport livestock throughout Tennessee. The company's first office was located in Livingston on the back porch of Bob's parents' home. During the 1970s Bob expanded the business by buying more trucks and hiring additional drivers and maintenance staff. However, before he was able to grow his business he had to convince bankers in the area to loan money to a trucking company, which was not common at that time due to the unstable reputation of the carrier industry.

In the 1980s Bob stopped hauling livestock and established a truck rental company called West Rents. As part of this business, he leased trucks, trailers, drivers, and maintenance staff. Soon after, the rental business boomed. In 1997 Bob sold West Rents and 1,000

pieces of equipment to Penske Corporation for a significant profit in an effort to concentrate on building R.E. West Inc. and its long-distance hauling services.

In a state that has few railroads, the Tennessee community and economy long have depended on trucks for goods and services, like food, cars, milk, and gasoline. Today, with its corporate office in Ashland City, R.E. West Inc. prides itself on being dependable and on time to ensure that clients receive their shipments. The company's dedicated team of professionals transports all types of freight—from water heaters, tractors, and bulldozers to food, and shoes,—to all continental 48 states and Canada.

Left to right: Robert West Jr., Reita West, son Bill West, and daughter Jenny West.

Throughout the last four decades the trucking industry has experienced somewhat of an evolution. From the introduction of interstate highways to deregulation and technology—all have contributed to the current success of R.E. West Inc. One of the major changes in the trucking industry occurred in 1980 with deregulation. With this change, trucking companies were allowed to travel most anywhere, increasing competition with other similar U.S. companies. Before deregulation, trucks in Tennessee were permitted to carry a certain type of freight from one specific location to another and service businesses on that route only. With deregulation, R.E. West expanded its services to include both intrastate and interstate trucking. The development of the interstate highway system in the late 1980s also brought along with it great advances to the trucking industry. With sophisticated roadways to carry shipments between states, there were more business opportunities for carriers. However, there also was significant competition and high fuel prices with which to contend.

Lebanon, Tennessee location.

Technologic advances have revolutionized the trucking industry. With the advent of satellite communications in all of R.E. West trucks, the company has been able to use the tracking hardware and software to monitor cargo. For example, a satellite computer system allows drivers to record the date, time, weight, piece count, etc. of shipment deliveries—all in real time. This system increases efficiency because the drivers do not need to call back to the main office to verbally report the information and it is accessible to all interested parties at any time. Increased technology in the trucks also provides drivers with helpful information, like fuel locations, mileage databases and the most direct routes, to make their trips consistent and ensure on-time deliveries. Technology also expedited the billing process. Previously, after drivers delivered shipments, the customers would be billed weeks later. Now drivers scan the bills at their delivery location and present them to customers on the same day, allowing for faster and more accurate billing procedures.

The trucks themselves have changed considerably during the last two decades. Specifically, conventional cab trucks were standard in the 1970s. In conventional cabs the drivers sat behind the engine. These trucks were replaced by Cab Over Engines (COE), in which drivers sat on top of the front axle and the engine. Conventional cabs gained popularity again in the early 1980s when trucks were allowed to be longer in length, thus drivers did not need to sit on top of the engine to conserve space.

One of Bob's first trucks, a 1979 cab over Peterbilt with a cattle trailer.

The dependability and comfort of trucks has increased as well. Today, R.E. West Inc. takes great pride in its specialized fleet of equipment used to transport cargo. For instance, a higher cube trailer allows drivers to haul more goods and a heavy hauling flat bed trailer has more axels, which accommodate a larger load.

Giving back to the Tennessee community that supported him throughout his career always has been important to Bob West and his family. He remembers his parents working to raise money for him and his classmates to play school sports. Now to relieve parents of such a big role as fundraisers, Bob has built softball fields, and sporting equipment as well as maintained buses for different sports teams in the area. R.E. West Inc. employees also are active in the National Chamber of Commerce, along with different local chambers. The company also remains active within the trucking industry and belongs to the Tennessee Trucking Association, which represents more than 500 trucking companies and industry vendors, the Farm Equipment Manufacturers Association and the Specialized Carriers and Rigging Association.

While R.E. West Inc. began with one employee, the company now employs 155 people, ranging from drivers to customer service representatives. Bob takes great pride in his staff and expects them to take the same amount of pride in their work. R.E. West drivers cannot have any DUI charges or felonies on their record and they undergo intense training, which includes a six-week course for new drivers. The company also requires that a trainer accompany new drivers for their first month on the road. Upon completion of training, an R.E. West employee who is a third party tester for the state of Tennessee, determines whether drivers are equipped to handle the roads.

After nearly 40 years, R.E. West has experienced many changes, but the strong values and ethical business practices that are most important to Bob West, have remained the same. The future of R.E. West Inc. looks promising as the third generation of Wests is involved in the daily operations of the business. Bob's wife, Reita and their children, Jenny and Bill Bob, personally know each employee's name, where they attended school and in many cases, they even know their parents. "We've worked really hard to maintain the honesty, loyalty, and family atmosphere that is so important to the company," said Bob.

Ashland City, Tennessee location.

SEWANEE: THE UNIVERSITY OF THE SOUTH

In an era of specialization, it is counter-intuitive to uphold the broad-based, humanistic ideals of liberal education as a surer means to success. Yet at Sewanee: The University of the South, the adherence to outstanding liberal arts education and enduring traditions of honor, community, and respect have transformed many generations of students, and have earned the abiding loyalty and support of alumni who are enjoying lives of integrity, leadership, and service.

"We believe that broadly educated men and women are ideally suited to address the complexities of life and work," says University vice chancellor Joel Cunningham, who assumed his position in 2000. "Sewanee graduates are better able to perceive connections among disciplines, to think creatively, and to communicate with others. These are the essential characteristics of citizenship and leadership, and we do a better job than most in achieving them."

As the university celebrated the 150th anniversary of its founding in 2007–2008, it looked back on a rich history and forward to new opportunities for the next generations. With a spectacular natural setting, a collaborative scholarly community, and a commitment to educational excellence that has made it one of the top liberal arts institutions in the nation, The University of the South faces a new era confident in its mission and its capacity to adapt to changing circumstance.

Sewanee was founded in 1857 by clergy and lay delegates from Episcopal dioceses throughout the south. They selected a site in Sewanee, atop the Cumberland Plateau about 50 miles west of Chattanooga, and local landowners and the Sewanee Mining Company donated nearly 10,000 acres for the enterprise. On October 10, 1860 the founders laid the cornerstone for a campus that would eventually grow to house 1,500 students on 13,000 forested acres.

Its planned opening delayed by the onset of the Civil War, the University successfully opened its doors in 1868 with the help of generous benefactors in America and England who supported the vision of a new Episcopal university in the southern United States. The first Opening Convocation on September 18, 1868 boasted a total of nine students and four faculty. (Sewanee continues to have

an outstanding student-faculty ratio today, with only 11 students per faculty member.)

The university struggled during Reconstruction, but by the turn of the century was firmly established with a preparatory school, college, and seminary programs, as well as professional programs. Successful athletic teams and a thriving cultural life testified to its emergence among mainstream colleges and universities.

Sewanee eventually abandoned its professional programs during the first few decades of the 20th century, and it persevered through the difficult years of the Great Depression and both world wars. The growth of higher education following World War II opened doors for many people seeking educational opportunity. Sewanee shared in the nation's newfound optimism and interest in higher education, and enjoyed a surge in enrollments that laid a foundation for the judicious growth that has continued to the present day.

Today Sewanee holds a place among the top liberal arts institutions in the nation, drawing students from around the nation and the world. The university remains purposefully small and dedicated to building a sense of community. All classes are taught by professors, not graduate teaching assistants, and close faculty-student interaction ensures that each student enjoys a rich and personal educational experience.

The result of such individualized education is clear in the academic success

St. Luke's Hall (1878) was home to the School of Theology for more than a century. In 1955 the interior was extensively renovated, and an addition was built on the east side. Following the seminary's move to the Sewanee Military Academy campus in 1984, St. Luke's continued to serve as an academic building for undergraduate courses, with dormitory space on its top floor. From 2005 to 2006 it was remodeled and refurbished to serve exclusively as a university residence hall.

of Sewanee students and alumni. The university has had 25 Rhodes Scholars—a number that puts Sewanee in the top four nationally among American liberal arts colleges—has been home to 26 NCAA Postgraduate Fellows, 36 Watson Fellows, and dozens of Fulbright Scholars, and has an acceptance rate to graduate and professional schools that far outpaces its peers.

Sewanee offers 36 majors, 27 minors, and 15 special programs, along with pre-medicine, pre-nursing, pre-law, and pre-business. More than 40 percent of students participate in study abroad programs, and a comprehensive endowed program that provides financial support for summer internships has greatly strengthened career development for undergraduates.

The university has an exceptionally strong literary tradition, with the nation's longest-standing literary review, *The Sewanee Review*, and a yearly writer's conference supported through an endowment established by playwright Tennessee Williams. The tradition permeates the entire curriculum, and Sewanee graduates are known for their facility with the written word. Emerging strengths in the physical and life sciences, including environmental sciences, are being supported with new facilities. Spencer Hall, a state-of-the-art addition to Woods Laboratory, opened in 2008 with more than 47,000 square feet of sophisticated laboratories, classrooms, and faculty offices.

The distinctive campus architecture borrows from the Gothic tradition of Oxford and Cambridge, with native sandstone buildings and garden pathways nestled into a wooded landscape, soaring bell towers, and—at the spiritual and physical center of the campus—the majestic All Saints' Chapel, modeled on the great European cathedrals. The campus, the curriculum, and the sense of respect that permeates personal relationships at Sewanee have given rise to unique traditions. Faculty wear academic gowns to class, and many of the students whose academic performance qualifies them to become members of the Order of Gownsmen likewise wear gowns to class.

The University Domain, as the campus and surrounding area is known, also is a remarkable academic and recreational resource, inviting students to become

Situated atop Tennessee's Cumberland Plateau, The University of the South provides an inspirational setting for one of the nation's leading liberal arts universities. The 10,000-acre Domain of the University is a rich educational resource as well as a place for outdoor recreation.

involved with nature and to engage in careful study of the natural environment. Rock-climbing, caving, cross-country running, and mountain biking are popular among students and faculty, and one of the university's strategic goals is to be a national leader in environmental studies and sustainability.

Sewanee remains committed to the humanistic traditions of education, providing a place to build lasting, personal relationships in an environment of exploration and learning. Sewanee alumni are close-knit and supportive, having shared the experience "on the Mountain," and they often maintain lifetime friendships with one another and with their professors. Their loyalty extends to the institution that made such relationships possible, strengthening Sewanee's reputation and making possible a remarkable record of fundraising, including the successful completion in 2008 of the record-breaking *Sewanee Call* capital campaign, which exceeded its $180 million goal.

"The essence of Sewanee is consistent from generation to generation," says Cunningham. "We are a university dedicated to liberal education, to time-honored traditions, and to our commitment to serve our students and this nation. We have been successful in advancing our mission, and I believe we have the resources and the will to ensure that Sewanee's best years are still to come."

The majestic All Saints' Chapel, at the physical and spiritual center of campus, takes its architectural inspiration from the great European cathedrals. Constructed of native stone from the area and featuring a stunning array of stained glass windows that tell the story of the University's history, All Saints' hosts regular worship services, musical concerts and the pageantry of the University's formal academic events.

SOUTHERN BAPTIST CONVENTION

The Southern Baptist Convention was founded in 1845 as a means for Baptist Christians in the South to connect through their faith in Jesus Christ and to fulfill their mission of spreading Jesus' message and legacy of service. Since that time, the term Southern Baptist Convention has come to encompass both the denomination as well as its annual meeting. Since its inception, the group has grown to more than 16 million members who worship at over 44,000 churches throughout the United States. This represents the largest Baptist association in the world as well as the largest non-Catholic denomination in the United States. Working through over 1,100 local associations and 42 state conventions and fellowships, Southern Baptists share basic core beliefs about the Scriptures as well as a commitment to proclaim the Gospel of Jesus Christ to the world through one unified voice.

The Southern Baptist Convention is unique in that independent churches affiliate with the organization at their discretion. In order to be part of the Southern Baptist Convention, a person need only join a church affiliated with the Southern Baptist Convention. Church membership is celebrated through the Christian rite of baptism, performed

Southern Baptist Convention Annual Meeting, Saint Louis, Missouri, June 1947.

through a ceremony that includes full water immersion of an individual who has professed his or her faith in Jesus Christ as Savior and Lord.

The part that individual churches play is vital in the Southern Baptist Convention, which is primarily Congregationalist in organization. Each local church is fully autonomous and is able to develop its own community personality within the general bounds of the denomination's beliefs. This gives individual churches leeway to conduct their own internal affairs and determine the amount of support they extend to SBC programs and groups.

The Convention, which has its central administrative offices in Nashville, Tennessee, meets annually for two days. The meeting, which is usually conducted in June, is held in a different host city each year. Host cities are proposed years in advance by the SBC's Committee on Order of Business, which seeks out cities that have ample services to accommodate 12,000 to 15,000 attendees. The committee regularly recommends the location move around the country to make it easier for people in

each area to participate in the Convention. Host cities have included Indianapolis, Greensboro, San Antonio, Los Angeles, and Salt Lake City.

Anyone may attend the Southern Baptist Convention; all that is required is registration. But the largest group of attendees is church messengers—those chosen by individual churches to attend and represent their churches in conducting Convention business and through voting for resolutions. A resolution has traditionally been defined as an expression of opinion or concern, as compared to a motion, which calls for action. A resolution is not used to direct an entity of the Southern Baptist Convention to specific action other than to communicate the opinion or concern expressed. Resolutions are adopted during the annual Convention meeting and can be submitted for consideration by any member in good standing of a Southern Baptist church.

Though messengers are elected by their churches, they are not instructed by them; rather, they are free to vote their own conscience in Convention matters. The number of messengers allotted each church depends on the level of support and participation with the SBC, though no church may send more than 10 messengers. This rule helps equalize the power throughout the churches, allowing smaller, rural churches an equal footing with larger churches situated in population centers.

As part of its outreach mission, Southern Baptists sponsor more than 5,000 missionaries serving in the U.S., Guam and the Caribbean, along with more than 5,000 missionaries in over 150 nations throughout the world. A little known fact is that the Southern Baptist Convention is the third largest disaster relief organization in America, a testament to the organization's powerful collective effort. Through Southern Baptist Disaster Relief, SBC volunteers have been on-site at some of the most devastating disasters in

Southern Baptist Disaster Relief feeding unit prepares meals following Hurricane Katrina.

The Congregation of First Baptist Church,
Martin, Tennessee, celebrates the centennial of
the sanctuary, September 18, 2005.

recent history. Even before Hurricane Katrina made landfall, SBC teams were already en route to New Orleans to render aid. It is not uncommon for Southern Baptists to be first in and last out of disaster areas. Volunteers, from shower crews, food serving units, chainsaw crews, and chaplains among others, were still in Louisiana and surrounding areas helping restore the area for more than two years during its long rehabilitation process.

Yet this is only one aspect of the enormous mission effort spearheaded by the SBC. Opportunities abound for adults and students to make a difference in their communities and beyond through SBC programs.

The SBC produces a publication entitled *SBC Life*, which is sent out to approximately 55,000 senior pastors and church staff. The mission of the magazine is to inform readers on issues concerning Southern Baptists; interpret the policies of the SBC for readers; inspire readers, particularly in areas of ministry and outreach; and encourage pastors who may be struggling, with stories from others who have faced similar challenges and found strength and fortitude in God.

Another vital aspect of the SBC is its commitment to Christian education. The SBC oversees a large seminary program with six main campuses around the country. Southern Baptists subsidize seminary education for students who are members of Southern Baptist churches that have voted to commend them to a Southern Baptist seminary. While many degree programs are offered to students, the basic program is a master of divinity, a professional graduate degree, which consists of a three-year program of seminary studies.

Another area of emphasis for the SBC is public advocacy. The SBC takes an active role in areas where matters of religious interest and public policy intersect. Through its Ethics and Religious Liberty Commission, the SBC represents its sizable Convention by communicating with and advocating to governmental entities and leaders from a Biblical and Christian worldview.

As the Southern Baptist Convention continues well past its 150th anniversary, its basic ideals remain the foundation for the future. According to Roger S. Oldham,

vice president for Convention Relations, the SBC plans to "build on its history and heritage to plant new churches, to strengthen established churches, and to broaden ministries of compassion." This will be accomplished through a continuing mission to demonstrate the love of Christ by sharing his good news and performing acts of kindness through local churches in local communities. By seeking to strengthen the cycle of love, learning, and giving through Christ, the Southern Baptist Convention strives to serve as a model of Christian leadership for those of every faith throughout the world.

Southern Baptist Convention Building,
downtown Nashville, Tennessee.

A TIMELINE OF TENNESSEE HISTORY

10000 BCE
Approximate date of first human arrivals in what is now Tennessee, nomadic hunters called Paleo-Indians by anthropologists.

8000 BCE
Beginning of the Archaic culture, in which Native Americans were less nomadic, developed tools, made bowls and baskets, and used clay hearths.

1000 BCE
Approximate advent of the Woodland culture, in which Native Americans settled down in small permanent villages, began to practice agriculture, and built burial mounds.

1000 CE
Approximate beginning of the Mississippian tradition that may have been the ancestors of the Cherokees, Chickasaws, Creeks, and Shawnee Indians. These people lived in large permanent towns, had advanced political and social structures, and well-defined gender roles.

1540
Spanish explorer Hernando de Soto was the first European to set foot in what is now Tennessee with a force of 600 in a futile search for gold.

1673
Jacques Marquette, a Jesuit missionary, and fur trader Louis Joliet traveled the Mississippi River to claim the area for

Woodland Indians, 1000 BCE to 1000 CE., by artist Greg Harlin. Courtesy, Frank H. McClung Museum, University of Tennessee.

U. S. Army fort, Knoxville 1793, by artist Lloyd Branson. Courtesy, Thompson Photograph Collection, C. M. McClung Historical Collection.

France and probably camped near what is now the city of Memphis. English traders James Needham and Gabriel Arthur led a trading party into the Great Valley of Tennessee, lived for a time in the Cherokee town where Arthur learned the Cherokee language.

1757
Construction of Fort Loudoun on the Little Tennessee River by South Carolina militiamen and British regulars, intended to hold the area against the French during the French and Indian War.

1760
When the Cherokees turned against the British in the French and Indian War, they surrounded Fort Loudoun and forced it to surrender. Although the Cherokees guaranteed safe passage to the besieged people, on August 8, 1760 warriors attacked those who had surrendered approximately 15 miles from the fort. Twenty-six soldiers and three women were killed and the remainder were taken prisoner, some of whom were tortured and killed.

1769
William Bean built a cabin on the Watauga River in northeast Tennessee, becoming the first permanent Euro-American settler. Other settlers began making their way to the area from Virginia and North Carolina.

1772
The settlers formed their own government, which they called the Watauga Association. They drew up one of the first written constitutions in North America.

1775
The Transylvania Company purchased a large tract of land from the Cherokees and hired Daniel Boone to blaze a trail from Virginia to the Cumberland Gap, later called the Wilderness Road.

1779
Jonesborough became the first chartered town. In the same year, James Robertson and John Donelson settled on the Cumberland River and constructed Fort Nashborough, later Nashville.

1780
Led by John Sevier, a group of 900 "Overmountain Men" gathered at Sycamore Shoals and marched over the Great Smoky Mountains to King's Mountain, where on October 7 they defeated a force of British and loyalists.

THE WAR FOR THE UNION.

PHOTOGRAPHIC HISTORY.

1784

Frustrated by the lack of government in the area, the three counties of Washington, Greene, and Sullivan formed the State of Franklin, which seceded from North Carolina for four years. When North Carolina offered conciliatory measures and simultaneously moved against Franklin's leaders (Franklin Governor John Sevier was arrested), the independent state movement collapsed.

1786

White's Fort, established at the confluence of the French Broad and Holston Rivers, was named for founder James White. In 1792 the settlement was named Knoxville, which became the first territorial capital, and was the scene of the founding of Tennessee's first newspaper (*Knoxville Gazette*, 1791), and the creation of Blount College (1794), the first American non-denominational institution of higher learning, later to become the University of Tennessee.

1789

Formation of the Territory of the United States south of the River Ohio. William Blount was its first and only governor.

1796

Tennessee became the 16th state on June 2, 1796. John Sevier was elected the first governor.

1800

Congress set up a postal route along the Natchez Trace, an old trail between Nashville and Natchez, Mississippi.

1812

Beginning with early tremors in the Louisiana Territory (in present-day Missouri), the New Madrid earthquake struck western Tennessee in February 1812 and was one of the largest earthquakes in United States history, measuring perhaps as high as 12 on the Richter Scale. There was considerable destruction in the Louisiana Territory, Kentucky, and Tennessee. The quake also created Reelfoot Lake and caused the Mississippi River to experience tidal waves and to run upstream for a time.

1813

Tennessee's first public library opened in Nashville.

1815

Under General Andrew Jackson, a mixture of U.S. troops, state militiamen, and volunteers triumph over the British in the Battle of New Orleans, making Jackson a national hero.

1826

The state capital was located permanently in Nashville. In that same year, Scotswoman Frances "Fanny" Wright established Nashoba near Memphis, a settlement for freed African Americans. In 1830 Nashoba was moved to Haiti.

1828

Andrew Jackson was elected seventh president of the United States.

1834

Sixty chosen delegates met in Nashville to revise the state's constitution. Among

Civil War Nashville, 1864. Courtesy, University of Tennessee Special Collections.

the most important changes were a reform of the state tax system, a revision of the state judicial system, the removal of property qualifications for voting and holding office, and the simultaneous disfranchisement of African Americans.

1838

Under the command of General Winfield Scott, United States troops rounded up approximately 13,000 Cherokees and sent them to American territory in the West in what became known as the Trail of Tears. Over 4,000 Cherokees died along the way.

1844

James Knox Polk was elected 11th president of the United States.

1861

On February 9, 55 percent of Tennessee voters rejected a proposal for a state convention to have the state secede from the United States. After the firing on Fort Sumter on April 12, a second vote was scheduled and this time 69 percent of the electorate voted to secede from the Union. Andrew Johnson, who opposed secession, was the only southerner to stay in the United States Senate.

1861–1865

Approximately 187,000 Confederate and 51,000 Union soldiers from Tennes-

see (including a number of African Americans who volunteered for the Federal army) served during the Civil War, known in the North at the time as the War of the Rebellion and in the South as the War Between the States. Tennessee was the scene of a number of significant battles. President Lincoln appointed Andrew Johnson as the military governor of Tennessee.

The defeat of the Confederate army under General John B. Hood late in 1864 virtually eliminated open resistance to the Union in Tennessee. On February 22, 1865, with pro-southern voters boycotting the election, the vast majority of voters approved an amended state constitution and William G. "Parson" Brownlow, a Methodist minister and Knoxville anti-secession editor, was elected Tennessee's governor.

1865

With the assassination of President Lincoln, Andrew Johnson became the United States' seventeenth president. His presidential career was a stormy one and he was impeached in 1868, but the Senate fell one vote short of removal. In 1865 the Ku Klux Klan was founded in Pulaski, Tennessee, with former Confederate general Nathan Bedford Forrest as the first "Grand Wizard."

1866

Tennessee was readmitted to the Union, the third state to ratify the Fourteenth Amendment. That same year Fisk University was established in Nashville as an Institution primarily for African Americans. Also in 1866, Tennessee was permitted to receive higher education money under the 1862 Morrill Act (the funds went to the institution in Knoxville that ultimately became the University of Tennessee in 1879).

Gay Street Parade, Knoxville, World War I. Courtesy, Thompson Photograph Collection.

1869

In a statewide election, the Radicals were overthrown by pro-South Conservatives, marking the *de facto* end of Radical Reconstruction in Tennessee.

1870

A new state constitution was adopted that, with some changes, is the constitution that governs Tennessee today.

1873

Vanderbilt University, named after American businessman and philanthropist Cornelius Vanderbilt, was founded in Nashville.

1878

A terrible epidemic of yellow fever in Memphis took the lives of over 25 percent of the city's population.

1880

Englishman Thomas Hughes established the Rugby colony in Morgan County as a haven for young British aristocrats. He paid for the land through royalties from his popular book, *Tom Brown's School Days*.

1893

The Ruskin Cooperative Association, a "grass-roots socialist" colony, was founded in Dickson County, west of Nashville.

1894

On December 27, President Grover Cleveland signed legislation creating the Shiloh National Military Park to commemorate and preserve the site of the April 1862 Civil War battle in which approximately 20,000 from both sides were killed or wounded.

1897

The Tennessee Centennial Exposition was held in Nashville to celebrate the state's 100th birthday. Perhaps the most dramatic aspect of the celebration was the construction of a full-scale replica of the Parthenon in Athens, Greece, an edifice that still stands in the state's capital.

1898

Four regiments of Tennesseans served in the Spanish-American War.

1900

The railroad train on which Casey Jones was the engineer crashed on April 30, killing him. The song remembering the crash became one of the most famous ever written about a Tennessean.

1917–1918

Approximately 100,000 Tennesseans served in the armed forces during the Great War (World War I), the most celebrated of whom was Alvin York of Fentress County who was awarded the Congressional Medal of Honor because of his almost superhuman feats on October 8, 1918 when he single-handedly killed over 20 Germans and forced 132 others to surrender.

The worst train wreck in United States history occurred in Nashville on July 9, 1918, killing 101 and injuring 171.

1920

Tennessee became the 36th state to ratify the Nineteenth Amendment, giving women the right to vote.

1925

When the state legislature passed a law making it a crime to teach evolution in the public schools, some businessmen in

Well-known entertainers (left to right) Rod Brasfield, Red Foley, and Minnie Pearl at the Grand Ole Opry, Nashville. Courtesy, Tennessee State Library.

Dayton decided to "put the town on the map" by convincing high school teacher John Thomas Scopes to admit that he violated the law and holding the well-publicized trial of Scopes in Dayton. It was the first trial broadcast nationally on the radio. Scopes was found guilty, although the conviction later was reversed on a technical error.

The country music show "The Grand Ole Opry" begins broadcasting on the radio. It became a network radio show in 1939 and a television show in 1955.

The state legislature approved Governor Austin Peay's General Education Bill which dramatically increased funding for public education.

1930

"Twelve Southerners," the most well-

known ultimately being Robert Penn
Warren, published *I'll Take My Stand*
which attacked modern industrial society and praised the agrarian way of life.

1933

The Tennessee Valley Authority (TVA)
was established during the first 100
days of the Roosevelt Administration.
Ultimately, TVA pumped approximately $7
billion into the 205 counties in parts of
the six states served by the Agency.

1940

The Great Smoky Mountains National
Park was formally dedicated by President Franklin Roosevelt. It has become
the most visited national park in the United
States, playing host to over 11 million
visitors each year.

1941-1945

Over 300,000 Tennesseans served in the
armed forces during World War II, with
thousands of others working on the
home front in war-related industries.
Especially valuable were women workers who were employed in just about
every position once held exclusively by
men.

1942

The construction of a "secret city" at Oak
Ridge in Anderson County began. Its goal
was producing uranium to be used in one
of the atomic bombs that were dropped
on Japan in August 1945. Oak Ridge at
one time had a peak population of 75,000.

1948

WMCT-TV in Memphis, the state's first
television station, went on the air.

1950-1953

Approximately 10,500 Tennesseans
served in the Korean War.

1952

Sun Studio in Memphis made its first rock
and roll recording. Ultimately Sam
Phillips, the head of Sun Records, would
record Elvis Presley, Jerry Lee Lewis,
Carl Perkins, and Johnny Cash. Presley
first recorded for Sun in 1954.

1960

College students and others held sit-ins
in Nashville at downtown lunch
counters, which up to that time had not
served African Americans. The sit-in
movement spread to Knoxville in the
summer of 1960.

1968

While in Memphis to support a strike by
the city's sanitation workers, the Reverend Martin Luther King, Jr. was shot to

*Norris Dam, TVA's first dam, 1936. Courtesy,
Tennessee Valley Authority.*

*President Franklin Roosevelt at the 1940
dedication of the Great Smoky Mountain
National Park. Courtesy, Thompson
Photograph Collection.*

death at the Lorraine Motel. King's death sent shock waves throughout the nation and, in spite of President Lyndon Johnson's call for calm, rioting broke out in several cities.

1970

The Reverend Billy Graham held a religious crusade in Neyland Stadium on the University of Tennessee campus. When President Richard Nixon rose to speak one evening, the crusade was interrupted briefly by anti-war demonstrators.

1976

Tennessee author Alex Haley won the Pulitzer Prize for his best-selling book *Roots*, which chronicled Haley's ancestors' lives in slavery and freedom. In 1978 the author was sued for plagiarism and settled out of court. Haley died in 1992.

1977

Elvis Presley died at his home in Memphis at the age of 42. His home, Graceland, was opened to the public in 1982.

1982

Knoxville hosted a World's Fair with the theme "Energy Turns the World." The fair ran for six months and attracted over 11 million visitors.

1983

The Butcher banking empire collapsed. Eventually, brothers Cecil and Jake Butcher went to federal prison.

1985

General Motors announced that it would build a new assembly plant for a new line of automobiles, to be named Saturn, in Spring Hill. The facility began operations in 1987.

1987

Opryland Amusement Park opened in Nashville.

1991

The National Civil Rights Museum opened in Memphis on the site of the Lorraine Motel. In 2002 the facility underwent an $11 million expansion.

1994

Governor Ned Ray McWherter introduced TennCare, a major reform of the state's Medicaid system.

1996

Tennesseans celebrated the state's bicentennial in cities and towns throughout the state. A U.S. commemorative stamp was issued to mark the event.

1998

The University of Tennessee's football team won the NCAA National Champi-

onship with a Fiesta Bowl victory over Florida State University.

1999

The Women's Basketball Hall of Fame opened in Knoxville. By 2005 it was hosting 42,000 visitors annually.

2000

The Memphis Rock 'n' Soul Museum opened.

2007

The University of Tennessee Lady Vols basketball team won its seventh national championship with a victory over Rutgers University.

Sit-In, Chattanooga, 1960. Courtesy, Tennessee State Library.

Coach Pat Summitt, Coach of Lady Vols 2007 National Women's Basketball Champions. Courtesy, UT Lady Vols Media Relations

BIBLIOGRAPHY

Abernethy, Thomas P. *From Frontier to Plantation* (Chapel Hill, N.C., 1932; reprinted, University, Ala., 1967).

Abramson, Rudy, and Jean Haskell, *Encyclopedia of Appalachia* (Knoxville, 2006).

Alexander, Thomas B. *Political Reconstruction in Tennessee* (Nashville, 1950).

Arnow, Harriette. *Flowering of the Cumberland* (New York, 1963).

———. *Seedtime on the Cumberland* (New York, 1960).

Ash, Stephen V., *Middle Tennessee Society Transformed, 1860–1870: War and Peace in the Upper South* (Baton Rouge, 1988).

Atkins, Jonathan M., *Parties, Politics, and the Sectional Conflict in Tennessee, 1832–1861* (Knoxville, 1997).

Bailey, Fred Arthur, *Class and Tennessee's Confederate Generation* (Chapel Hill, 1987)

Baker, Thomas H. *The Memphis Commercial Appeal: The History of a Southern Newspaper* (Baton Rouge, La., 1971).

Bergeron, Paul H. *Antebellum Politics in Tennessee* (Lexington, Ky., 1982).

———. *Paths of the Past: Tennessee, 1770–1970* (Knoxville, 1979).

———. *The Presidency of James K. Polk* (Lawrence, Kansas, 1987).

Bergeron, Paul, Stephen V. Ash and Jeanette Keith, *Tennesseans and Their History* (Knoxville, 1999).

Biles, Roger, *Memphis in the Great Depression* (Knoxville, 1986).

Brown, Fred, *The Faces of East Tennessee: An Historical Perspective on the Counties of East Tennessee* (Knoxville, 1990).

Campbell, Claude A. *The Development of Banking in Tennessee* (Nashville, 1932).

Campbell, Mary R. *The Attitude of Tennesseans Toward the Union, 1847–1861* (New York, 1961).

Capers, Gerald M., Jr. *The Biography of a River Town—Memphis: Its Heroic Age* (Chapel Hill, N.C., 1939; reprinted, New Orleans, 1966).

Cartwright, Joseph H. *The Triumph of Jim Crow: Tennessee Race Relations in the 1880s* (Knoxville, 1976).

Chambers, William N. *Old Bullion Benton: Senator from the New West* (New York, 1956).

Cimprich, John. *Slavery's End in Tennessee, 1861–1865* (University, Ala., 1985).

Clark, Blanche Henry. *The Tennessee Yeoman, 1840–1860* (Nashville, 1942).

Cleveland, Catharine C. *The Great Revival in the West, 1797–1805* (Chicago, 1916).

Conkin, Paul K. *Gone With the Ivy: A Biography of Vanderbilt University* (Knoxville, 1985).

Connelly, Thomas Lawrence. *Army of the Heartland: The Army of Tennessee, 1861–1862* (Baton Rouge, La., 1967).

———. *Autumn of Glory: The Army of Tennessee, 1862–1865* (Baton Rouge, La.). *Civil War Tennessee* (Knoxville).

Corlew, Robert E. *A Short History of Tennessee* (Nashville, 1976).

———. *Statehood for Tennessee* (Nashville, 1976).

Cooling, Benjamin Franklin, *Fort Donelson's Legacy: War and Society in Kentucky and Tennessee, 1862–1863* (Knoxville: 1997).

Crofts, Daniel W., *Reluctant Confederates: Upper South Unionists in the Secession Crisis* (Chapel Hill, 1989).

Crutchfield, James A., *The Tennessee Almanac and Book of Facts* (Nashville, 1988).

Davidson, Donald. *The Tennessee: The Old River, Frontier to Secession* (New York, 1946).

———. *The Tennessee: The New River, Civil War to TVA* (New York, 1948).

Deadrick, Lucille, ed., *Heart of the Valley: A History of Knoxville, Tennessee* (Knoxville, 1976).

Dickinson, W. Calvin, and Eloise R. Hitchcock, eds., *A Bibliography of Tennessee History, 1973–1996* (Knoxville, 1999).

Doyle, Don H., *New Men, New Cities, New South* (Chapel Hill, 1990).

———. *Nashville in the New South* (Knoxville, 1985).

———. *Nashville Since the 1920s* (Knoxville, 1985).

Durham, Walter T. *Daniel Smith, Frontier Statesman* (Gallatin, Tenn., 1976).

———. *Nashville: The Occupied City, the First Seventeen Months—February 16, 1862 to June 30, 1863* (Nashville, 1985).

———. *Reluctant Partners: Nashville and the Union* (Nashville, 1987).

———. *Before Tennessee: The Southwest Territory, 1790–1796* (Piney Flats, TN, 1990).

Dykeman, Wilma. *Tennessee: A Bicentennial History* (New York, 1975).

———. *The French Broad* (New York, 1955; reprinted, Knoxville, 1965).

Egerton, John. *Visions of Utopia: Nashoba, Rugby, Ruskin, and the "New Communities"* (Knoxville).

Egerton, John, Federal Writers Project of the Work Projects Administration. *Tennessee: A Guide to the State* (New York, 1939; reissued, Knoxville, 1986).

Encyclopedia of Tennessee, The (New York, 1993).

Fisher, Noel, *War at Every Door: Partisan Politics and Guerrilla Violence in East Tennessee, 1860-1869* (Chapel Hill, 1997).

Folmsbee, Stanley J. *Blount College and East Tennessee College, 1794–1840* (Knoxville, 1946).

———. *Sectionalism and Internal Improvements in Tennessee, 1796–1845* (Knoxville, 1939).

———. *Tennessee Establishes a State University: First Years of the University of Tennessee, 1879–1887* (Knoxville, 1967).

Folmsbee, Stanley J., Robert E. Corlew, and Enoch Mitchell. *History of Tennessee. 2* vols. (New York, 1960).

Ginger, Ray. *Six Days of Forever: Tennessee v. John Thomas Scopes* (New York, 1958).

Glen, John M., *Highlander: No Ordinary School* (Knoxville, 2nd ed. 1996).

Goodstein, Anita Shafer, *Nashville, 1780–1860: From Frontier to City* (Gainsville, FL, 1989)

Govan, Gilbert E., and James W. Livingood. *The Chattanooga Country* (New York, 1952; reprinted, Chapel Hill, N.C., 1963).

Graf, LeRoy P., and Ralph W. Haskins (eds.) *The Papers of Andrew Johnson.* 6 vols. to date (Knoxville, 1967-).

Graham, Hugh Davis. *Crisis in Print: Desegregation and the Press in Tennessee* (Nashville, 1967).

Greene, *Lee* Seifert. *Lead Me On:* Frank Goad Clement and Tennessee Politics (Knoxville, 1982).

Greene, Lee Seifert, David M. Grubbs, and Victor Hobday. *Government in Tennessee,* 4th edition (Knoxville, 1982).

Groce, W. Todd, *Mountain Rebels: East Tennessee Confederates and the Civil War* (Knoxville, 1992).

Hamer, Philip M. *Tennessee: A History, 1763–1932.* 4 vols. (New York, 1933).

Harkness, David. *Tennessee in Literature* (Knoxville, 1949).

———. *Tennessee in Recent Books, Mu-sic, and Drama* (Knoxville, 1950).

Harper, Herbert L. (ed.) *Houston and Crockett, Heroes of Tennessee and Texas* (Nashville, 1986).

History of Tennessee: Containing Historical and Biographical Sketches of *Thirty East Tennessee Counties* (Greenville, SC, 1991).

Holt, Andrew D. *The Struggle of a State System of Public Schools in Tennessee, 1903–1936* (New York, 1938).

Honey, Michael K., *Southern Labor and Black Civil Rights: Organizing Memphis Workers* (Urbana, IL, 1993).

Horn, Stanley F. *The Army of Tennessee* (Indianapolis, Ind., 1941).

———. *The Invisible Empire* (Boston, Mass., 1939).

Hudson, Charles, *The Southeastern Indians* (Knoxville, 1976).

Isaac, Paul E. *Prohibition and Politics: Turbulent Decades in Tennessee, 1885–1920* (Knoxville, 1965).

James, Marquis. *The Life of Andrew Jackson.* 2 vols. (New York, 1933, 1937).

———. *The Raven: A Biography of Sam Houston* (New York, 1929).

Johnson, Charles W., and Charles O. Jackson. *City Behind a Fence: Oak Ridge, Tennessee, 1942–1946* (Knoxville, 1981).

Johnson, Leland, and Daniel Schaffer, *Oak Ridge National Laboratory: The First Fifty Years* (Knoxville, 1994).

Jones, Robert B., *Tennessee at the Crossroads: The State Debt Controversy, 1870–1883* (Knoxville, 1977).

Keith, Jeanette, *Country People in the New South: Tennessee's Upper Cumberland* (Chapel Hill, 1995).

Lamon, Lester. *Blacks in Tennessee, 1791–1970* (Knoxville, 1981).

Lee, David D. *Tennessee in Turmoil: The Volunteer State, 1920–1932* (Memphis, 1979).

———. *Sergeant York: An American Hero* (Lexington, Ky., 1984).

Lovett, Bobby L., *The Civil Rights Movement in Tennessee: A Narrative History* (Knoxville, 2005).

————, and Linda T. Wynn, eds., *Profiles of African Americans in Tennessee* (Nashville, 1996).

Luther, Edward T. Our *Restless Earth: The Geologic Regions of Tennessee* (Knox*ville).*

MacArthur, William J., *Knoxville: Crossroads of the New South* (Tulsa, OK, 1982).

————, *Knoxville's History, An Interpretation* (Knoxville, 1978).

McCormack, Edward M. *Slavery on the Tennessee Frontier* (Nashville, 1977).

McFerrin, John Berry. *Caldwell and Company, a Southern Financial Empire* (Chapel Hill, N.C., 1939; reprinted, Nashville, 1969).

McIlwaine, Shields. *Memphis Down in Dixie* (New York, 1948).

McKenzie, Robert Tracy, *Lincolnites and Rebels: A Divided Town in the American Civil War* (New York, 2006).

————, *One South Or Many? Plantation Belt and Upcountry in Civil War-Era Tennessee* (Cambridge, UK, 1994).

McMurray, Richard M. *John Bell Hood and the War for Southern Independence* (Lexington, Ky., 1982).

Majors, William R., *Change and Continuity: Tennessee Politics Since the Civil War* (Macon, GA, 1986).

————. *Editorial Wild Oats: Edward Ward Carmack and Tennessee Politics* (Macon, Ga., 1982).

————. *End of Arcadia: Gordon Browning and Tennessee Politics* (Memphis, 1982).

Maslowski, Peter, *Treason Must Be Made Odious: Military Occupation and Wartime Reconstruction in Nashville, Tennessee* (Millwood, NY, 1978).

Masterson, William H. *William Blount* (Baton Rouge, La., 1954).

Miller, William D. *Mr. Crump of Memphis* (Baton Rouge, La., 1964).

————. *Memphis During the Progressive Era* (Memphis, 1957).

Minton, John D. *The New Deal in Tennessee, 1932–1948* (New York, 1979).

Mooney, Chase. *Slavery in* Tennessee (Bloomington, Ind., 1957).

Noe, Kenneth, and Shannon Wilson, eds., *The Civil War in Appalachia: Collected Essays* (Knoxville, 1997).

Norton, Herman A. *Religion in Tennessee, 1777–1945* (Knoxville, 1981).

Owsley, Frank L. *Plain Folk of the Old South* (Baton Rouge, La., 1949).

Parks, Joseph H. *Felix Grundy: Champion of Democracy* (Baton Rouge, La., 1949).

————. John *Bell of Tennessee* (Baton Rouge, La., 1950).

Posey, Walter B. *Frontier Mission: A History of Religion West of the Southern Appalachians to 1861* (Lexington, Ky., 1966).

Putnam, A.W. *History of Middle Tennessee; or Life and Times of Gen.* James *Robertson* (Nashville, 1857; reprinted, Knoxville, 1971).

Ramsey, James G.M. *Annals of Tennessee to the End of the Eighteenth Century* (reprinted, Knoxville, 1967).

Remini, Robert V. *Andrew Jackson and the Course of American Freedom, 1822–1832* (New York, 1981).

Rothrock, Mary Utopia, ed., *The French Broad –Holston Country: A History Of Knox County, Tennessee* (Knoxville, 1946).

Satz, Ronald N. *Tennessee's Indian Peoples: From White Contact to Removal, 1540–1840* (Knoxville, 1979).

Scott, Mingo, Jr. *The Negro in Tennessee Politics* (Nashville, 1964).

Sellers, Charles G., Jr. *James K. Polk, Continentalist, 1843-1849* (Princeton, N.J., 1966).

————. *James K. Polk, Jacksonian, 1795–1843* (Princeton, N.J., 1957).

Shackford, James A. *David Crockett: The Man and the Legend* (Chapel Hill, N.C., 1956).

Shapiro, Karin A., *A New South Rebellion: The Battle Against Convict Labor in the Tennessee Coalfields* (Chapel Hill, 1998).

Spain, Rufus B. *Baptists* (Nashville, 1967).

Starkey, Marion L. *The Cherokee Nation* (New York, 1946).

Taylor, A. Elizabeth. *The Woman Suffrage Movement in Tennessee* (New York, 1957).

Terral, Rufus. *Newell Sanders: A Biography* (Kingsport, Tenn., 1935).

Tidwell, Mary Louise Lea, *Luke Lea of Tennessee* (Bowling Green, OH, 1993).

Tigert, John J. *Bishop Holland Nimmons McTyeire, Ecclesiastical and Educational Architect* (Nashville, 1955).

Tucker, David M. *Memphis Since Crump: Bossism, Blacks and Civic Reformers, 1948–1968* (Knoxville, 1980).

Vanderwood, Paul J. *Night Riders of Reelfoot Lake* (Memphis, 1969).

Waldrep, Christopher, *Night Riders: Defending Community in the Black Patch, 1890–1915* (Durham, NC, 1993).

Waller, William (ed.) *Nashville in the 1890s* (Nashville, 1970).

————. *Nashville, 1900 to 1910* (Nashville, 1977).

West, Carroll Van, ed., *The Tennessee Encyclopedia of History and Culture* (Nashville, 1998).

Wheeler, Marjorie Spruill, ed., *Votes for Women! The Woman Suffrage Movement in Tennessee, the South, and the Nation* (Knoxville, 1995).

Wheeler, William Bruce, *Knoxville, Tennessee: A Mountain City in the New South* (Knoxville, 2005).

————, and Michael J. McDonald, *TVA and the Tellico Dam, 1936–1979* (Knoxville, 1986).

White, Leonard D. *The Jacksonians: A Study in Administrative History, 1829–1861* (New York, 1954).

White, Robert H. *Development of The Tennessee State Education Organization, 1796–1929* (Nashville, 1929).

White, Robert H. (ed.) *Messages of the Governors of Tennessee.* 8 vols. to date (Nashville, 1952).

Wiley, Bell 1. *The Plain People of the Confederacy* (Baton Rouge, La., 1944). Williams, Frank B., Jr. *Tennessee's Presidents* (Knoxville, 1981).

Williams, Frank B., Jr. *Tennessee's Presidents* (Knoxville, 1981).

Williams, Samuel Cole. *Beginnings of West Ten-nessee in the Land of the Chickasaws, 1541–1841* (Johnson City, Tenn., 1930).

————. *History of the Lost State of Franklin* (Johnson City, Tenn., 1924).

————. *Tennessee During the Revolutionary War* (Nashville, 1944).

Williams, Samuel Cole (ed.) *Early Travels in the Tennessee Country* (Johnson City, Tenn., 1924).

Wilson, Charles Reagan, and William Ferris, eds., *Encyclopedia of Southern Culture* (Chapel Hill, 1989).

Winters, Donald, *Tennessee Farming, Tennessee Farmers: Antebellum Agriculture in the Upper South* (Knoxville, 1994).

Wolfe, Charles K. *Tennessee Strings: The Story of Country Music in Tennessee* (Knoxville, 1977).

Young, Thomas Daniel, *Tennessee Writers* (Knoxville, 1981).

INDEX

General Index
Italicized numbers indicate illustrations.